GUINNESS'S BREWERY
IN THE
IRISH ECONOMY

THE SECOND ARTHUR GUINNESS, 1768–1855
Painted by J. C. Miles in 1845: Guinness Collection

PATRICK LYNCH & JOHN VAIZEY

GUINNESS'S BREWERY

IN THE
IRISH ECONOMY

1759-1876

CAMBRIDGE
AT THE UNIVERSITY PRESS
1960

CAMBRIDGE UNIVERSITY PRESS
Cambridge, New York, Melbourne, Madrid, Cape Town,
Singapore, São Paulo, Delhi, Tokyo, Mexico City

Cambridge University Press
The Edinburgh Building, Cambridge CB2 8RU, UK

Published in the United States of America by Cambridge University Press, New York

www.cambridge.org
Information on this title: www.cambridge.org/9780521283311

First published 1960
First paperback edition 2011

A catalogue record for this publication is available from the British Library

ISBN 978-0-521-05615-1 Hardback
ISBN 978-0-521-28331-1 Paperback

Additional resources for this publication at www.cambridge.org/9780521283311

CONTENTS

ILLUSTRATIONS

PLATES

FIGURES

*The following two figures are available for download from
www.cambridge.org/9780521283311*

*The signature which appears on the title-page is that of
the first Arthur Guinness*

PREFACE

THESE are the conditions under which this book has been written. The authors have been guaranteed by Arthur Guinness, Son & Company, Limited, complete freedom of inquiry, and every assistance has been afforded them. They have had, too, freedom of expression, and it is hardly necessary to say that neither they, nor the firm, would have wished otherwise to be associated with the work.

Some preparatory work was done at the request of the Board of the firm by Dr Maurice Craig, Dr Brian Inglis and Mr R. G. Morton. The material was sorted and catalogued by them, and some preliminary excursions were made into the history itself. The Board then asked Patrick Lynch and John Vaizey to write the history. The period since 1876 was given to Professor S. R. Dennison and Dr Oliver MacDonagh to write as a second book.

Many people have given us their time and energy with great generosity and good humour. The Guinness family have helped us, particularly the Earl of Iveagh, K.G., C.B., C.M.G., the Countess of Iveagh and Lord Moyne.

The Board of the Company have been considerate, forbearing and helpful. Our grateful thanks are due to Sir Hugh Beaver, K.B.E., D.Litt., D.Econ.Sc., Dr C. K. Mill, and Dr A. H. Hughes, who is the director in charge of the history and who has been a very good friend. Professor George O'Brien has been invaluable in his own person and through his books. The basic economic histories of Ireland are his three books: *The Economic History of Ireland in the Seventeenth Century*, *The Economic History of Ireland in the Eighteenth Century*, and *The Economic History of Ireland from the Union to the Famine*. These unique and pioneering books are outstanding. They are well documented, and beautifully written, with a carefully expressed viewpoint, with which, however, in certain respects we venture to disagree.

The brewers have been unfailingly generous in help, especially Mr D. O. Williams, Head Brewer at St James's Gate, who wrote a memorandum which is the basis of the technical chapters of the history, and who has been unsparing in his critical advice. Mr L. McMullen has been a most valuable guide in difficult territory,

Preface

and Messrs L. E. Hudson and M. Ash have also done much to help us. We are indebted as well to Messrs D. Carrick, W. Dresser, F. E. James, H. Murdock, W. C. A. McKenzie, D. F. Strachan and the Misses M. Malone and J. Nell.

We have been assisted in various ways by Mrs N. Christie, Mr D. E. Grey, Reverend P. Lynch, Mr R. G. L. McCrone, Miss K. Northcott, Mr W. O'Sullivan and Miss P. Rowan.

Our thanks are also due to Mr R. A. French for help on legal matters and for discovering some important documents, and to the librarians of the Cambridge University Library; Bodleian Library, Oxford; British Museum; National Library of Ireland; Northern Ireland Public Records Office, Belfast; Bristol Central Library; Liverpool Central Library and Manchester Central Library. For certain advice or help on source material we thank Mr Garret FitzGerald, Mr Kevin McCourt, Mr León Ó Broin, Mr Walter Smithwick, K.M. and Mr D. B. Walsh, and we are indebted to Dr Conor Cruise O'Brien and Mr Thomas Woods for constructive criticism, not always accepted, of our interpretation of Irish economic history.

There is a fraternity among professional scholars which we have abused by sending our work for criticism and comment. In particular we are grateful to Professor James E. Beckett, Mr S. Brittan, Dr K. H. Connell, Dr P. L. Cook, Mr G. Cyriax, Professor Dudley Edwards, Dr R. M. Hartwell, Dr Hugh Kearney, Mr P. Mathias, Dr K. Nowlan, Mr Sean O'Sullivan, Professor J. Purser, Professor E. A. G. Robinson, Professor Brinley Thomas, Professor R. M. Titmuss, Mrs Maureen Wall and Professor T. D. Williams.

Above all, Miss Violet Anderson has been indispensable as friend, researcher, secretary and typist.

PATRICK LYNCH

JOHN VAIZEY

Dublin and London, 1960

INTRODUCTION

FROM THE HILLS above Dublin the Welsh mountains may be seen on a clear day, but often clouds and fog obscure the view. Guinness's steamers sail regularly between Dublin and England; sometimes the journey is stormy and difficult. Thus it has been in the political and economic relations of the two islands, linked by the migration of people and capital, sharing common markets and techniques, speaking a common language, but often torn asunder by religion, politics and local economic interest.

The growth of Guinness's in the century-and-a-quarter after its foundation in the year 1759 from a little Dublin brewery to a firm whose public issue in 1886 excited the London Stock Exchange is in part the story of the economy that grew up around the ports on both sides of the Irish Sea. On a small scale the Irish Sea mirrored the development of the Atlantic economy. A short sea-passage separated Dublin from Liverpool, Cork from Bristol. The ships that sailed between these ports carried passengers and cargoes to whom the political entities of 'Ireland' and 'England' meant little. The absence of any great economic or political division had important repercussions on the nature of the economy in which the firm of Arthur Guinness grew, and consequently on the problems analysed in this book. Guinness's brewery can no more be considered solely in an Irish context than can the Irish economy be considered as an autonomous unit. Guinness's grew to straddle the Irish Sea. The first Arthur Guinness almost took his brewery to Holyhead in Anglesey; his descendant, the second Earl of Iveagh, built a brewery in London. Britain and Ireland are so interconnected that the story of a Dublin business is part of the history of both countries.

The history of a business is the history of men and their decisions, which taken together form a narrative of growth. The evolution of Guinness's brewery as a great firm reflects the remarkable capacity of its proprietors and the men whom they employed; without these men there would have been no firm. The context within which they worked is more especially the historian's concern; it determines the broad limits of their actions. But their actions themselves alter the

Introduction

context, and the historian must try to indicate, however inadequately, the springs of action which moved the people in the story.

This book surveys at some length the economic background against which the Guinnesses built their business. The narrative is analytical as well as descriptive, but the compass of general economic history is confined to what is necessary for an intelligible account of the Irish brewing industry and of Guinness's emergence as the dominant firm in it. The work has been designed to show the relationship between men and business and their response to economic forces.

It would be tempting to describe the development of Irish brewing in a series of simple stages, but economic growth is a Protean concept, and the Irish brewing industry is no exception. The competition of the British brewers in the Irish market and the popularity of illicit distilling were formidable obstacles to the advance of Irish brewing; to attribute its advance exclusively to the removal of these obstacles, however, would be an incomplete explanation, if only because of the timing of the phases of development. Again, it is sometimes suggested that the brewing industry owed more to politics than to economics. But this is an error rather than an explanation. Obsolete legislation certainly harassed the brewers until relief came in the last decades of the eighteenth century, and the reform then achieved was of great importance. Fluctuations in the fortunes of the brewing industry have, indeed, reflected the course of taxation; public policy as expressed through fiscal and administrative practice elucidates part of the story—but only part of it, for there were great fluctuations unconnected with fiscal changes. A defective fiscal policy may frustrate enterprise and impede efficient organization, as it did in Ireland for most of the eighteenth century, but an enlightened fiscal system merely creates the conditions of progress, it does not of itself promote progress if enterprise and initiative are lacking.

During the first half of the eighteenth century the Irish brewers were reasonably well off, though they were more heavily taxed than their British rivals. Then in 1741 the Irish customs duties were raised; and further duties on imports from Britain were imposed in 1789. Despite these measures, however, imports of British beer increased from 5000 barrels in 1741 to 125,000 barrels in 1793. Even equal burdens of duty would, in effect, have been a form of discriminatory taxation since the competitive position of the Irish brewers was inferior to that of their British rivals. Because their market was limited, the Irish brewers were not yet able to take advantage of the economies of large-scale production. These economies had been available to certain London brewers since the beginning of the eighteenth century, and were consolidated when these brewers began to specialize in the production of porter.

None of the Irish brewers achieved the critical minimum size necessary for efficient production or specialized in the manufacture of a single product—porter—until the end of the eighteenth century, very many years after their London rivals. As a result, the London brewers were able to undersell Dublin brewers in their own city in the second half of the eighteenth century. Indeed, Dublin, a compact market, offered the British brewers admirable opportunities for remunerative selling of marginal units of output. The raising of the Irish customs duties in 1741 was, therefore, a response to threats of competition which the Irish brewers had already felt or appre- hended. But the attempts at equalization of taxation failed to impede the flow of imports and additional Irish duties were imposed in 1789. For four more years, however, British imports continued to grow. Then in the ten years after 1793 imports fell by half and dwindled to insignificance by 1813.

Taxation changes favourable to the Irish brewers are not in themselves a sufficient explanation of the decline of British beer imports into Ireland after 1793. No doubt the Irish legislation of 1795, which reformed the whole Irish system of taxing beer, played a part in creating conditions favourable to the Irish brewers. But ever since 1791 the British brewers had been handicapped in their own country by the restrictions, shortages and increased transport costs caused by the French wars. As yet Ireland had barely been sensible of these disabilities. Moreover, the inflation after 1797 increased demand in Dublin and enabled Irish brewers to expand the scale of their operations, thus improving their productive effi- ciency. Soon Guinness was beginning to specialize in the manufac- ture of porter and meeting the needs of customers who previously had been served mainly by the London brewers. In short, therefore, a conjuncture of many causes explains the growth of Irish brewing after 1795; no single answer is satisfactory, just as no single factor accounts for the earlier vicissitudes of the industry.

The more important Guinness records begin in 1797. A man

Introduction

looking at Ireland then would have seen two worlds—one with an economy closely linked with that of the rest of the British Isles, with resurgent industries and a settled commerce, the other a rural subsistence economy, based on the potato, where the population and the area under cultivation were expanding rapidly. One society was modern, and the other remote from modernity; one was destined to survive and the other, in less than fifty years, to collapse.

In the maritime fringe the towns were linked by sea and by canal. A visitor would have found the country not markedly different from what he had seen in England—except that there was no equivalent of the industrial north, with busy coalmines, rising factory chimneys and glowing iron foundries. Dublin and the other towns had a few factories—mainly breweries; there was a small coalfield; and a Guinness was a partner in an iron foundry. In general, however, the industrial changes of the age had not yet reached Ireland.

Politically, Ireland was on the eve of ferment. The 1798 rising was being organized and fomented while the College Green Parliament—an independent deliberative assembly with no executive power—was in its hey-day: most of its members were unaware that its extinction was imminent and that the republican rising would seal its fate. Parliament, with the consent of the executive, had voted two years earlier for a reduction and simplification of the excise duties on beer, and the brewing trade was again beginning to prosper. This was typical of a number of industries to which fiscal encouragement had recently been given and from which, in a few instances, returns were already showing. A percipient business man, however, would have said that the two greatest influences on trade were the growth of population and the war with France. The population of the British Isles was increasing rapidly and new consumers and new workers were being added to it daily. The war was becoming more violent and desperate; government expenditure was expanding, and with it economic activity and employment, and prices rose.

This then was Ireland in 1797. One economy was growing; the other, peopled largely by moneyless country folk, usually Irish-speaking and sometimes downtrodden, was largely static. The maritime economy was thriving, under the impulse of population growth and war; politically the outlook was unsettled and often stormy. For the most part, however, domestic political events were irrelevant to the economic developments that were taking place.

4

Introduction

As the first Arthur Guinness, then seventy-two years old, rode from Beaumont, his house on the northern shore of Dublin Bay, to his brewery at the western edge of the city, and to his mills beyond, his eye could light upon a considerable range of family relations in business, politics and religion. Grattan was still at College Green. Three of Arthur Guinness's sons, Arthur, Ben and William Lunell, were at the brewery; his eldest son Hosea was a curate at St Werburgh's; his wife was related by marriage to Edward Smyth, minister of Bethesda Chapel; his own Sunday School was eleven years old and flourishing. His family connexions were the strength of his business, and they were not unimportant for the Dublin brewing trade as a whole. Henry Grattan had been influential in securing the legislation of 1795 that gave the brewers such considerable fiscal advantages. The positions which Guinness and his sons held were signs of their prestige in their industry and the importance of the brewers in Dublin.

Already the Guinnesses were prosperous. Their brewery was one of the biggest in the city—though none of the breweries was very big and few of them sold beer outside Dublin. The Guinness family also had the flour-mill. The brewery—which is to be the main concern of this history—was bigger than it had been thirty-eight years before when Arthur Guinness first acquired it; it still made ale as well as porter; its main market was still in Dublin. Already, however, some casks were going along the canals to towns in the centre of Ireland, but few were going to England or to towns along the coast of Ireland.

Inflation was becoming intensified in Britain. The English and Irish pounds went off the gold standard. Paper money became widespread, business flourished; and as the inflation was faster in Ireland than in Great Britain there was a depreciation of the Irish currency in terms of the British pound sterling. As a result, Irish exports were encouraged and imports discouraged. Trade began to penetrate into rural Ireland.

From 1797 to 1814 the war-time boom based on a currency no longer tied to gold led to a great expansion of trade in maritime Ireland, and spread back into the rural areas, along the canals and round the coast. The pattern of Guinness's sales reflected these changes. In this prosperity the passing of the Irish Parliament in 1801 took place with less lamentation than might be supposed: its

5

disappearance made little real difference to the groups who sought commercial benefit from the legislature whatever their apprehensions may have been beforehand. Then, in 1815 the war-time demand for goods and services ended and a policy of 'sound money' was introduced. Maritime Ireland was depressed, unemployment rose, prices fell and trade, which had been extending in rural Ireland, receded.

The effects were at once seen in the brewing trade. Helped first by the legislation of 1795, and then by the war-time boom, the sale of beer had increased. The brewing industry was also helped by the suppression of legal distilleries from 1808 to 1811. But the depression from 1815 to 1821 was extremely serious for the brewing trade; it almost destroyed Guinness's. The expansion of beer sales after 1821 is explicable by the growth of trade to Britain (materially helped by steamship transport for the cross-Channel passage), the recovery of the maritime Irish economy from the slump, and the decline of illegal distilleries.

Guinness's took a leading part in the recovery and expansion of Irish beer-sales. Its agents in Bristol, Liverpool and London were responsible for a rapid development of its British trade, which represented the greater part of its output until 1845; trade in rural Ireland was negligible. Mainly because of its British trade Guinness was now Ireland's leading brewery. Compared with the big London brewers, however, it was still a small concern, though it had already entered the London market through its agent Henry Tuckett.

These successes of Guinness's were attributable in part, at least, to the efforts of its agents as salesmen. In England, Samuel Waring, Antisell, Tuckett and Sparkes Moline had a good product to sell. The quality of the beer was possibly due to the two Pursers—John Purser, junior, and John Tertius Purser, who were partners of the Guinnesses at James's Gate. The second Arthur Guinness succeeded his father in 1803, and was helped by his two brothers Benjamin and William Lunell. When Benjamin died and William Lunell retired, Arthur Guinness's own two sons Benjamin Lee and Arthur Lee took their places in the business. In 1840 Arthur Lee Guinness left the firm, and the second Arthur virtually retired. By 1845 the brewery was run by Benjamin Lee Guinness and the two Pursers. They were all good brewers and Benjamin Lee Guinness was an excellent business man.

6

Introduction

The second Arthur had been in many respects the architect of his firm's fortune. The brewery was probably not his main concern though he supervised it closely. He was a leading banker, and as such was partly responsible for the post-1815 economic depression in Ireland that nearly ruined his brewing business. Nevertheless, under his direction the brewery's trade revived, and he was especially successful in leading his firm along a narrow, but carefully mapped path through a sometimes politically disturbed country.

In 1845, with the appearance of the potato blight the Irish rural economy fell into a great catastrophe. But Guinness's brewery had already experienced over twenty years of steady growth. The second Arthur Guinness was an old man; Benjamin Lee Guinness was in his prime; and the brewery was well placed to take advantage of the changes that the Great Famine was about to produce.

The tragedy of the Great Famine is the central fact of modern Irish history. Paradoxically, its consequences for the brewing industry were not an unmitigated disaster; it marked the end of the old subsistence economy and the assimilation of the Irish hinterland into the maritime economy of the rest of the British Isles. Its consequences for the brewing industry, therefore, were decisive; a new market appeared of country people with money to spend on beer. The government relief measures and other expenditure during the Great Famine introduced into rural Ireland the economy which previously had been confined mainly to the eastern seaboard. In due course the increase there in income per head created opportunities for the sale of beer from which Guinness's derived more advantage than did any other Irish brewer. In this, again, their agents, Atkinson, Barrett, Kennedy and Rourke, played a role of outstanding importance.

Why did a single brewery emerge to dominate the industry in Dublin and not in London or Burton or Edinburgh? Did the Guinnesses have a peculiar genetic genius denied to so many others? Perhaps, because they were always prolific and long-lived there was in each generation a wide choice of candidates from whom the head of the brewery could be selected. They certainly showed wisdom and skill in choosing men to work for them and in learning from their own mistakes. Did the Guinnesses succeed because they wisely decided to specialize in making a single product when their brewery had achieved a size sufficiently large to permit of its efficient

7

manufacture?[1] Or, was it because they were primarily devoted to business and avoided conspicuous consumption, unlike other merchants and traders, who so often drained their business of working capital to invest improvidently in landed estates or squander their substance in creature comforts? This book attempts to answer some of these questions.

The brewery was privately owned by the Guinness family from its establishment in 1759 until its incorporation as a public Company in 1886. But the association of the Guinness family with it continued to be as close after 1886 as before. As far as the history of the brewery is concerned the crucial change had taken place ten years earlier when Edward Cecil Guinness bought out his brother Arthur and became sole owner. It is because of this special significance of 1876 in the history of the brewery that this book ends in that year.

[1] When the first Arthur Guinness was an old man an entry was made in one of the firm's brewing books: 'Today, April 1st 1799 was brewed the last ale brew.'

8

[1]

The Economic Background

The evil in Ireland is not a deficiency of food for the year, or even
of a particular description of food, potatoes; but the great and supposed general deficiency of that description of food operating upon
the social condition of Ireland; the habits of the great body of the
people...who have not the pecuniary means, and if they had the
pecuniary means are not in the habit of purchasing their food in the
markets. (*The Duke of Wellington to Sir Robert Peel, in 'Memoirs,
Published by Lord Mahon and the Rt Hon. Edwd. Cardwell, M.P.
1828–1846' (London, 1856), vol. II, p. 199.*)

THE MARITIME ECONOMY

IRELAND in the eighteenth century could be divided into two parts.
About three-quarters of the population lived in a rural, and mainly
subsistence, economy which occupied the greater part of the country.
On the eastern coastal fringe extending from Belfast to Cork, and
in the towns of Limerick and Galway there was a separate cash
economy linked to England by ties of trade and credit and by a
constant traffic in people. Although Dublin, the centre of this
maritime cash economy, was a capital, it was economically a provincial city of the British Isles, like Bristol or Norwich, and its mercantile
relations were mainly with London rather than with its Irish background. Its citizens got their living from the Castle and from the
official and military establishment like those of any other garrison
town. Wealthy people and the middle class lived on rents from their
country estates or on receipts from the funds, and created employment for a host of domestic trades and services, among which was
brewing. Some of their purchases were of goods from England or
abroad. Some were of food from rural Ireland. Their relation with
the areas beyond their hinterland, however, was no more than that
of people in any big town drawing upon outside areas for simple
labour and basic foods, because their main highway was the sea
and their outlook was maritime.

The peculiar social structure which evolved in the eighteenth
century in this maritime economy was most fully realized in Dublin.

9

The Economic Background

A society came into existence whose members produced the leaders of rank and fashion in the country. The conflict of their political and economic interests with those of England strengthened their independence of outlook. Their pride in their city found expression in the stately Parliament House in College Green, elegant public parks, well-proportioned houses, wide streets, dignified squares and seemly churches. The conditions of life of those who were excluded from their society—the great majority of the city's inhabitants—remained wretched.

Why did the advanced cash economy of the maritime region take so long to penetrate and assimilate the subsistence economy? The problem is not a unique one, save in its scale, because in all the Celtic fringes of the British Isles an older way of life survived well into Queen Victoria's reign. In the Highlands of Scotland the Gaelic culture continued until it ended, too, in famine.[1] Since much of Ireland was more remote than Wales or Scotland, it endured as a place apart, a separate system; but the Irish economy was potentially so big and so important a field for capitalist initiative that its isolation is not self-evidently explicable.

THE SUBSISTENCE ECONOMY

In 1700 the population of Ireland was over 2·5 million, and that of the rest of the British Isles over 6·0 million. By 1800 it had grown to 5·0 million, when that of Great Britain was over 10·0 million. It rose from 6·8 million in 1821 to 8·2 million in 1841. The growth of population was the dominant social and economic fact of the period. In sixty years, from 1781, the Irish population rather more than doubled. The rise appears to have been shared by town and country, and since the country was the larger part of the island most of the increase was in rural population.[2] At a rough estimate, perhaps rather more than 6·0 million people lived in the subsistence economy when the Great Famine came in 1845, and about 2·0 million in the maritime economy around Dublin, Belfast, Cork, Waterford, Limerick and Galway.

The custom of early marriage was closely related to the structure of Irish rural society.[3] Poverty led to the early foundation of a

[1] Malcolm Gray, *The Highland Economy, 1750–1850* (Edinburgh, 1957).
[2] K. H. Connell, *The Population of Ireland, 1750–1845* (Oxford, 1950), p. 33.
[3] *Ibid.* ch. 3.

family, because a family was an insurance against disaster, not a hostage to fortune. The standard of living could not fall by having children who were easily fed from the cow and the potato patch. It was low partly because the system of land tenure discouraged improvement,[1] but the ease of acquiring a smallholding made it possible to feed everybody at least to subsistence level. The religion of the majority also encouraged early marriage, and the division between man's and woman's work made a wife as essential to a man's domestic economy as to his felicity. The masses had no hope of rising by saving or by exertion from the low estate to which they were called.

Outside the towns most Irish people from about 1770 lived mainly on potatoes. 'It was of quite fundamental importance in permitting and encouraging the rapid growth of population in the sixty or seventy years before the Famine.'[2] For not only was the potato associated with the digging up of pasture land, the reclamation of the bog and barren hillsides, the subdivision of holdings and the increase in early marriage, but its nutritional adequacy reduced disease and so lowered mortality rates. The countryman lived longer than the town dweller and the infantile mortality rate was much lower in the country than in the towns. Medicine and vaccination had little influence, and the potato and milk diet seems to have been an important element affecting these rates of mortality.

The lack of money in Ireland outside the big coastal towns is well attested. In Mayo during the 1823 distress, 'There was no price for corn.... In short, there was plenty for everyone; there was no deficiency of anything, but the means of buying.'[3]

Campbell Foster, an exceedingly percipient and accurate observer, was correspondent for *The Times* at the beginning of the Great Famine and his *Letters* give a dramatic picture of a subsistence economy on the point of breakdown.[4] Sometimes the people knew so little of the commercial value of money that they pawned it.[5] The retailing system was primitive. Travelling salesmen are mentioned often in contemporary narratives. There was little or no specialized

[1] See below, p. 15.
[2] Connell, *The Population of Ireland, 1750–1845*, p. 159.
[3] P.P. 1823 (561), vol. VI, p. 380, i. *Report from the Select Committee on the Employment of the Poor in Ireland*, cited by Connell, *The Population of Ireland, 1750–1845*, p. 142.
[4] T. Campbell Foster, *Letters on the Condition of the People of Ireland* (London, 1846), pp. 313–15 and also pp. 391–3.
[5] George O'Brien, *The Economic History of Ireland, from the Union to the Famine* (London, 1921), p. 527.

merchanting. Even if the people had wanted to buy beer, or other commercial products, they had neither the money to pay for it nor was there the commercial organization to bring it to them.[1]

This was a society without a market. Campbell Foster gave a remarkable instance of an improving landlord—Lord George Hill— who introduced a market economy into a Donegal estate, at Gweedore. In 1837, in a village of over 9000 people, there was 'one cart, one plough, 20 shovels, 32 rakes, 2 feather beds and 8 chaff beds. They had no clocks; there was not a looking-glass in the whole parish above 3*d*. in price; they had no garden vegetables or fruits of any kind, but potatoes and cabbage.'[2] Ten shillings was the highest rent paid, and the tenants owned a leg of a beast rather than the whole beast; twenty-six people owned one half-acre field between them. Lord George bought the estate and opened a shop and a corn store, and built a road, an inn and a quay. The level of amenity rose immediately. Lord George enclosed the farms and encouraged the building of houses—all against the most tremendous resistance by the local people to change, so powerful were the forces of tradition. But by 1845 the people had crops of oats and turnips and so could avoid the Great Famine.

The majority of the Irish population in the eighteenth century consisted of small farmers and their families holding a tenuous and temporary interest in the patch of land whose rent they paid by working as labourers for bigger farmers. In England the rural worker was paid in money for his labour; in Ireland in land or goods. The countryman was only vestigially in contact with a money economy. The squalid conditions of his existence may have been among the forces that drove him to be thriftless and unproductive. Apart from adequate food he was without the frugal comforts of peasant communities in other countries. His alcohol was cheap locally distilled spirits; he rarely drank beer except when he sold something in a market town. These subsistence conditions were always threatened by the risk of bad harvests; when famines occurred the precariousness of a non-monetary economy which was normally unnoticed became apparent with startling rapidity. Grain was little known in many parts and there were few granaries to store what

[1] P.P. 1816 (436), vol. IX, p. 73, *Report from the Select Committee on Illicit Distillation in Ireland.*
[2] Campbell Foster, *Letters on the Condition of the People of Ireland*, pp. 116–25.

The Subsistence Economy

was not immediately required for food. Techniques were backward or primitive and scientific knowledge lacking. In spite of the absence of land taxes and poor-rates and the presence of cheap labour, the average Irish crop of wheat and barley (and possibly oats) was smaller than in England, inferior in quality and dearer than English corn which could undersell the home product in the Irish market. There was not in Ireland any of the experimentation and development which was making East Anglia one of England's main sources of food, and especially a source of barley-malt for the London brewers.

The growth of national wealth in Britain was marked during the latter part of the eighteenth century. Because of the larger and richer market the sales of products of all kinds rose rapidly. There were recessions and panics, booms and enthusiasms, but the general trend was unmistakable. This is the period that has come to be called the Industrial Revolution because of its conjunction of rising population, new techniques, more abundant capital, and expanding foreign trade. From this time can be traced the growth of cotton and woollen firms, potteries and iron foundries, collieries and banks, on a modern scale. One of the first industries to be affected, probably, was brewing. In London, in the early eighteenth century, a number of breweries introduced modern industrial methods, and operated on a large scale, using big financial resources. The reasons are not far to seek. Their methods were simple, and the advantages of brewing on a large scale were many. The market was expanding and the cash was there.

In England, as the population grew, the supply of capital grew faster and so income per head in general rose. In Ireland, on the other hand, the growth of population often outstripped the supply of capital arising from savings, and consequently from time to time real income per head fell. The most that could be said of the Irish rural economy was that its members grew no poorer; indeed, some of them probably became better off because usually they had ample food except when periodic harvest failures caused near-famine. In general, however, they had little money. The rural economy was founded on subsistence farming and barter. Coin of the realm was scarce. The majority of the population provided no market for the industrial goods now beginning to come with increasing abundance from British manufacturers, or for the agricultural surpluses that the new farming methods were producing in eastern England.

13

The Economic Background

In any process of economic growth there must be the opportunity of profit, a supply of labour, capital, business ability and technical competence. Without these economic development is not possible. Many factors affect each of them, but in Ireland in the eighteenth and early nineteenth centuries it is possible to sort out the main influences.

The opportunity for investment in the eighteenth century was mainly dependent upon the exploitation of a fertile soil and accessible mineral wealth, situated near good ports and easy markets. Much of Ireland's soil is less fertile than that of many parts of England and there is little known mineral wealth. Without these two advantages the opportunities given by good ports and a growing population were insufficient to lead to prospects of quick and steady profit. Almost all Great Britain's new industries grew on coalfields. Ireland had only small resources of coal. The inducements to invest in Ireland were considerably weaker than those in Great Britain.

Ireland had an abundant supply of labour, and healthy and strong young men and women became her chief export. The Irish formed a major part of the labour force of industrial Lancashire and the Clyde, and at a later stage in British development they helped to build the railways. A considerable number migrated permanently and even more spent a few years, or a few months every year, in Britain. Many came from the country into the Irish towns, which were no healthier than other towns at the time, and which were therefore dependent for their growth upon a rate of absorption of country people that overtook the heavy urban death-rate. This pattern of migration from the countryside to industrial districts and big towns was typical of all the rural parts of the British Isles, and Ireland was not a special case. It differed, however, from the other reservoirs of labour. Its people tended to be more mobile than those from within Great Britain itself, where the typical migrant was one who moved ten or fifteen miles but no more. The Irish migrant in Great Britain was more foot-loose.

The efflux from Ireland was an eighteenth-century characteristic, and thirty years before the Great Famine many thousands of Irish had settled permanently in London and its neighbourhood, and in

The Two Economies

Glasgow.[1] So, too, had Irish migratory labour been common in the south and east of England and south-west of Scotland.[2] They became agricultural labourers, navvies, or road builders.[3] Many of the Irish were unemployed handloom weavers, as well as surplus agricultural labourers. They formed the most depressed part of the army of the redundant in the British Isles. The Irish were driven from Ireland mainly because their numbers exceeded the capital available; it was not because the great flow of British manufactures drove them out of employment.[4]

The subdivision of Irish land and the extension of the margin of cultivation up the hillsides and out into the bogs was the result of the social system and the absence of a market. There was little improved agriculture in Ireland, no big enclosure movement to impel the country folk off the land and turn them into wage-labourers, no pouring of capital into hedges and ditches and stock-raising and seed experiments. Most farmers were tenants at will with a life interest in the estate of a rack-renting landowner who was sometimes an absentee. The landlord raised rents to the limit of his tenants' capacity to pay (which was their subsistence level) instead of allowing the prosperity of his tenants to fructify the land and yield him greater dividends per acre. The landlord himself was often merely a link in a complex system of mortgage and common indebtedness. The level of agricultural technique was elementary and simple conditions of exploitation existed. Many landlords who were absentees had often no interest in their land or in their tenants and the duties and obligations of ownership meant little to them. They took their rents and spent and invested them in England or in the towns on the east coast of Ireland.

Some of the capital to finance British economic development may have come from Ireland. Had the money stayed where it was made the rate of Irish population growth might even have been accelerated. It is likely that existing social trends would have been intensified rather than that the people would have been given the opportunity

[1] J. H. Clapham, *The Economic History of Modern Britain*, 2nd ed. (Cambridge, 1930), vol. I, p. 57.

[2] *Ibid.* vol. I, pp. 57–8.

[3] Barbara M. Kerr, 'Irish Seasonal Migration to Great Britain, 1800–1838', *Irish Historical Studies*, vol. III (1942–3), p. 365.

[4] In 1851 half the English population was rural, and the proportion was considerably higher in 1831. Clapham, *op. cit.* vol. I, pp. 65–8.

to invest in or to improve their holdings. It was in England that the economic return on investment was highest, so in the circumstances funds inevitably flowed to England from the periphery. Part of the capital certainly went to build Dublin. Some of it went in rich living. This expenditure provided work and incomes in the towns for people from the rural hinterland. The rents from the rural economy were the impetus behind some of the rural emigration.

In general the growth of population was not overtaken by a growth of capital accumulation in rural Ireland; and the rate of growth of the maritime economy was insufficient to take enough people off the land to effect this. As labour was so plentiful it was cheaper to extend the cultivated area with elementary techniques than to cultivate the land more intensively with higher techniques.

The insufficiency of economic growth must be attributed mainly to a lack of profitable opportunities to invest in Ireland arising from the absence of a market. Some of the other conditions for investment were available—a growing potential market, and an adequate labour force—but there was little effective demand. There were some small traders and business men, but, on the whole, no industrial and mercantile classes comparable with those to be found in the rest of the British Isles. The country was divided into peasants and labourers, and landowners, of differing religious and social allegiance. This division was inimical to the growth of that middle-class society which was associated with the rise of industry and town life in Great Britain. Dublin, Cork, Belfast, Waterford, Wexford and Kilkenny, with their deeper settlement of prosperous people, were virtually the only exceptions to this generalization. These cities and towns were surrounded by hinterlands where improving landlords were common.

In 1842 and again in 1845 Nassau Senior, the economist, attributed the poverty of the Irish in part to the lack of fixity of tenure for the tenant and an absence of the middle class. 'There are many parts of Ireland in which a driver and a process-server form regular parts of the landlord's establishment.' The poor were impoverished by their lack of legal right and by their ignorance.

The ignorance...which marks the greater part of the population of Ireland is not merely ignorance of the moral and political tendency of their conduct...but ignorance of the businesses which are their daily occupations. It is ignorance, not as citizens and subjects, but as cultivators and labourers.

The Two Economies

The indolence of the people appalled him—

From the time that his crops are sown or planted until they are reaped, the peasant and his family are cowering over the fire, or smoking or lounging before the door—when an hour or two a day, employed in weeding their potatoes or oats, or flax, would perhaps increase the produce by one-third.

Nassau Senior saw no future in gradual self-improvement; only an influx of capital would help the country. But terrorized as it was by revolutionaries and groaning under the impositions of the Church, Ireland was not a likely field for investment. He advocated a removal of Irish abuses; but in general he despaired.[1] In this he was not alone.

In the growth of a country with two economies, one capitalist and the other subsistence, the primacy of the maritime capitalist economy with a heavy bias towards exports is a well-established historical phenomenon. The problem is to explain the lack of contact between the two. Where contact is limited the main exporting industries in the maritime zone tend to be those with a high capital/output ratio, often using relatively advanced techniques. Indeed there is usually a gap in the hierarchy of techniques corresponding to the boundary between the zones—in the maritime the level of techniques is high; in the subsistence it is very elementary. In Ireland, brewing —situated in the maritime economy—was an industry with a high capital/output ratio, using relatively advanced techniques, and Ireland is, to this extent, one of a generality of cases.

At first sight the cheap supply of labour available from the subsistence economy might seem to militate against an industry such as brewing by making it cheaper to use labour-consuming techniques. Where the skill of the labourers is low, however, the best industry to adopt may be one in which the need for labour is not great. As there was little effective demand for the products of the subsistence economy because of the dearth of purchasing power, the ability of the brewing industry to generate growth in rural Ireland was severely restricted, especially as the incomes of the brewers were relatively large and their tastes metropolitan. Their profits were a large proportion of their total incomes, and their consumption tended to have a high import content.

[1] Nassau Senior, *Journals, Conversations and Essays Relating to Ireland* (London, 1868), vol. I, pp. 45–7.

The Economic Background

In Dublin, as in the provincial cities of England in the eighteenth century, there were bankers and business men, speculative builders and merchants, who catered for the needs of the expanding city. The connexions of the banks were with London and other British cities and not with rural Ireland, just as Trinity College, Dublin, looked to Oxford and Cambridge and not to the Irish hedge-schools for its inspiration. The closest analogy to eighteenth-century Irish town life is with the settlements in the American colonies—their economies and their culture were linked with Britain, while behind them lay a different and unexplored society.

The analogy holds, too, in the sphere of government. Ireland had its own Viceroy and was garrisoned with British troops. The masses, of course, were no more represented in the Irish Parliament than they were in the American Assemblies or at Westminster. The Parliament at College Green was a gathering of the established. It helped to bring trade and influence to Dublin, but it was deeply committed to the maintenance of existing society. The great land-lords were generally in control, although occasional concessions were made to the burgesses of Dublin and the bigger towns, and to the Church of Ireland. The influence of the Castle was usually decisive.

One cause of English economic growth in the eighteenth century was the peace that reigned from the end of the Civil War in 1647. Ireland was a striking contrast. Cromwell devastated it. Then forty years later the Glorious Revolution was followed by the Williamite Wars. The eighteenth century opened with a devastated and occupied Ireland lying beside a prosperous, peaceful and successful England. The nature of the political settlement in Ireland was such that probably a higher proportion of the national income was taken in taxation than that of the rest of the Kingdom. These fiscal disadvantages might have been offset if heavy government spending had created trade and encouraged business; but the character of eighteenth-century government was such that a considerable part of the expenditure went to placemen and hangers-on whose expenditure was often concentrated on London and the fashionable resorts. On the other hand, the jobbery associated with the Irish Parliament helped to attract some trade towards Ireland, and the troubled condition of the country led to

18

higher military expenditure there than elsewhere. The political dependence of Ireland, therefore, had adverse economic effects on the
fiscal arrangements between the two countries, but probably to a
lesser degree than has commonly been supposed.

The existence of a separate Irish Parliament in the eighteenth
century led to a separate corpus of legislation which, it is often held,
was more favourable to Irish economic development than the legislation which later applied to the whole United Kingdom. If true,
this proposition may be a clue to the allegedly inadequate development of the Irish economy after the Union during a period of rapid
growth in English and Scottish enterprise. Attempts were certainly
made to promote economic improvement, especially in regard to
canal construction and drainage. Economic betterment, however,
was not the characteristic contribution of the Dublin Parliament to
Irish life. Politically, its power to pursue an independent policy
was limited by the narrow room for manœuvre left it by the Parliament at Westminster, and by its own members' notions of what
might be achieved by legislation. Politics in the eighteenth century
were about the spoils of office, not the improvement of society. The
significance of the Irish Parliament was social, not sociological; it
represented interests and adjusted them.

Restrictions on trade between the two countries aroused Irish
grievances. These were aggravated by the increase in British demand
for Irish agricultural products. The Irish sought to meet that demand,
and the British farmers wanted to keep the market to themselves.
Agitation in Britain led to the prohibition of imports of Irish provisions in 1778. Gradually, opposition grew in the Irish House of
Commons to these and other government measures, and in 1779 the
government, preoccupied with war in America and anxious to
avoid acute trouble nearer home, made substantial concessions to
the Dublin Parliament. Most of the economic restrictions were
removed, though a condition was imposed that Irish import and
export duties on trade with the colonies should be maintained at
the same levels as in Britain. The Dublin Parliament took advantage
of these possibilities to support home industries. The motive may
often have been to derive private profit from public funds, but sometimes the consequences were more widely beneficial. Protection
could not, however, remedy the inherent disadvantages with which
geography and history had saddled Ireland.

The Economic Background

The Irish Parliament, where these differences between the kingdoms were debated, produced a number of outstanding parliamentarians, among them Henry Grattan (1746–1820), well-known to the second Arthur Guinness, a Dubliner and a graduate of Trinity College who practised at the Irish Bar. In 1775 Grattan had become a member of the Irish House of Commons on the invitation of Lord Charlemont. He identified himself with the opposition to the restrictions on the Irish export trade, and was soon demanding that the Irish Parliament should be wholly independent of Westminster. He urged the repeal of Poyning's Law by which all Bills passed in the Irish Parliament, except money Bills, were subject to concurrence by the Privy Council. He also supported the repeal of the Declaratory Act of 1720 that gave Westminster the statutory right to legislate for Ireland.

By 1782, just before the end of the American war, Grattan carried a vote in the Dublin Parliament on these issues, and with the fall of Lord North the Irish proposals were accepted. In this House, Grattan's influence sprang greatly from what the Duke of Rutland called 'the most beautiful eloquence ever heard': he was closely associated with the Whigs at Westminster, and when they were in office his influence was great. He was an outstanding champion of the Irish brewing industry.

A majority of the Irish House of Commons tended to favour Irish separation, religious emancipation and tithe commutation, issues on which the government usually differed from them. But the government managed to regain control of the Commons, and in 1800 succeeded in gaining the passage of the Act of Union which abolished the Irish Parliament. The reasons for the Union were many. Among them were the fears inspired by the republican rising of 1798 that Ireland would provide a landing ground for the French. There were also the apprehensions of British manufacturers and farmers that a privileged enclave with special tariffs would grow on their doorstep. The majority of Irish manufacturers and landowners opposed the Union. The unestablished hierarchy supported it in the belief that its consummation would lead to better treatment of their flock and allow them to penetrate England. In any event the bishops had the greatest detestation of Irish republican aspirations inspired by the French Revolution. The Church of Ireland thought that the Union would strengthen its position by uniting the forces against religious emancipation. Eventually the Union was passed with little real opposition—and its passage was helped by lavish compensation to the borough-mongers and the politicians.

IRISH TRANSPORT AND IRISH INDUSTRY

What was the character of the commercial and industrial life that flourished fitfully in the Irish littoral in the late eighteenth and early nineteenth centuries?

At a level below that of parliamentary legislation and political activity there was a complex commercial organization. The crafts and trades of Dublin, Cork and Belfast were organized in guilds, which claimed the right to control conditions of entry and work of employees, training of apprentices and the supervision of the quality of the goods. Some of the guilds were very old, others were of Tudor origin, and some—the brewers, the maltsters, and the coopers— received their charters in the seventeenth century. The power of the guilds declined in the eighteenth century. As they and their traditions faded new organizations such as the Dublin Society appeared. All these had their importance because it was through them that commercial experience and industrial expertise were communicated.

The Dublin Society, founded in 1731 and better known since 1820 as the Royal Dublin Society, addressed itself to the advancement of agriculture, manufacturing and the arts in Ireland. It was the outcome of an intellectual movement that may be said to have begun in 1720 with Swift's pamphlet 'A Proposal for the Universal Use of Irish Manufacture'. The Irish Parliament gave active and practical support to the Dublin Society.

As a result of parliamentary action considerable improvement in methods of transport took place. The number and quality of the roads increased. Canals were built. In England, canals followed trade; in Ireland it was hoped that trade would follow the canals. The hope was only partially fulfilled, for outside Dublin the new canals served few areas of commercial or industrial importance. The earliest legislation on canals was enacted in 1715 and was directed towards the drainage and improvement of bogs as well as the easing of inland carriage. But the system was slow to get under way; it was clumsily and improvidently administered and frequently paralysed by incompetence and corruption.

The Economic Background

The Grand Canal and the Royal Canal were the two most important, though their economic effects were limited to Leinster. Traffic between Ulster and Munster and Connaught and Dublin had the choice of a slow and expensive journey by cart of over a hundred miles or a passage by sea.

The Grand Canal, south of the Liffey, played a considerable role in the development of the Irish economy, and the Company's records reflect the extension of trade in central Ireland from 1780 onwards. The canal was begun in 1756 by the Inland Navigation Authorities, but a group of influential business men, including Sweetman the brewer, the leading members of the Dublin Corporation and members of the House of Commons, in 1772 formed the Company of the Undertakers of the Grand Canal to expedite its construction. The Company was given government support, and began its work on the canal in 1774. By 1779 the first stretch of water was opened from the canal harbour in Rainsford Street near James's Street to Robertstown. Over the next few years the canal was extended, at great cost, to Edenderry, across the Bog of Allen. In 1784 a link from Canal Harbour across James's Street to the Liffey was begun but never finished. The first twenty miles of canal cost £190,000 and took fourteen years to complete. The abortive link to the Liffey cost £30,000.

The traffic in the early years was mainly of gravel and coal from Kilkenny to Dublin, and of dung from Dublin to the farms along the canal. Passenger traffic was very small and at first travellers had to lie on their faces as they went under three of the bridges. The Royal Canal, to the north of the Liffey, was engaged mainly in agricultural traffic, and in 1789 the directors of the Grand Canal wrote to the directors of the Royal Canal suggesting a junction at Kinnegad, 'thereby [the Royal Canal Company would obtain] the most advantageous junction with the Kilkenny collieries near Athy an object of great importance in the carriage of coal of those collieries for fuel and manufacture and culm for burning lime for manure'. The canal traffic was already important. Parliament realized this. The coal traffic was encouraged by a government bounty of 2s. a ton on fuel brought to the city of Dublin by inland navigation or along the coast. The Canal Company favoured the granting of this bounty to turf—the name given in Ireland to peat—and sought other aid. In 1789 the Company was given £57,100 to extend the canal to the

22

Shannon; the remainder of the money was borrowed on debentures at 5 per cent, and by 1790 the total expenditure was over £300,000. Land belonging to a subsidiary canal, the Circular Road Canal, was bought in 1790, providing a new harbour at Rathmines to which the first lock was linked. This canal was dug by the Grand Canal Company at a cost of over £70,000. The years 1789–95 marked the peak of activity in Irish canal building. The Royal Canal was also being constructed in a line towards the Shannon above Athlone: the two companies were rivals for trade and for water, but the Grand Canal won continually.

The canals were beautifully built, and had harbours, quays and storehouses at all the main points. There were hotels for passengers, and sometimes police stations to protect the workers. The Grand Canal Company was allowed to carry passengers but not goods; consequently the commerce was carried by agents.[1] These were merchanting firms owning boats on the canal, with warehouses of their own at the ports.

In 1804 the Grand Canal reached Shannon Harbour[2] near Banagher on the Shannon (where Anthony Trollope was later to be a Post Office surveyor), and subsidiary routes were built as relief schemes. The most important of these reached Ballinasloe in 1827. The river Shannon was crossed by a ferry drawn by a winch; the horses crossed on the ferry itself and the barges were towed. The Grand Canal had a leading part in the growth of Guinness's trade, and Shannon Harbour became a great distributing centre.

Though the results of Irish canal construction in the eighteenth century were fairly disappointing, their construction reflected the concern of the Dublin Parliament with economic development, particularly in Dublin. Other enterprises had more enduring consequences. With the growth of population the city began to expand first, for a short time, westwards and then eastwards, and the civic authorities undertook the building of additional bridges over the Liffey. Quite early in the century the quays were improved, the North and South Walls were extended, and by 1762 the configuration of the harbour, practically entirely man-made, was completed. These works, together with great schemes for reclaiming tidal lands,

[1] This situation was changed by an Act of Parliament in 1850, when the Grand Canal Company itself became the carrier.
[2] Shannon Harbour is two locks above the Shannon, because in winter flood-waters cover the lower reaches of the canal. See below, p. 203.

were major stages in the commercial expansion of Dublin. The first Custom House was built as early as 1707, and the present building— Gandon's—on a different and more commanding site, is perhaps the city's greatest legacy of the commercial aspirations and architectural distinction of the eighteenth century.

The Georgian charms of Dublin are a result of the decision of the eighteenth-century Parliament to establish the Commission for Making Wide and Convenient Streets. This body had powers of compulsory purchase of houses which obstructed their plans for improving narrow and congested streets. At first the fashionable residential area extended from Capel Street, Mary Street, and Mountjoy Square, across the river to College Green and Dame Street. Later it developed south-eastwards in a leap-frog when the Duke of Leinster built Leinster House, and Grafton Street, Kildare Street, Molesworth Street, South Frederick Street, Fitzwilliam Street and Merrion Square became the new centre of the city. Expenditure on elegant capital cities is an often-remarked feature of poor economies.

There was a flourishing banking system in Ireland linked with London, Bristol and Manchester. In the seventeen-eighties a number of banks were founded including the Bank of Ireland, and soon the maritime economy had an elaborate credit structure of its own. Domestic industries produced goods of quality and repute in Dublin. Cabinet-making, glass, pottery, porcelain and silver were prominent. There was book-binding of distinction and many makers of musical instruments.

The linen industry, the most important Irish industry in the eighteenth century, was localized in the north, chiefly around Belfast. Dublin, because of its market, was the great distributing centre for the industry, the drapers making their purchases in Ulster markets, transporting them to Dublin and selling them there to buyers from England. But Dublin began to lose this trade with the growth of Belfast as a port and the establishment of direct commercial communications with Liverpool and Glasgow. During the late decades of the eighteenth century the textile industries and some others in Britain were beginning to introduce new processes and mechanical improvements. Ireland for the most part clung to old-fashioned methods whose efficiency was not increased by the protective subsidies devised by the Dublin Parliament for their encouragement. The industries which were being fostered were often economic anachronisms. There was one big exception to this generalization. Brewing became a thriving industry.

SLOW GROWTH OF THE MARITIME ECONOMY

The dissolution of the Irish Parliament and the Union with the rest of the United Kingdom under one legislature have invested the year 1801 with a symbolic importance. It may be doubted whether that year had in reality the economic significance sometimes given to it. The two economies of Ireland continued to grow. In the one, the largely maritime economy of Belfast, Dublin and the other towns, the development was healthy. In the rest of the country the subsistence economy continued its expansion under the stimulus of readily available land and the pressure of a population growth at a rate greater than that in the rest of the British Isles. The increase was divided between the two regions, but it was concentrated numerically in the subsistence part; its effect on the demand for manufactured products was negligible because of the lack of connexion between the two.

There were links but they were slight and tenuous, as the division between the economies was fairly sharp. Along the canals, for instance, there was a commercial life connected with the towns. A day's cart-journey from any town the use of money was rare and the conditions of life were very different from those on the farms producing cash-crops. Landlords collected crops and marketed them for cash, much of it being spent outside Ireland, but some going to Dublin. Irishmen went as seasonal labourers to the cash-crop farms in the east of the island and in Great Britain, to earn money to pay the rents for their family holdings. In this way the cash economy extended tentacles into subsistence Ireland, but the penetration was neither deep nor broad. This remoteness, indeed, from the economic mainstream enabled the subsistence economy to continue its career until the disaster of the Great Famine. Its significance is mainly that of the dog in Sherlock Holmes's case, whose significance was that it did *not* bark; the Irish subsistence economy plays a passive role in history until it appears on the stage quite suddenly in 1845.

Around Dublin, Cork and Waterford and in Belfast an economy

The Economic Background

evolved that was closely linked to Britain. It provided the background to the growth of Guinness's brewery. In this environment Guinness's found their market and their finance, their technical knowledge and their business skill, their influence and their reputation.

MONEY AND FINANCIAL RELATIONS BETWEEN IRELAND AND GREAT BRITAIN

There are three reasons why monetary and banking history is crucial to this study.[1] Without a sound monetary system the Irish maritime economy could scarcely have survived. Next, in the early years of the nineteenth century, there was a considerable devaluation of the Irish currency at a critical moment for the encouragement of the Irish export trade. Lastly, the second Arthur Guinness became the Governor of the Bank of Ireland in the year in which the stability of the currency was finally guaranteed. His family and his business were intimately concerned with this process. After 1815 a severe deflation revalued the Irish pound, and at a critical time the spread of the method of payment for labour by money wages was arrested for thirty years. By the suppression of paper money in 1826 the tragic effects of the Great Famine twenty years later were made inevitable.

As usual, there were variations in local circumstances. The province of Ulster (except Donegal) was largely exempt from the worst features of the Great Famine. The system of land tenure there was different from that prevailing elsewhere in rural Ireland. In Ulster gold was the sole circulating medium, and there were hardly any banks until after the inflation in the Napoleonic Wars. Ulster suffered less from the inflation and from the subsequent deflation than the rest of the country. Elsewhere, in the coastal towns and their hinterlands, and more especially in and around Dublin, the circulating medium was partly gold and partly bank-notes.

The smallness of the monetary circulation tended to isolate the Irish monetary economy from the commercial crises that characterized England in the eighteenth century, although there were occasional irruptions in the social fabric which appear to have been similar to those in England and to have occurred at the same time. Credit crises were matters more of commercial than industrial signifi-

---

[1] This section relies heavily on F. W. Fetter, *The Irish Pound* (London, 1955), and F. G. Hall, *History of the Bank of Ireland* (Dublin, 1949), and the sources they cite.

cance, and affected most of all the terms on which government could get credit. The Irish Government could always at a pinch cover its deficits by borrowing from the British Government, so that there was an insulator between London's crises and Ireland's—indeed the protection for Ireland added to Lombard Street's difficulties by causing periodic drains of gold from the Bank of England to boost the Irish exchequer. There were close financial ties with Britain despite the separate governments and currencies. London was the central money market for the country; Dublin and the other cities dealt directly with London for all matters of foreign exchange, except those with Portugal during the Peninsular War, and the connexions of the Irish banks were with London, not with the Bank of Ireland. This bank might well have been an embryonic central bank for Ireland; it was in fact a highly competitive commercial bank.

The main factor in the economic relationship between Britain and Ireland was almost certainly capital movements. It has been assumed in many analyses that there was a drain of capital from Ireland to England of several million pounds a year in the rents paid to absentee landlords.[1] There was, of course, a transfer of some kind for these purposes, but in the present state of knowledge it is impossible to say how great it was. Further, the objections to the payment of these rents may have been confused with a separate issue. There was probably also a loss of gold on current account in some years to finance an excess of imports into Ireland over the yield of Irish exports. There is, moreover, a number of reasons for doubting the figures hitherto presented of the drain of gold caused by the payments to absentees. Many of them are evidently wild guesses, and they vary erratically from year to year and from author to author, and they all clearly grossly exaggerate, because, for instance, in 1797 the gold circulation in Ireland was only £5 m. If there had been a drain from the country on the scale suggested by contemporary polemicists this currency in circulation would have vanished. In fact it had been increasing during the period when the drain had allegedly been taking place. As the economy of the areas where the absentee landlords had their estates was almost exclusively of a subsistence kind, the rents paid in money cannot have been substantial in absolute terms, whatever they were relative to total money

[1] O'Brien, *The Economic History of Ireland, from the Union to the Famine*, p. 516.

27

The Economic Background

incomes. A drain of money capital on the scale suggested would have driven the rural economy to a money basis very quickly because it would have been necessary to finance the loss by sending exports to earn cash in Britain. In fact it is known that the growth of the market economy and the use of money was slow and tenuous. The spread of the market, as Professor Postan has remarked, is one of 'those subtler historical changes which led men away from domestic self-sufficiency and directed them towards shops and market places'.[1] Finally, there is some evidence which suggests that there was a net capital import into Ireland.[2] The outflow from the provinces may have been offset by an inflow from England into the eastern towns of Ireland. Whether the balance of capital import into Ireland as a whole was negative or positive, it was small either way.

THE MARITIME PRICE-RISE

The outbreak of the war with France was the main cause of a rise in prices in the last years of the eighteenth century. The Irish budget became unbalanced, generating an internal boom, partly because of the heavy expenditure associated with the repression of the republican rising of 1798, and partly because of the expenditure voted to fight against France. Price-rises, too, were imported from England, and the demand for Irish exports increased. The breweries, Guinness among them, participated in this boom. The Irish situation became more inflationary than the British and there was a flow of specie to Ireland between 1795 and 1797, which was one of the reasons for the suspension of gold payments by the Bank of England in February 1797. The Bank of Ireland followed suit on instructions from the Lord Lieutenant, and by May 1797 specie payments by all the Irish banks had stopped.

After 1797 the monetary economy became subject to a fairly marked price-rise which was accompanied by a shortage of specie, an increase in bank-note circulation, a rapid increase in prices and

[1] M. M. Postan, 'The Rise of a Money Economy' in E. M. Carus-Wilson, (ed.), *Essays in Economic History* (London, 1954), p. 8.
[2] P.P. 1826-7 (245), vol. VI, pp. 101-3. Evidence of Robert Marshall, Inspector General of Imports and Exports of Ireland, *Report from the Select Committee of the House of Lords to Inquire into the State of the Circulation of Promissory Notes under the Value of £5 in Scotland and Ireland*, reprinted 26 May 1826. There is also a letter from Sir Robert Peel to the Marquess of Anglesey, Anglesey Papers, Northern Ireland P.R.O., Belfast, 26 July 1828, saying that Ireland had received £2·4 m. from Britain, in aid, since 1823.

28

a depreciation of the Irish currency relative to the English. The effects of this were substantially to expand the market for goods in Ireland. That is why the Union of 1801 itself took place against a general background of prosperity although the classes likely to be most vocal were also those who suffered most during the price-rise—the people dependent on money rents and the classes with relatively fixed professional incomes. The Union and the price-rise have been confused and the Union has been blamed for the difficulties felt by some sections of the community which were due in fact to the price-rise.[1]

With the abandonment of the gold standard in 1797 the link between the two currencies, formerly fixed at a ratio of 12:13, was broken.[2] Both currencies became bank-note currencies, and after 1797 the Irish currency continued to depreciate faster than the English. As a result of the inflation, coin of the realm became very scarce in Ireland. Business houses issued I.O.U's and a number of concerns issued token coins. The government took a hand and imported tokens from England. The use of tokens led to a rapid extension of credit arrangements as a means of financing the expansion of business. This was a direct consequence of leaving the gold standard. The use of money substitutes and credit spread rapidly. Another important consequence was that by September 1803 following the rapid inflation in Ireland the Irish pound stood at a discount of 20 per cent to the English pound, except in Ulster where the value of the currency was maintained by disregarding the obligations of the law which restricted the issue of specie. In effect, in Ulster, the use of the Scottish and English currency was general. The use of gold diminished when good banks were established.[3]

The rise in imports in the period 1797–1803 drove the visible trade balance into deficit. The 1798 republican rising in Ireland destroyed confidence, while the Union may have induced the migration of some persons of substance to London. The fears that the Union might not be accomplished or might be overthrown were also discouraging.

---

[1] According to Silberling, the English price-index (1790 = 100) was 170 in 1800 and 174 in 1801: N. J. Silberling, 'British Prices and Business Cycles, 1779–1850', *Review of Economic Statistics* (October 1923), Prelim. vol. v, suppl. 2, pp. 232–5. The Irish index was probably higher.
[2] £100 British was equal to £108. 6s. 8d. Irish.
[3] Foster Papers, Northern Ireland P.R.O., Belfast, D.o.D. 562/2074.

The Economic Background

The Irish pound fluctuated in terms of the English pound according to the state of demand in the two Kingdoms. Usually it remained well below par. In 1804 it picked up as a result of the Treasury transfer to Dublin of the proceeds of an Irish loan, and it rose particularly from 1811 to 1815. This suggests heavy payments into the Irish economy arising from capital imports because the recorded balance-of-trade figures show a substantial deficit which would have been magnified in the balance-of-payments figures by payments for invisible imports. The gap was filled by net capital imports; these were highly probable at a time when the war effort was at its height and the high level of activity at home would have deterred the export of rents. There is occasional evidence of a drain of gold from London which makes the inference a likely one. Gold was so scarce that the transfer of the silver tokens raised problems for the Treasury in London.

The consequences of the inflation were several. Among them was the increase in economic activity. This overflowed into subsistence Ireland. The demand for food in England was growing rapidly and Ireland became England's supplementary granary. All classes save three tended to benefit. The exceptions were the paupers, who were affected by the rise in commodity prices and the consequent scarcity of food for those without cash, some professional persons and the landlords, whose rents appear initially to have risen less fast than prices so that their real incomes tended to fall. The experience of the Irish economy was on the whole one of fairly rapid development. The extension of urban activities and the promotion of industries providing consumer goods might have been expected. The boom in Guinness sales from 1810 to 1815, which are analysed later, was taking place therefore in a prosperous Dublin.

The economic growth of towns was a marked feature of Irish life during the latter part of the eighteenth century and the first part of the nineteenth. Of Dublin Dr McDowell writes: 'The eighteenth century stately and spacious architectural tradition had not snapped with the Union, and in the decades immediately following, in addition to sedate new residential quarters, a number of impressive public buildings and monuments were erected.'[1] The urban expansion was accompanied by employment for builders and shopkeepers

[1] R. B. McDowell, *Public Opinion and Government Policy in Ireland 1801–1846* (London, 1952), p. 41.

The Maritime Price-rise

and the manifold traders and artisans who are necessary for urban life. Parliament voted money to improve roads and port facilities. In most respects many of the war years were years of rising employment for those concerned with the paraphernalia of urban consumer life, no less after the Union than before it.

The depression of the hand-trades, in which Ireland was strong, has been ante-dated. In England the year 1830 marked the greatest employment of handloom weavers.[1] The collapse or decline of the craft trades was a process that began in the textile industries towards the end of the Napoleonic Wars, and continued in other trades throughout the nineteenth century. The small trades flourished in Ireland under Foster as they were flourishing in England under Pitt, and their decline in maritime Ireland is almost contemporary with their decline elsewhere, for the Irish maritime economy was in almost every essential a part of the rest of the British Isles economy. The logic of the situation was that the industries of any region flourished until technical change, aided by falling transport costs, led to the eventual triumph of manufacturing industry. Since manufacturing industry was based largely upon coal and iron and upon the ability of entrepreneurs, it was to be expected that most of its growth was in the north of England and the midlands, rather than in Ireland or elsewhere in the United Kingdom.

For the ordinary Irish consumer these developments meant better and cheaper goods. The standard of living of those who lived in the maritime economy depended partly upon local produce and partly upon imports from England. The influx of cheap imports meant the collapse of many local manufacturers and a consequent decline in employment. There are three issues raised by this chain of events, two of which have often been discussed before and one that has not. First, how far is it true that the failure of Irish manufactures after the end of the war was due to a policy of free trade pursued by the United Kingdom Parliament? Next, how far was the lack of industrial development due to natural or political handicaps, and how far did it reflect the low degree of economic organization in Ireland at that time? Lastly—and this is the point that has been neglected—how far was the establishment of a sound currency based on sterling

[1] In the Anglesey Papers, Northern Ireland P.R.O., Belfast, III, 2 (22), there is a letter from George Howell of Dublin to Lieut.-Col. Gossett, 29 November 1830, saying that 'Celbridge factory is advertising for 100 weavers', showing that the woollen trade had not fallen off 'as mentioned by agitators'.

an important factor in retarding internal economic growth in Ireland?

These three issues are aspects of one problem. Ireland was geographically part of the British Isles, but in some respects it stood apart from the other island. There was insularity but viability was lacking because geographical, cultural and economic frontiers did not coincide.

The alleged 'collapse' of Irish industry after 1815 was in part a replacement of hand-methods of production in wool and cotton by imports from England. The eventual elimination of the greater part of these trades in the maritime economy was effected by cheaper manufactured imports from England, the severe post-1815 depression, and that of 1826, and by the reduction in cross-channel transport costs after 1830 brought about by the introduction of steamships in 1824. Shipbuilding, linen, building and brewing, on the other hand, continued to grow during this period. So did a host of ancillary trades. Those whose livelihoods had depended upon employment in the declining trades were inevitably plunged into poverty unless they found alternative employment. On the other hand, those whose money incomes were unaffected benefited from the flow of cheaper goods. As in England, this process was associated more with the period from 1820 to 1840 than with the twenty years immediately after the Union.[1] Ireland's economic miseries were not the consequence of the Union. One reason why the use of money did not spread far into rural Ireland before the Great Famine was the arrest of growth in the maritime economy after 1815. This was largely due to a restriction of credit, and for that the cause must be sought in the monetary controversies of the time.

DEFLATION AND DEPRESSION

The sudden end of the war in 1815 was followed after a brief interval by a serious depression in the United Kingdom. Probably some 300,000 or more men were discharged from the armed forces. War contracts were cancelled. Employment and output fell. Late in 1815 and early in 1816 there was a short-lived boom, followed by a slump intensified by the high prices of a bad harvest, and the depression

---

[1] It is perhaps significant, however, that the protective duties which survived the Union ceased to operate in 1825.

Deflation and Depression

when it came was severe.[1] From May 1815 to January 1816 the Irish pound went into a further depreciation. This moderated the distress in Ireland arising from falling prices in the British market, by maintaining internal prices to some extent. The depression beginning in 1816 was intensified by the poor harvests of 1817 and 1818, which gave high prices without the high incomes of the wartime boom.[2] These years were among the worst of the nineteenth century.[3] After 1819 there was an increase of economic activity culminating in the boom of 1824–5.[4] From 1820 through the early months of 1825 there was a fairly continuous increase in output and employment.

From 1815 to 1825, the revaluation of the Irish pound depressed exports, and it took a decade to readjust trade to the new currency conditions. Maritime Ireland in the years after Waterloo experienced what Britain was to experience in the twentieth century after the return to the gold standard in 1925.

The situation in Dublin is to some extent unclear. The Irish potato crop failed in 1817, in 1819 and in 1822, and there was widespread distress, but how far Dublin was affected there is little direct evidence.[5] Dublin is not excepted by contemporaries from the general run of the country, and a number of contemporary accounts speak of distress in the year 1819. William Lunell Guinness was on the Managing Committee of the Association for the Suppression of Mendicity in Dublin which reported that in 1819 'an epidemic, brought on by want and improper food during a period of scarcity' had killed many people.[6] The boom of 1819 apparently never reached Ireland.

There was serious agrarian trouble between 1820 and 1828, and

[1] T. Tooke, J. J. and W. Newmarch, *A History of Prices and of the State of the Circulation During the Years 1793–1856* (London, 1838–57), vol. II, p. 11, and p. 15 for the bad harvest of 1816.

[2] W. W. Rostow, *British Economy of the Nineteenth Century* (Oxford, 1948), pp. 32–6. This account relies on Tooke and is perhaps inclined to over-emphasize the importance of harvests.

[3] E. J. Hobsbawm, 'The British Standard of Living 1790–1850', *Economic History Review*, 2nd series, vol. x, no. 1 (August 1957), p. 56.

[4] Rostow, *op. cit.* pp. 110–12, and p. 116.

[5] McDowell, *Public Opinion and Government Policy in Ireland 1801–1846*, pp. 37–9 and pp. 71–3. P.P. 1819 (409), VIII, p. 457, *Second Report from the House of Commons Select Committee on the State of Disease, and Condition of the Labouring Poor, in Ireland*.

[6] *Second Report of the Association for the Suppression of Mendicity in Dublin* (Dublin, 1820), p. 7. This evidence conflicts with that of bank-note circulation as a sign of distress in Dublin in that year.

The Economic Background

a number of Dublin industries and trades collapsed.[1] The reduction in the size of the army particularly affected Dublin. On the other hand, there is no positive evidence that Dublin remained in its post-Napoleonic depression after 1820, and there is evidence that some other parts of the Kingdom prospered. Between 1815 and 1825 the slump in Irish export prices was considerable. Irish butter which had varied between 110s. and 138s. a hundredweight from 1808 to 1815 fell rapidly, to a low level of 73s. in 1823, and remained at about that price for a long time.[2] This is suggestive of a general slump in the maritime economy.

The explanation for the continued depression lies in the severity of the collapse after 1815, a collapse usually associated with the delayed effects of the Union on Irish industry, but really attributable to the deflation following the end of the war, with the reduction in military expenditure, and with the attempt to put the Irish pound on a 'sound' basis which restricted credit inordinately. 1819 was a year of near-famine because of the failure of the potato, and this had the effect of reducing the supply of food to Dublin and so of raising prices. The rise in prices caused a drain on Irish balances in Britain because of the attraction of imports and depression of exports. This tended to depress the exchange as well as causing a drain on gold in the Bank of England; this in turn led the Bank of Ireland to reduce lending in Dublin as soon as it reasonably could and so to intensify the depression.[3]

From 1814 to 1819 the circulation of Bank of Ireland notes and post bills was stagnant or fell; in 1819–20 it rose sharply and then stagnated again. Trade, employment and exports were all down. Between 1817 and 1819 the Irish pound rallied. The Bank of Ireland redeemed some notes in gold. This was deflationary. As opposed to the earlier period, the crisis was being treated not by capital imports but by deflation in Ireland, and by 1820 the depreciation was almost ended.[4] There were bank failures, attributable in part to restriction

---

[1] O'Brien, *The Economic History of Ireland, From the Union to the Famine*, p. 386.

[2] Tooke and Newmarch, *A History of Prices and of the State of the Circulation During the Years 1793–1856*, vol. II, p. 408, gives butter prices *ex* Waterford.

[3] The statement in the text must be modified to some extent because there was a rise in the circulation of notes and post bills in 1819. This rise was, however, attributable to the replacement of gold withdrawn from circulation. The delay of a few months between the repayment of gold to London by gold withdrawn from circulation and the withdrawal of gold substitutes modified the force of the credit squeeze.

[4] Fetter, *The Irish Pound*, pp. 53–8.

34

Deflation and Depression

of credit by the Bank of Ireland and to bad trade. Gold, by February 1821, was at a discount to Bank of Ireland notes, and gold payments were resumed in June. The Irish pound settled at its usual discount to the English pound of about nine points, and the Bank of Ireland adopted a policy of exchange stabilization that lasted until the assimilation of the two currencies in 1826.[1]

The second Arthur Guinness and his connexion William Peter Lunell, were the two directors of the Bank deputed in 1826 to explain this policy of exchange stabilization to the Select Committee of the House of Commons on Promissory Notes in Scotland and Ireland, and were presumably closely connected with the administration of the policy. The Committee were strongly prejudiced against paper money and their questions were directed to show that it was of no advantage to business and that its use was in itself inflationary and led to unsound credit. Benjamin Lee Guinness wrote to his correspondent in Liverpool in 1826 that his father was 'much occupied with bank business'. The Bank of Ireland was conceived of by them as an agent for maintaining a steady link with London. The policy of assimilation was inevitably extremely deflationary for the Irish maritime economy. It is ironical that the policy with which Arthur Guinness was associated as a banker was one of the causes of his ten bad years as a brewer.

His views were strongly held. The Committee inquired:[2]

'Are you of opinion, that if a law was passed, after due notice, prohibiting the issue of all notes under £5, any considerable inconvenience would arise to the commerce and general pecuniary transactions of Ireland?'

'I conceive, that after due notice, and some considerable time being given, such a change in the circulation of the country might be effected without prejudice to the general commerce of Ireland; but I am of opinion, that it would be attended with some inconvenience in the smaller pecuniary transactions....'

'Do you, or do you not conceive that there would be benefit arising from such prohibition that would more than counteract any inconvenience that might arise from the want of the small notes?'

'I conceive that a wholesome circulation is essential to the permanent prosperity of the country, and that such a prohibition is calculated to correct and improve the circulation; but in the present instance I do

[1] *Ibid.* pp. 58–61.
[2] P.P. 1826–7 (245), vol. VI, p. 400. *Report of the Select Committee of the House of Lords to Inquire into the State of the Circulation of Promissory Notes under the Value of £5 in Scotland and Ireland.*

35   3-2

not think such a corrective so essential as it might be under other circumstances.'

'Would there not be less likelihood of a run upon you, in case of alarm, or a general derangement in the country, if a considerable proportion of the circulation was in the precious metals, rather than in small paper?'

'I think, if the circulation of England was placed upon the footing now proposed, the state of the exchange between England and Ireland, which is extremely sensible, would in a great degree correct the circulation in Ireland; but at the same time I admit that we might be more exposed to fluctuations than we should be if we were precisely assimilated to the state of England. I however conceive those fluctuations can never be excessive, for the reasons already given.'

The ultimate consequences of the revaluation of the currency and the restoration of specie in Ireland were of the greatest political and economic significance. It is possible, indeed, that the reduction of the circulating medium in this period was a major factor in limiting the growth of the use of money in rural Ireland, and that the depression of demand resulting from the pressure on credit was a cause of many of the ills attributed later—and mistakenly—to the Union. That this depression would have occurred even if Ireland's Parliament had remained in College Green cannot reasonably be doubted.

[2]

The Irish Brewing Industry Before 1772

To consider in what manner it might be expedient to give encouragement for the establishment of good public breweries in different parts of this Kingdom. (*A resolution of the Dublin Society appointing a committee in 1771.*)

INTRODUCTION

THE COMPARATIVE advantages of the average producer in the Irish food and drink industries in the early eighteenth century were not substantially less than those available in England. A number of breweries were firmly established in Ireland in the first decades of the century. An adequate supply of barley was at hand, although the quality of Irish malt frequently evoked criticism. Transport was improving and technical skill could be imported relatively easily. Gradually commercial brewing was able in some cases to outgrow the domestic form of organization, especially in Dublin and Cork, and some of these breweries achieved a considerable degree of technical development. In Dublin the growing population of the city afforded a market, increasing in size but geographically limited, in many respects ideal for the economic distribution of a non-keeping beer, brewed for early consumption. The industry suffered a setback, however, about the middle of the century from which it did not recover for twenty years. Brewing failures were common. The businesses which weathered the depression, however, emerged stronger and more efficient.

Brewing was one of Dublin's principal industries and the affluence of the brewing families was sufficient to enable them to enter society early in the eighteenth century. The Leesons left their brewery to become Earls of Milltown, but it soon became possible to move in society without having to give up the trade. By the end of the century brewing was an occupation consistent with high social position. Brewers, some with native names like Farrell or Byrne, came to live in the most fashionable parts of Dublin. The use of the description 'an eminent brewer' in contemporary writing testifies as much to the extent of the craft as to the general esteem of the person on whom it

37

was conferred. Brewing was a prosperous occupation and one of the few successful forms of Irish industrial enterprise. In Dublin particularly it was the outstanding and most lasting industrial enterprise of the eighteenth century. Its progress owed much to the maintenance of long-established standards in the manufacture of its produce, in business relations and in concern for its customers. The survival of these less tangible, but no less distinctive, aspects of achievement in the eighteenth century is evidence quite as conspicuous as that preserved in stone of the discrimination and accomplishment of Georgian Dublin.

The increasing amount of legislation concerning Irish brewing reflected the importance of the industry in the eighteenth century, but more significantly, perhaps, it was evidence of the proliferation of controls which the law imposed on the brewers. The list of restrictions was as varied as it was long. It ranged from investigations by the House of Commons into the by-laws of the Brewers' Corporation to penalties on brewers' dray-men for abusing 'by ill-language, or otherwise, any person passing by'.

The question that the historian must pose is: to what may be attributed the rise of the Dublin brewing industry? Was its rise due to cost and price advantages springing from technical progress and good local raw materials? Or was the quality of Dublin beer exceptionally good? Was its growth a response to a rapidly expanding urban market with cash to spare to buy manufactured drink? Was its rise due to political favouritism by the Irish Parliament? Before answering these questions it is necessary to glance at the position of brewing in the mid-eighteenth century when the first Arthur Guinness came to Dublin to set himself up as a brewer.[1]

THE DRINK

In England, and especially in London, at the beginning of the eighteenth century there was already a variety of exceptionally strong beers with such names as 'Pharaoh', 'Huff-cup' and 'Knockdown'. Some of these brews were so strong that their retail price was double that of ordinary beer. They were described as 'stout', and the enthusiastic if critical opinions of contemporary English writers suggest that high standards had been attained in their manufacture in the two decades after 1700.

[1] See *The Complete Brewer* by *A Brewer of Extensive Practice* (Dublin, 1766).

The Drink

Mixtures of ale, beer and 'twopenny'[1] became popular in ale-houses and taverns in the eighteenth century. Customers who favoured a mixture of ale and beer called for a quart of 'half and half'; those who wanted a portion of 'twopenny' added asked for 'two-thirds' or 'three-threads'. Andrew Campbell states that another kind of 'three-threads' included a stronger beer which having achieved maturity in cask was called 'stale'. A brewer named Harwood, in Shoreditch, East London, is said to have produced from a single cask in 1722 a beer with the characteristics of this kind of 'three-threads'. This innovation dispensed with the necessity of drawing three liquors from separate barrels, yet combined the flavour and qualities of the three in a manner that immediately satisfied popular demand. The character of the dark brown component of the 'three-threads' was introduced by the employment of a considerable propor-tion of highly dried 'brown malt' in the mixture of malts used for brewing. The new drink was called 'entire' or 'entire butt' because it was drawn from a single butt or cask. Subsequently it was called 'porter' because many of its consumers were porters or manual labourers. There are references long before 1722 to porters' beer and ale, which presumably were mixtures of more than ordinary strength. From this time onwards, however, the word 'porter' was increasingly used to designate the new beverage 'entire' which is believed to have been first sold in 'The Blue Last' in Shoreditch. The word 'stout', sometimes used as a synonym for porter or 'Extra' porter, may be an adaptation of the earlier term for unusually strong and very dark beers.

The new drink was highly hopped, stronger than ordinary beer but weaker than ale. It differed from pale ale because of its darker colour and because it was brewed with soft rather than hard water. Brewed specifically to keep, its flavour actually improved on keeping. It had great public appeal, and as it could be kept in stock it led to savings for the brewers and opened the way to mass production. Areas outside a localized market around the brewery could now be supplied as soon as suitable transport was available. It was later discovered that a considerable saving in extract could be obtained by replacing the brown malt used for porter by a much smaller propor-tion of a more highly coloured malt made by drying at a much higher temperature than the brown malt. The new malt was known as 'patent brown malt'.

[1] 'Twopenny' was a third classification of beer.

39

The advantages of commercial brewing were that these products could be given a consistent quality, and the economies of brewing in bulk could be passed on to the consumer by making it cheaper for him to buy beer than to make it, and to the retailer by making it cheaper for him to buy wholesale than to run his own brewhouse. The quality of commercially brewed beer seems to have been better and more reliable than that of the publican brewers.

There were doubts about the quality of Dublin beer in the eighteenth century. In the early decades, and perhaps even later, it was almost certainly a brown beer brewed with a highly coloured malt. A ballad of 1725, 'The Old Cheese', is unflattering:

> This beer is sour—thin, musty, thick and stale,
> And worse than anything except the ale.

Standards of brewing improved as production passed into the hands of the common or commercial brewers, who had become incorporated in 1696.

LOCATION

The contiguity of Dublin and Cork to barley-growing areas was an important element in determining the situation of the Irish brewing industry, because it was possible to use local raw materials and it was somewhat more expensive to import English malt. Wexford, Kilkenny, Cork, Offaly, Leix, Tipperary, Louth and Kildare, counties with low soil acidity, became the barley-growing counties. In the eighteenth century, when land transport was slow and primitive, breweries were established as close as possible to their market and their principal raw material. The demand of the breweries for barley encouraged the cultivation of the crop in the surrounding areas. Brewing helped to bring these farming districts into the cash economy of which they formed an important part.

The advance of brewing might have been more rapid in eighteenth-century Ireland but for the enormous resistance to change of the subsistence economy. The counties beyond the maritime hinterland neither bought beer nor supplied barley to be malted. Malt was the basis for the manufacture of illicitly distilled spirit which, because of its cheapness, was then the national drink. It was extremely concentrated and so fairly easily transported. It was also sold in the maritime economy for cash and helped to pay the rent. A deterrent to tillage, and so to barley growing, in the maritime economy was the exemption after 1735 of pasture-land from tithes. Parliament made several attempts to stop the decline in tillage during the half-century that followed. Little success was achieved until after 1759 when an Act was passed to provide bounties on corn transported from all parts of the country to Dublin.[1] The condition that corn had to be brought to the capital to qualify for bounty may have increased the subsequent cost of corn to the consumer outside the capital, but it ensured that supplies were always available in Dublin. In this way the bounty conferred on the Dublin brewers a benefit unintended by the legislature. The bounty helped to turn the tide in favour of tillage although its effects did not become fully apparent until the last decades of the century.

There was a close connexion, therefore, between the growth of the Dublin brewing industry and the development of Irish agriculture. Further, an important part of the cheapening of beer was the removal of the duties on hops. There was a continual failure to grow hops in Ireland although the Dublin Society offered prizes for their cultivation. In a letter from John Foster to Sir R. Heron on the subject of taxation (31 August 1779) the following remark is made:[2]

For our Breweries—by exempting from the additional duties, all Beer and Ale brewed on *Hops of Irish Growth*—while we depend for Hops on another Country, our Brewery rests on a very precarious Footing, and exclusive of a consideration for the Brewery I know nothing more likely to encrease the Plantation of Trees.

[1] Arthur Young described this act as 'one of the most singular measures that have anywhere been adopted; that is giving a bounty on the inland carriage of corn from all parts of the Country to the Capital'. At first it provided that the corn should come from more than ten miles from Dublin, but an amending Act of 1767 fixed the distance at five miles. The rate of bounty for malt was 2½d. per mile for 5 cwt. and for barley 1½d. per mile for 5 cwt. Arthur Young, *Tour in Ireland*, vol. II.

[2] John Foster, the last Speaker of the Irish House of Commons (1740–1828), was a Dubliner who represented first Dunleer and then County Louth, and became Chancellor of the Irish Exchequer in 1784. During his year of office, before he became Speaker, he introduced the corn law which bore his name, imposing duties on the import of corn and bounties on its export. This law was a mark of his high ability as a financier. He was a loyal member of the government party until in late 1798 (after the republican rising) the government proposed the union of the Parliaments, when Foster came out strongly against Pitt. For four years he was an opponent of Pitt, until in 1804 he again became Chancellor of the Irish Exchequer, a post he held until 1811 except for the period of the Ministry of All the Talents in 1806–7. Later he became Lord Oriel. His opinions, recorded in his papers, are of great value; he has many claims to be a most considerable figure in Irish history.

41

The Irish Brewing Industry before 1772

The Dublin breweries in the early decades of the eighteenth century served the same localized market as the bakers. They bought their barley from the adjoining counties and imported their hops from England. For the most part they were maltsters as well; the differentiation between brewers and maltsters had not yet taken place. Most brewers were publican brewers. The market was evidently the crucial factor in location.

BREWING TECHNIQUE

As the century advanced the more successful brewers expanded the scope of their operations and gradually began to absorb their less enterprising competitors; they discovered that by brewing porter, which was a robust product, there were advantages in enlarging the scale of their production within a single plant; for brewing, unlike other industries, did not have to await the application of steam before large-scale production was possible. Once the malt had been elevated and extracted—and all this needed was power to raise the malt and hot water and machinery which could be worked by hand to grind the malt and mix the mash—the process could be continued (in a tower brewery) without any further use of power as long as each succeeding vessel was situated below the one before it. No single new invention was necessary to enable the brewers to cater for the expanding market. Capital was needed to finance bigger plant but the use of bigger vats did not involve a proportionate increase in the number of workers. In this way substantial cost savings could be made, just by the application of elementary principles of commonsense technology—provided that the market was big enough to absorb the extra output. As costs fell so did prices and this helped to extend the market. It was possible in the brewing industry, as in no other, to achieve industrialized manufacture on a large scale by harnessing the forces of gravity. And since specialization is limited by the extent of the market, the growth of the market was vital. An increase in the scale of production realized economies which could not readily be secured in the production of solid goods until the adoption of steam power.

The first great scientific inventions were not applied in the brewing industry until late in the eighteenth century. The thermometer did not come into general use in Britain before 1780, although Combrune

42

introduced it in his own brewery in France nearly twenty years earlier. Before this the brewer relied on his thumb as a means of judging temperature. Four years after the general acceptance of the thermometer John Richardson gave a detailed description of the saccharometer, by the use of which it was possible to determine the specific gravity of the wort (or unfermented liquor). Exact regulation and calculation were made possible by the use of these two instruments. In particular the saccharometer made it possible to brew beer of the same strength from day to day and thereby take advantage of the higher extract of the better malts. Before this a given amount of malt was used to produce a given amount of beer: if the malt was better the beer was stronger; if it was worse the beer was weaker. As the scale of production in breweries grew, precision in measure became more possible. It also became more necessary to the making of profits by cost savings.

In Dublin, however, in the eighteenth century the brewers were at a much earlier phase in the evolution of the industry. They had access to two of their raw materials—barley and water; hops, for a time, they were able to import on advantageous terms, because of the benefit of the drawback payable on exports from Britain. They had the stimulus of a growing market, which could be served by economical transport arrangements. They were less burdened by taxation than British brewers. Yet throughout the century consignments of beer from London, Bristol and Liverpool were, despite transport costs, able to secure a market in Dublin and present the Dublin brewers with serious competition in the second half of the century. The superiority of English beer and its cheapness is the only adequate explanation of the failure of the Dublin brewers to cater satisfactorily for the city's demand for beer at that period. They lacked knowledge of developments in the technique of brewing; and they were too small to buy bigger capital equipment. Nor was there a tradition of experimentation. These disadvantages set limits to their progress for a large part of the eighteenth century. The consequences were perhaps best demonstrated by the failure of Irish brewers to exclude British competition from their domestic market when the Irish system of taxation conferred positive benefits on them.

The Dublin Society encouraged technical advance in the brewing industry. As early as 1744 it granted premiums to brewers who used the greatest quantities of Irish hops. In 1764 the Society granted premiums to persons who sold by retail the greatest quantity of Irish porter. In October 1765, Thomas Andrews of New Row, Dublin, on the River Poddle, was awarded £62. 6s. 6d. (representing 1d. a gallon) for 14,958 gallons of porter brewed by him since 1 June 1764. Andrews was, presumably, the first Dubliner to brew porter sufficiently reputable in quality to attract the favourable attention of responsible people.

The Society appointed a committee in 1771 'to consider in what manner it might be expedient to give encouragement for the establishment of good public breweries in different parts of this Kingdom'. In its recommendations in March 1772 the committee's report emphasized the need for discouraging the consumption of gin and poteen which 'were equally damaging to health, morals and manufactures'. The way to do this was to build breweries throughout the provinces. They proposed that a premium of 4s. a barrel 'should be given on the first 1000 barrels of ale of the value of 30s. per barrel (first cost to the retailer) which shall be made and sold out of any one brewery which shall be erected after 25 March 1772'. The Society adopted these proposals subject to the condition that no brewery within twenty miles of the city of Dublin should be eligible. The campaign launched by the Dublin Society did not have widespread success and twenty years later beer had achieved little popularity outside the larger towns.

In 1772 the Society corresponded with the French brewer, Michael Combrune, then settled in London and widely known as the author of *The Theory and Practice of Brewing*. The naivety of the correspondence is an indication of the backwardness of the industry at that time. Combrune explained that there was no royal road to good brewing, but that there were certain general principles: bad beer might be brewed from good malt, but the foundation of brewing good beer was good malt. He rejected the view of certain Irish brewers that the defects in Irish porter were due to bad hops and bad barley; he attributed the defects to bad malting. With proper materials, suitable utensils and a skilful 'artist' it would be possible, he said, to brew in Dublin porter similar to that brewed in London.

Combrune's reputation both as a theoretician and practitioner was high. His theory was mostly wrong and he can be looked on as the last of the brewing 'alchemists'. Nevertheless he was himself a successful brewer, possibly because he did not follow his own theories.

44

THE INDUSTRY'S ORGANIZATION

The Brewers' Corporation enabled the Dublin brewers to mobilize their influence and resources effectively. They had a representative on the Dublin City Council and they maintained vigilant relations with Members of Parliament, especially with Members who exposed their grievances, supported the brewers' interests or served what the brewers regarded as the public good. They made a practice during the eighteenth century of rewarding their friends with the Freedom of their Corporation or with presentations. William Pitt became a Freeman in recognition of his endeavours to check corruption, and Sir Lucius O'Brien received their thanks and a gold box for his 'disinterested conduct' in Parliament. They also addressed themselves to more general aspects of public policy, advocating for instance the expenditure of Exchequer funds on canals to improve the transport of fuel; their concern for the public good may or may not have been as disinterested as the conduct for which they commended Sir Lucius O'Brien.

The most useful and rewarding work of the Guild was performed when they directed their experience and practical knowledge to the problems of the brewing industry. Their usual practice was to appoint committees of their members to investigate and prepare reports on fiscal grievances, threats from the distilling industry or foreign competition, and on proposals for desirable reforms. When these reports were considered the Corporation, if they thought fit, made representations to Parliament. Pressure on Parliament was gradually intensified during the difficult decades in the second half of the century. In June 1767 the Guild gave consideration to one of the most fundamental questions affecting the industry, when they debated whether or no the excise tax on beer and ale should be replaced by a tax on malt.

Throughout the period the majority of breweries in giving their official style and title did not differentiate between their products; it may be assumed, therefore, that a number of them manufactured some porter in addition to other kinds of beer. Many of these breweries were no doubt small, and some of them short-lived, but throughout Guinness's concern grew in size and importance.

45

The Irish Brewing Industry before 1772

At the beginning of the eighteenth century the annual output of Irish beer was about 600,000 barrels. By 1772 it had fallen to 433,000 barrels, and imports which had averaged about 300 barrels a year in the seventeen-twenties were now approaching 50,000 barrels a year. The year 1772 was, in fact, that in which Irish brewing began to recover from the twenty-year-long depression.

For decades the brewers had been spasmodically presenting complaints to Parliament without achieving results. Their declining fortunes in the seventeen-fifties impelled them to adopt a more consistent and single-minded approach. Competition from British brewers was their main concern. By 1745 porter in England was being linked with bread as one of 'the two great pillars of life', and as, 'from nearly universal usage, an indispensable beverage'. It was certainly not yet an indispensable beverage in Dublin, though the complaints of the city's brewers left little doubt of its growing popularity. The Dublin brewers Joseph and Ephraim Thwaites told as much to the Irish House of Commons in 1763.[1] Their brewery, which had paid over £100,000 in revenue since 1743, had at great expense tried to manufacture Irish porter and had at last perfected the process. But British competition was threatening their enterprise. They urged restrictions on imports which, they said, would give an assured future to the Irish brewing industry. The revenue would gain as well; as the excise was much heavier than the customs duty, increased consumption of Irish porter would benefit the Exchequer.

Two years later the Brewers' Corporation were pointing to the increased consumption of spirits as their enemy. However much force there may have been in these contentions, it would seem that the poor quality of Irish beer at this time was largely to blame for the brewers' troubles. According to an official memorandum,[2] Irish malt liquor was 'scarcely drinkable;...if the brewers improve their beer and ale, it will greatly increase the consumption; for it is notorious that in the County of Wexford, and other counties, where the beer is of good quality, no other liquor is drunk by the commonalty...'. One thing is clear—the excise returns had been falling steadily, from £146,000 in 1762 to £96,000 in 1772.

---

[1] I.C.C. vii, 212 (1796 ed.).
[2] *Home Office Papers*, Col. 1766–69. Sec. v, 436, pp. 60, 61.

The Trend of the Industry

The market for commercial beer at this period was restricted to the towns, and to the better-paid classes in the towns. The drink of the majority and of nearly all rural drinkers was spirits or home-brewed beer. In writing the history of the industry of that time, therefore, the focus of attention is several social classes higher than that of a similar study in the later nineteenth century. Guinness's porter even at 4*d.* a quart was expensive for a working man earning at most between 5*s.* and 10*s.* a week, with a big family and irregular employment, and it was quite impossible as a drink for the almost moneyless peasantry. The important market in Ireland for commercially brewed beer in the eighteenth century was the better-off section of the Irish population—the artisans and their betters. These social classes were largely confined to the maritime economy at that time. It was therefore natural that the Irish brewers should look across the Irish sea for markets where essentially similar social classes were to be found with adequate incomes and a taste for commercially brewed beer.

The emergence of the working class as beer drinkers was a profoundly important change in the nature of the demand for beer. It occurred first in England, and it was helped by temperance legislation against the gin trade. The changing social pattern with the emergence of a prosperous middle class and a well-paid artisan class, and the expression of public disapproval of spirit consumption, was the background of the growth of commercial brewing. The market was available and increasing, therefore, soon after 1750. A variety of considerations determined the response of the brewers. Most important, perhaps, was the development of a retailing system for distributing the beer.

RETAILING

The number of publicans in the Irish towns was very large. Some were themselves brewers. Their products were often bad, but if they were at all successful they usually became common brewers and supplied other publicans. In rural Ireland, however, the number of publicans in anything approaching the modern sense of the word was very small; the usual source of supply in that almost moneyless society was the fair, or the travelling vendor. Such shops as there were sold everything. Publicans and the licensing-system were to be found only in the towns where the monetary economy was established.

47

The effect of the licensing-system was to reduce the number of publicans by making it more expensive to enter the trade and to remain in it. This restricted the possibility of competition, and put a premium upon close relationships between the common brewers and the licensees whom they supplied, because the brewers wished to reduce the retailers' margins in order to keep prices down. This they could only do by controlling the retailers. Because the licensing-system was less rigorously enforced in Ireland than elsewhere the premium arising from restricted entry was not so high as in Britain, and therefore one important element in the development of the tied house—the publican who sold only one brewer's beers—was absent.

In Ireland the licensing-system originated much later than in England. The first statute in the reign of Charles I required that alehouses and tippling houses be licensed annually by commissioners who were justices appointed for each county, with other persons selected by the Lord Deputy. Two beds, at least, for travellers had to be provided—a condition designed to meet the scarcity of inns in Ireland. The licence-holder was required to enter into recognizances for the good conduct of his house and pay a licence duty of 5s. 6d. The administration of the law was lax, however, and illicit retailing of beer and ale, as well as wines and spirits, continued for more than two centuries.

The first recorded reference to the tied house is in 1780 when the Brewers' Corporation complained to Parliament that a few brewers had cut prices 'which means a falling off in the quality' of their porter. In an attempt to undersell one another these brewers were, according to the petition, 'setting up sundry persons in different parts of the town to retail their porter at 3d. per quart, whereby the publicans' profit is much reduced...'.[1] But it was only in the early decades of the next century that reference became frequent to attempts by brewers to control publicans.

It was a custom among Irish brewers in the eighteenth century to offer 'douceurs' or free gifts to retailers as bribes to sell a particular kind of beer. The practice was illegal, but the prohibition was almost impossible to enforce. The law could be flouted by a resourceful brewer. Gifts were mostly given when trade was bad. A distiller named Brophy, giving evidence before a Dublin Parliamentary

---

[1] *Journals of the Irish House of Commons*, x, p. 100, 22 April 1780.

Retailing

Committee in 1792, blamed douceurs for the decline of brewing; but it seems more than likely that he was confusing cause with effect.[1]

The distinction between the giving of douceurs and other trade practices such as allowing credit, the granting of rebates for cash or quantity, is not easy to draw. A retailer might be promised a drawback if he settled his accounts before Christmas, or a brewer might offer a customer a quarter-barrel 'on trial'. Any douceur, gift or unauthorized rebate, however, was a breach of the regulations.

The peculiarity, then, of the licensed trade in Ireland was that there was a large number of publicans, and probably because of this the incentives to a tied-house system were less strong there than in England. This had a significant effect on the growth of the Guinness trade which came to be based on a conscious withdrawal from retailing. It might easily have been otherwise.

SPIRITS

In Ireland in the early eighteenth century whiskey became the staple drink of the peasantry. It was easily made, needed no hops, took very much less time to produce and contained a great deal more alcohol than the strongest beer. The last recommendation was probably not the least important.

At the beginning of the century less than 200,000 gallons of spirits were known officially to be distilled annually, and annual imports amounted to something over 300,000 gallons. By 1762 both imports and home production were officially recorded as having trebled. By 1768 imports were more than 2,400,000 gallons, and they continued to increase year by year. During the first half of the century the duty was only 8d. a gallon in Ireland, and malt was not taxed.

In addition to the amounts of spirits on which duty was paid there were quantities distilled by small distilleries on which no duty was paid, and the quantity manufactured illicitly was almost certainly larger again. During the first half of the century distilleries were established in great numbers all over the country. A widespread demand for whiskey was satisfied legally and illegally, and this more than anything else except the poverty·of the mass of the people was

[1] *Irish Parliamentary Register*, xii, p. 258.

responsible for the comparative insignificance of the brewing industry. In the impoverished country illicit distilling was widely practised and beer was practically unknown. The authorities were quite unable to restrict illicit distilling, and as taxation was so low on the legal distillers—8*d.* a gallon until 1760, then 10*d.* a gallon—the government were in fact encouraging the industry. Moreover, the landed gentry were bitterly opposed to any attempts to hamper an industry which maintained a steady demand for corn.

GOVERNMENT POLICY

The taxes on beer varied greatly during the eighteenth century, but generally they were higher in England than in Ireland. For the greater part of the century the tax on a barrel of strong beer in England ranged from 5*s.* to 8*s.*; in Ireland, from 2*s.* 6*d.* to 4*s.* 6*d.* The lighter burden of domestic taxation in Ireland might have been expected to place the Irish brewers in a more advantageous position than that of the British brewers. But the Irish brewers were constantly complaining that, even taking the costs of freight and insurance into account, British beer could undercut the native product in Dublin as a result of drawbacks and bounties. In 1741 an Irish revenue duty of 2*s.* 6*d.* a barrel on imported beer tended to equalize the fiscal burdens. There were, however, still grievances. British malt was sold in Dublin, though imports of Irish malt were prohibited in England, thus handicapping those Irish brewers who were also maltsters. As hops were not grown in Ireland, the Irish brewing industry was entirely dependent on imports. After 1710 Britain acquired a monopoly of this trade as the importation of foreign or colonial hops into Ireland was prohibited. The Irish brewers were particularly aggrieved when a drawback was withdrawn in 1720 and a British export tax was imposed. At first this duty was 1*d.* a lb. on hops, but it was increased by 5 per cent in 1739 and again in 1750. Another cause of complaint was the bounty which came into force after 1760. After good harvests there was a bounty of 1*s.* a barrel paid on British beer exports when barley was under 24*s.* a quarter. Early in the eighteenth century there was also a tax on coal.

Adam Smith's views on taxation played an important part in leading to the simplification of the taxation on brewing. In essence,

Government Policy

he regarded all taxation as falling ultimately on consumers, but differing in its effects on industry by the means of its imposition. In his chapter on taxation he wrote: 'It must always be remembered, however, that it is the luxurious and not the necessary expense of the inferior rank of people that ought ever to be taxed. The final payment of any tax upon their necessary expense would fall altogether upon the superior rank of people.'[1]

Brewing he regarded as a particular muddle. First, private people who brewed were exempt from taxation: 'It is difficult to imagine any equitable reason why those who either brew or distil for private use should not be subject to a composition of the same kind.' Secondly, by a number of different 'excises' upon beer, cider and spirits, the opportunity for evasion was substantial, particularly in the distilling of spirits where 'the opportunity on account of the smaller bulk and greater value of the commodity, and the temptation on account of the superior height of the duties' was much greater than in brewing. By imposing a lighter duty on malt the excise would be easier to collect, and less liable to evasion.

According to Smith, by a single duty neither the brewer, maltster nor the barley-grower would pay more in tax than before, because 'no tax can ever reduce, for any considerable time, the rate of profit in any particular trade which must always keep its level with other trades in the neighbourhood. The present duties upon malt, beer, and ale do not affect the profits of the dealers in those commodities, who all get back the tax with an additional profit in the enhanced price of their goods.' He estimated that on the average the duties on malt, beer and ale amounted to 24s. or 25s. 'upon the produce of a quarter of malt'.[2] He suggested that if the various duties on beer and ale were removed and the malt tax trebled, a greater revenue might be raised from this single tax than from the more numerous taxes on brewery produce that then existed.

In short, during the first sixty years of the eighteenth century the English beer duty ranged from 5s. to 8s. a barrel while in Ireland it averaged 4s. a barrel on 'strong' beer. In England in addition there was a tax on malt which increased from 6½d. a bushel to 1s. 4½d. a bushel between the beginning of the century and 1780. A malt tax

[1] Adam Smith, *Wealth of Nations*, Book v, ch. 2.
[2] He calculated that a quarter of malt was seldom brewed into less than two barrels of 'strong' and one barrel of 'small' beer, or into two-and-a-half barrels of 'strong' beer.

of 7*d.* a bushel was introduced in Ireland in 1786. In 1761 a London brewer paid a beer tax of 8*s.* a barrel, and in addition a tax of almost 2*s.* a barrel on the malt content. Without taking into account the small levies on hops and coal he paid almost 10*s.* a barrel to the Exchequer on his output of 'strong' beer. A little later the total taxation levied on the Irish brewer was about 6*s.* a barrel (Irish). But the firmly established English brewing industry could sustain a burden of heavy taxation better than the Irish industry could sustain a lighter burden. What really mattered was the price at which English beer could be sold in Ireland and the relative merits of the products of the two countries.

IMPORTS

When Guinness bought his brewery in 1759 the Irish brewing industry was, in fact, faced with growing competition from British imports. In 1719 about 600,000 barrels (Irish) were brewed in Ireland, and only 299 barrels (Irish) were legally imported while 6408 barrels were exported. By 1761 output had fallen to 588,000 barrels and legal imports had risen to 18,837 barrels while exports had fallen.[1] Henceforward imports, which had exceeded 10,000 barrels a year for the first time in 1747, increased until the last decade of the century. Exports after 1761 remained stationary for about ten years and then began to dwindle. Imports had increased from less than an average annual amount of less than 300 barrels in 1720 to 1988 barrels in 1740; around 1760 imports averaged 13,500 barrels and increased to 47,736 barrels in 1772. In 1764 the average annual amount of Irish 'strong' beer on which duty was paid exceeded 622,000 barrels; in 1772 the amount had fallen to 433,160 barrels.

The import duty on British beer coming into Ireland was only about 10 per cent *ad valorem* whereas the duty on Irish beer imported into Britain was prohibitively high. This no doubt discouraged Irish beer exports, but the comparatively low duties charged on imports of British beer into Ireland are not sufficient explanation of the failure of the Irish brewers to meet the requirements of their home market. Indeed they had been much more successful in achieving this aim in the first half of the eighteenth century before their relative fiscal

---

[1] Samuel Morewood, *A Philosophical and Statistical History of the Inventions and Customs of Ancient and Modern Nations in the Manufacture and Use of Inebriating Liquors* (Dublin, 1838), pp. 707, 726, 727.

disadvantages were eased by the raising of import duties. Irish writers complained vociferously about the unfairness of the fiscal exactions. According to them English beer exports were reaching Ireland in such quantities as almost to ruin domestic brewing. It seems that in the decades after 1750 these exports were a response to a demand for beer of a quality that the Irish brewers could not produce. Not only was beer imported but also malt, suggesting that one fault lay in the quality of local barley and malt (as Alexander, the Norfolk maltster, later pointed out)—indeed the large imports of British malt ultimately benefited Irish brewing by giving it access to good raw materials when its techniques improved.

[3]

The Critical Years: 1773–1795

I will show that the brewer has been sacrificed to the distiller, and to the obstinate and insane whimsies of the revenue empirics. (*Speech by Henry Grattan in the Irish House of Commons.* '*Parliamentary Debates of Ireland*', *2 February 1792*, XII, *p. 52*.)

THE YEARS 1773–95 were critical and decisive for the Irish brewing industry. By 1773 the growth in spirit drinking and the competition of the London porter brewers brought the industry to the verge of collapse. The brewers demanded a repeal of the beer duties as a further aid to their industry, but despite the persistence of their demands they were unsuccessful for more than twenty years. Relief was to come in 1795, but in the meantime the industry was saved by adapting itself to meet popular taste in Dublin for porter. The process of adaptation was inevitably slow, but henceforward many of the brewers who had previously brewed ale were describing themselves as porter brewers. For centuries 'ale' had been brewed from malt only. When hops were introduced the new drink was called 'beer'. With the passage of time the words 'ale' and 'beer' had come to be used indiscriminately, but when certain black beers containing a proportion of roast malt came to be known as 'porter' the word 'ale' was reserved for beers not coloured in this way. Most of the Dublin porter brewers, Guinness included, continued for some years as manufacturers of ale as well, but certainly by 1796 porter became their biggest and most typical product.

In 1773 a Committee of the Irish House of Commons found that the revenue from beer had fallen by £51,000 a year 'not owing to any temporary accident, but to a gradual decay in the trade' and they found that imports had risen and would have risen more but for a bad corn harvest in 1772.[1] According to Thwaites, the Dublin brewer, a quarter of the brewers had failed in the previous ten years, mainly because the high price of raw materials had led them to reduce the use of malt and hops and the drink was less good. Their

---

[1] *Journals of the Irish House of Commons*, IX, App. CLIV, Report made 10 December 1773.

difficulty was that they could not raise prices because of the competition of English porter—'the London brewers have now nearly engrossed the whole trade in Dublin, and send their own factors to sell here to the retailers'. Andrews, another brewer, said that he 'had a mind to set up a brewery at Holyhead' to take advantage of the excise law in England and Wales, and so undersell the Irish brewers. Arthur Guinness, 'another considerable brewer', said that he also had intended 'to set up a brewery at Carnarvon or Holyhead, if he could get a brewery ready built there; and he went to Wales in search of a brewery, and that he would at this day settle there, and build a brewery, if he could be sure that the laws would stand as they are, for seven years'.

The year 1775 was important because the duty on Irish beer was reduced by 5*d.* a barrel. This began a process of legislative encouragement for the trade.[1] The relief helped the industry, though in 1776 the Dublin brewers complained that a clause had been introduced into the Revenue Bill of the previous year 'which if passed into law, must infallibly put a total stop to the brewing in Ireland'. This was a clause forbidding common brewers to brew small beer under the value of 16*s.* a barrel. The object of the clause was to prevent tax evasion. But it was another instalment in the system of regulations which irked all brewers, and particularly handicapped the enterprising ones. The brewers argued that to deprive the industry of the right to sell small beer would prevent it from manufacturing strong beer cheaply enough to attract customers because their breweries had been equipped 'at considerable expense' to produce both types of beer. As a final threat they told Parliament that if the restriction were enacted brewers would emigrate to England which 'might in time prove a very profitable change to them, yet must extremely ignore the poor, who would be thereby deprived of cheap beer or even milk, which in this great city depends upon the grains produced by the brewery'. The claim that the city was indebted to the brewers for its milk supply was a novel one, but in any event the small-beer brewers were reprieved. Soon, however, they were again petitioning Parliament about other tribulations. In 1783 they informed the Commons that it was ruinous for them to face the disparity between the increasing prices of their raw materials

[1] Although a proposal that the duty on imported liquors—including beer—be increased by 2*s.* a barrel was rejected.

and the fixed prices at which they were compelled to sell their product.[1] Even the cost of coal and fodder for horses had gone up. They urged that the law be amended to allow them to sell at 10*s*. 10*d*. a barrel when malt sold for more than 12*s*. a barrel, or hops over 5*s*. a hundredweight, and that hucksters be permitted to sell small beer for 1¼*d*. a quart. Immediate action was required, they said, to save the brewing industry from bankruptcy. The House of Commons—possibly impressed by the force of their arguments— ordered preparation of a Bill to enable small-beer brewers to raise prices when costs of materials rose above certain specified levels.

This action is significant for two reasons. It shows the beginning of the collapse of the old system of state regulation of industry—by fixing prices and qualities, for instance—at the same time as Parliament was endeavouring by fiscal means to encourage some industries and discourage others. The effectiveness of the new mechanism depended on the excise man, while the older system depended on the force of public opinion in a small society, ready to act and to inform if the common rules were broken. The old order was collapsing, and the new order had to wait for a growth in the efficiency of the excise to be effective.

The regulations were, no doubt, vexatious, but some problems of the Irish brewers were more apparent than real. In a Report of the Irish House of Lords in 1784[2] two English brewers—Robert Barclay and Joseph Delafield from Mr Wentbreed's brewery (evidently Whitbread's)—whose houses 'export near four-fifths of the whole' of British exports to Ireland—claimed that the British export trade to Ireland was diminished by an Irish Act regulating retail prices which had reduced their retail profit margins. Further, there was no duty—and at certain prices even a bounty—on malt exported to Ireland which gave the Irish brewers an advantage over the English, who had to pay malt duty. The witnesses were asked directly:

If beer brewed in Ireland was allowed to be imported into England, subject to the duties equal to the excise duties payable on such beer brewed in England, would the English brewer have any reason to apprehend a competition in the market of England?

From the present state of the brewery in both countries, we apprehend there would be no material competition, especially in the article of porter.

[1] *Commons Journal Ireland*, xi, 147.
[2] Report of the Lords of the Committee of Council...on two questions, Dublin, 29 March 1784. *Lords Journal Ireland*, v, 474.

The Critical Years: 1773–95

But if skilful brewers should remove from hence to Ireland, indeed from the present advantages of procuring and manufacturing English malt and hops, free from duties paid by the English brewers, as well as from the low price of labour in Ireland, it is very probable a dangerous competition might in time arise unless Irish beer imported into this country should not only pay our inland excise on beer, but also a further duty, proportionable to the duties paid in England on malt and hops; on both of which, the duties are drawn back on exportation to Ireland, and even a bounty given on malt when barley is under 22s.

The Irish brewers drew little solace from another attempt to help them when the import duty on British beer was levelled up by an increase of 5s. a hogshead in 1789. The flow of imports was hardly affected. The new imposition 'caused a little suspense in the Trade', said Robert Barclay and Joseph Delafield, 'but it soon reversed itself'.[1] These imports, they added, originated mainly in London, though small quantities came from Bristol, Liverpool and Scotland. Freight and insurance charges amounted to 4s. a barrel, or 18 per cent, in 1785, and had fallen to 3s. 6d. a barrel, or 15½ per cent in 1791. As there was a duty in respect of malt and hops of 2s. 6d. a barrel (on which the British exporter received no drawback) the London brewers claimed that their products met their Irish rivals at a disadvantage of 6s. a barrel in Ireland.[2]

After 1775 the Irish Parliament acted—according to its lights—continually in the interests of the Irish brewers. Grattan himself was at the heart of its concern, and as early as 1791 he came out against the government regulation of the trade and against the excise duty on beer. Whether it was an entirely disinterested move it is impossible to say. The *Freeman's Journal* hinted strongly in 1795 that Grattan was in the pay of the brewers and 'upon the honesty of the brewers must be depended in a principal degree the success of Mr Grattan'. It is impossible on the evidence available to make a judgement. One possible explanation lies in his recognition of the strength of the Dublin Brewers' Corporation as a political force. They, in their turn, were well aware of their debt to Henry Grattan, but subsequent events proved their memories to be short or their sense of gratitude to be limited. As early as 1792 they formally thanked him for his support

[1] Evidence to Council of Trade, 11 February 1791. British Museum Add. MSS. 38393 of 24.
[2] Letter of Committee of Council of Trade to Lord Grenville, 8 March 1791. British Museum Add. MSS. 38394 of 141 (ff.).

of the industry and offered him the freedom of their Guild.[1] Five years later Grattan expressed his sentiments towards the Guild:

Gentlemen: The health of Ireland and the prosperity of her brewery I consider as intimately connected. I have looked to your trade as to a source of life and a necessary means of subsistence. I have considered it as the natural nurse of the people and entitled to every encouragement, favour and exemption.

It is at your source the Parliament will find in its own country the means of health with all her flourishing consequences and the cure of intoxication with all her misery.

My wishes are with you always. My exertions such as they are you may ever command.
I have the honour to be,
Your sincere and humble servant,
Henry Grattan.

Whatever his motives, Grattan's arguments about brewing were valid. In his speech in 1791 he held that Parliament for years had sought to encourage brewing, but had not done so in fact. 'It is not so much the duties as the regulations and the methods of enforcement that trammel the industry....It is admitted that the brewery industry in Ireland has declined in the previous thirty years by one-third, whereas every other manufacture has increased.' Excessive regulation was the cause of decline in the quality of the Irish beer. The original complaint was that Irish breweries made weak beer and in an attempt to check this Parliament prescribed specified prices and minimum quantities of hops and malt. 'The effect of the regulations was mischievous; it was to corrupt the malt liquor of the country, and make the beer and ale not strong, but abominable.' The consumers were forced to pay £100,000 a year extra for bad drink while the brewers, not the restrictions, were blamed for it. The removal of some of the restrictions in 1791 had done some good: that should be a reason for removing all the restrictions. The Chancellor of the Exchequer, Beresford, had said,

what he wants is, that Parliament by some law should make the brewers brew good drink. Sir, that interference is the thing that will prevent it— because the brewer, like every other manufacturer should be perfectly free, unrestrained as to the kind of manufacture he shall make, unrestrained as to the quantity, and unvisited by the excise man.

Adam Smith himself could not have spoken more clearly.

---

[1] A gold Freedom Box presented to Grattan by the Guild was bought from Grattan's heirs by Arthur Guinness, Son and Company, Limited, in 1948. It is now on loan to the National Museum of Ireland in Dublin.

The Critical Years: 1773-95

John Beresford[1] became a Commissioner of Revenue in 1770 and, after an advantageous second marriage to Lord Townshend's sister-in-law, he rose to what his biographer calls 'an almost unlimited, though an unobtrusive and hidden, authority in Irish affairs'.[2] As First Commissioner of the Revenue he arranged for the building of the Custom House, helped the work of the Wide Streets Commission, and eventually, under the younger Pitt, was the chief manager of Irish affairs. His biographer suggests that his was the chief influence behind the Union, and there is no doubt that it was his fiscal arrangements which both helped to make it possible and were important in making it work. Consequently it seems probable that his attitude to the revenue should be interpreted in the light of his role as a manager of political matters as well as of a statesman with a budget to balance, and while it might have suited him, as it suited Grattan, to encourage home industry (for which the more astute reader will substitute the words Dublin brewers) he had also to protect the revenue and discourage the opposition to the maintenance of lawful authority. In one year it might be better to fortify the revenue and deny some important interests, in another to deny the revenue and uphold the brewers, as is suggested in a letter from Lord Fitzgibbon to Mr Beresford, 2 March 1795:[3]

On Friday last Mr Forbes came down and moved a string of very absurd resolutions upon the Treasury business....The said Mr Forbes, having thus saddled his ass, proceeded to resolve the House into a Committee of Ways and Means, when and where he abolishes the Excise duties on ale and beer, and proposed an additional tax on malt and spirits....
I believe that you will agree with me that by this most salutory financial operation he has eased the subject of taxes to the amount of £100,000 in the current year.

The debate in the Irish Parliament in 1791 had caused quite a stir in London and embarrassed the government. The British Secretary for Foreign Affairs, Lord Grenville, in a private letter to the Lord Lieutenant of Ireland, the Earl of Westmorland, on

---

[1] John Beresford (1738-1805), the second son of the Earl of Tyrone and the Baroness de la Poer (both in the peerage of Ireland), sat from 1760 to his death as Member for Waterford in the Irish House of Commons and then in the Imperial Parliament after the Union.
[2] *Dictionary of National Biography.*
[3] W. Beresford, *The Correspondence of the Rt Hon. John Beresford, Illustrating the last thirty years of the Irish Parliament, selected from his original papers, and edited, with notes, by his grandson, the Rt Hon. W. Beresford*, 2 vols. (London, 1854), pp. 76-7.

3 February 1791 made a sharp reference to the Irish proposals for combating British beer imports:[1]

I heartily wish that the question about English beer had not been stirred ...I find the difficulties here are thought to be almost insuperable as to the two proposals you suggest, either of withdrawing the bounty here or agreeing to the imposition of any countervailing or protecting duty there. In truth it is not easy to find any reason for doing either of the two last on the subject of beer, which might not be used with equal force on that of any other manufacture which Ireland wished to establish against Great Britain. It is perfectly evident that this cannot be necessary for the sole object of discouraging the sale of spirits, because this would best be done by making *all* beer cheap, whereas the measures now proposed are contrivances for making Irish beer cheap and English beer dear. The business has, however, as its importance required, been sent to the proper Offices for their reports....

In his reply of 8 February 1791 to Lord Grenville, the Earl of Westmorland explained that the debate in the Dublin Parliament had left the Irish Government with no option but to make some concession in favour of remodelling the duties on beer. He had raised the question of the bounty with Grenville so as to be briefed with the opinion of his London authorities on the matter. He went on to say that his proposals, a copy of which he enclosed, had recognized the interests of British brewers in the Irish market. He added:[2]

You will observe...that the English barrel of beer will have an advantage of ten pence (Irish money) over the Irish barrel; it has at present thirteen pence. In conformity to your wishes of not stirring the question, I mean not a word should be said upon the shilling bounty paid in England on the export of a barrel, but that it should be proposed to leave the import duty on English beer exactly as it now stands. By our silence perhaps the present duty may be continued without observation, whereas if we should attempt to continue the preference of English beer over Irish beer thirteen pence, as it now is, by reducing the duty the proportional three pence, we should draw the attention of the Opposition to that point. You must, I am convinced, see that it would be impossible in argument to resist them; and perhaps the clamour upon the injustice and absurdity of giving English beer a preference, at the time that our pretext is to encourage the Irish brewery, [may] make such a preference more unpopular and difficult than the thing is worth. I am in great hopes, as there is some difficulty in understanding the duties, that patriotism will be silent. I would recommend to the English brewers not to open their lips, for you

---

[1] Historical Manuscripts Commission, *Fourteenth Report*, App. Part v, vol. ɪɪ (London, 1894), p. 27.

[2] *Ibid.* p. 30.

The Critical Years: 1773–95

must be sensible that the more the matter is discussed, the more difficulty will be found in making the proposed preference of ten pence in the English barrel; and should it be warmly contested, it will be too unreasonable to desire Parnel or Beresford to expose themselves, and to be abused, with the argument so plain against them for such a trifle; and I am sure the proportioned duties on spirits will fully make amends to the English brewers, by the increased consumption, for the diminished preference of three pence per barrel; or if we should be compelled (which I trust we shall not), the full thirteen pence preference they enjoy at present.

The Foreign Secretary was reassured by the determination of Dublin Castle to leave the import duty on British beer as it stood, and to maintain a discreet silence on the British export bounty.[1] Writing again to the Lord Lieutenant in Dublin on 16 February 1791 Grenville said:

If you can continue the present import duty on English beer, without adverting to the bounty, I as an individual, do not think that any great harm will be done...but I fairly own to you that I think it absolutely necessary for you to resist the idea of laying on any additional duty, or stipulating for our taking off the bounty. You will observe, first, that our bounty is not constant, but is only paid when a bounty is also paid on the export of barley, which is the raw material. And, secondly, that it is a bounty in the nature of a drawback, but by no means a complete drawback of the duties paid here. And, therefore, that nothing can be more unfair or incorrect than to suppose that the bounty operates as a preference *pro tanto* in favour of English beer over Irish. If our brewers were to make up a similar account to that which you sent me, they would state more justly the whole amount of duty paid by them here, and the difference between the bounty and the import duty, as opposed to the 3s. 10d. to be paid in Ireland on Irish beer. I hope, however, these questions will not be stirred, and, if the import duty is not augmented, nor the bounty discontinued, I think our people will be wise enough to be silent.

While these exchanges were taking place between Dublin and London the Committee of the Council of Trade in London were also considering the problem.[2] On 3 February 1791 Grenville had sent them a copy of the Lord Lieutenant's letter containing the proposals for the withdrawal of the bounty on British exports or the imposition of a countervailing or protective duty in Ireland. The Lord Lieutenant had made it quite clear that the effect of the British export bounty had been to retard the development of the Irish brewing

[1] *Ibid.* p. 34.
[2] British Museum Add. MSS. 38394 of 141 (ff.).

61

industry. He had also pointed out that the Irish legislature had the right to demand equality between native beer and British beer sold in Ireland.

The Committee replied to Grenville on 8 March 1791. They repeated the argument that when account was taken of the duties on malt and hops and of freight and insurance charges, British beer in Ireland met the local product at a disadvantage of 6*s*. a barrel. If, however, the Irish Parliament insisted on equality the Committee would recommend the withdrawal of the bounty rather than the imposition of an Irish import duty, which would operate at all times, whereas the bounty had effect only in certain circumstances. The Committee added: 'The share which the beer of Great Britain has at present in the Irish market is solely imputable to the better quality of our malt and to the present superiority of the British brewer in the art of brewing.' They were 'not able to state the precise quantity [of British beer exports to Ireland] from the Custom House Accounts, as They have discovered a very capital Error in those Accounts'. They estimated, however, that between 60,000 and 80,000 barrels were exported annually, and that the total tended to increase.

Grattan attributed the decline in the Irish brewing industry to many causes: the dearness and inferiority of Irish barley; the prohibition on imports of hops from Flanders; the superior quality of imported British malt liquors; the high duties which burdened the industry; the complexity of excessive regulation. The excise duty on strong beer was 4*s*. 6*d*. a barrel, on small beer 10*d*. a barrel, and the excise duty on malt was 2*s*. 6*d*. a barrel. Grattan proposed the removal of excise duties from ale and the imposition of a further duty on malt with the aim of raising the level of taxation on spirits. 'Whatever is adopted with regard to spirituous liquors would be imperfect, indeed, if nothing was done in advancement of the breweries.'

Grattan's proposal that excise duty should be taken off beer was not accepted, but certain concessions were made to the brewers. The excise duty on strong beer was reduced to 2*s*. 6*d*. a barrel;[1] the old regulations were replaced by a less cumbrous code, and revised price limits for beer were fixed. Most important of all, perhaps, was the adoption by Parliament of several resolutions against the excessive use of gin and whiskey, and suggesting that preference

[1] 31 Geo. III, c. 1.

should be given to breweries over distilleries by changing the duties in their favour.

Grattan was thus only partly successful in 1791 and 1792. The Chancellor of the Exchequer replied to his charges and displayed a certain wholesome realism: 'it was as clear as the sun at noon-day that the backward state of the brewery did not arise from the increased consumption of spirits, nor from the increased importation of English beer', but from the bad quality of the drink produced in Ireland. He suggested that the brewers wanted to stop competition by shutting up the market against all good foreign drink so that they might go on making such liquor as the people would not drink while they could get any other. There was a certain amount of truth in what he said.

The following exchange illuminates both Grattan and Beresford— the fiery eloquence of the one and the down-to-earth sense of the other:[1]

Grattan: I will show that the brewer has been sacrificed to the distiller, and to the obstinate and insane whimsies of the revenue empirics.

The Chancellor of the Exchequer: It is of very little consequence to the morals of the people (if they will get drunk) what they get drunk with; it is however the duty of the legislature as much as in them lies, to make the means of intoxication as difficult to come by as they possibly can: this can only be done by laying duties as high as the article will bear. For if you lay a duty amounting to a prohibition, or beyond a certain point, you defeat your own purpose—you indemnify the risque of the smuggler— the article so taxed is produced in greater plenty than ever—the people's morals are corrupted in a double sense by the practice of fraud and the practice of intoxication, and you collect no revenue at all.

The brewers carried on with their campaign. On Tuesday, 14 February 1792, in the Irish House of Commons, Arthur Guinness,[2] brewer, of James's Gate, was examined: he had been for thirty years in the brewing trade, and had never known it in a worse state than at present; of its declining state he supposed the three principal causes were, the encreased consumption of spirits, the consumption of English malt liquors, and the high price of malt. The distillery, he said, at present enjoyed an advantage it had never done before; for by the late parliamentary regulations the consumption of foreign spirits had greatly decreased, by which the consumption of the home spirit was encreased; the wholesale price of spirits was therefore encreased, but the price of the naggin continued

---

[1] *Parliamentary Debates of Ireland,* 2 February 1792, XII, p. 52.
[2] *Ibid.* pp. 121–2.

the same, because the retailer deteriorated its quality. He thought the best mode to encourage the brewery was to imitate the sister country, whose brewery was the first in the world; first, by laying a heavy duty on distillation, by protecting the Irish brewer against the foreign brewer, as England had done, where there is a duty of 25*s.* a barrel on beer imported. The consumption of spirits in Dublin he stated to have encreased 97,177 gallons, in the three quarters ending December 1791, above the three quarters ending December 1790.

Mr J. G. Kennedy, ale brewer, was examined as to the state of the ale trade; by whose testimony it appeared to be declining very fast, the decrease in consumption of the nine months previous to December 1791, being 2452 barrels, compared with the consumption of the corresponding nine months of the year 1790. The best mode of encouraging the trade, in his opinion, would be to remove the excise from the ale, and place it on the malt.

Then on 27 February an attack of a different kind was averted when the House of Commons examined:[1]

Mr Fisher, an Englishman, superintendant of a brewery in this city. The sum of his evidence was, that he had come to Ireland in order to engage in the brewing business, if he found it advantageous, but that not finding due encouragement he had not entered into the trade; that as good beer could be made here as any imported, by using a greater quantity of material; that his opinion, and that of all the English brewers with whom he had conversed, was, that the present flourishing state of the English brewery was owing to the suppression of the use of gin in that country. On being asked, by Mr John Beresford, whether there was less or more spirit distilled at present, in England, than previous to the passing of the gin act? He answered, that in his opinion there was less. (This opinion Mr Beresford declared unfounded, as the quantity of spirit distilled at present, in England, was considerably greater than previous to the passing of that act.) Mr Fisher believed that the sale of malt liquor in this country, depended on the quality of it. The quantity of materials used to a hogshead of porter, he stated at fourteen stone of malt and six pound of hops. The expense of manufacturing a hogshead of porter, he said, was from eight to nine shillings.

Beresford then interrupted:

Mr Beresford thought this charge so extravagant, that he wished Mr Fisher to state the particulars that constituted this expense; which, he said, he was at present unprepared to do minutely: in general, however, the expense consisted in labourers wages, keeping of horses, fuel, rent, and wear and tear of brewery. The weekly sale of the brewery, in which he was concerned, was one hundred and ten hogsheads; the number of horses eight; that of labourers eighteen, at seven shillings per week.

[1] *Parliamentary Debates of Ireland,* 1792, XII, pp. 251–2.

The Critical Years: 1773-95

The Parliamentary Record then continues soberly:

Mr Fisher's examination was here interrupted by the confused noise of persons on the roof; the House was alarmed: Mr Thornton, the clerk, went up to examine what had happened, and in a few moments gave notice from above, that the roof was on fire, and that the dome would probably fall within five minutes. The Speaker instantly resumed the chair, and put the question of adjournment, which passed, *nem. con.*

Notwithstanding every possible assistance was immediately given, the progress of the fire was so dreadfully rapid, that in less than two hours the House of Commons, whose beautiful architecture and disposition had been since its construction the admiration of Europe, was burned to the ground.

Meeting in the coffee room, the House had a full-scale debate on 5 March 1792.[1] Grattan in unmeasured terms repeated his point of view, and then the Chancellor of the Exchequer spoke. He

did not controvert the position that the home-brewery should be supported against imported liquor—but the reasoning did not apply to this instance —for the object of the regulations was to diminish the consumption of spirits by promoting that of malt liquors;—the first was the primary object —the other was but secondary and subservient;—it was therefore right for the committee to compound the imported with the home-brewed beer in their enquiries;—he granted indeed it would be better if the whole consumption were of Irish beer—but it was better it should be of any beer, foreign or home-made, than that the people should still continue in the use of spirits. To prove that the profits of the brewer were fully adequate to enable him to make good drink he recited a record from Chancery, by which it appeared that four partners entered into the brewing business, three or four years back—one of them having a capital borrowed from the others, for which he paid interest—the capital of the company was £6000, and on sharing profits at the end of four years, it was found that the poorer partner's share of profits was £1200 besides his having paid £180 yearly for the interest of his debt. Another shortly died after, and his profits on a capital of £1500 amounted to £2500; thus the profits it appeared were 46 or 50 per cent.

Unfortunately the witness had testified to the great variety of profits being earned by brewers, and this point was not a good one.

For nearly four more years the brewers continued to pursue their campaign with patience and persistence, and helped by the advocacy of Grattan and others they gradually brought the House of Commons to accept their case. A major argument they advanced was that drunkenness in Ireland was dangerously increasing, and according to them whiskey was the real culprit, the instigator of turbulence, the

[1] *Ibid.* p. 269.

inspiration of faction fights—and worse. Beer seemed a wholesome alternative to whiskey. Thus with whiskey exposed as a menace to manners and morals, the brewers found political allies who in their detestation of spirit drinking were prepared to regard the brewing industry as an instrument of social reform. In other centuries and other countries the same battle has been fought with varying degrees of success.

In February 1795 the Dublin brewers reminded the House of Commons of the resolutions they had adopted four years earlier. As the measures already taken had proved 'totally inadequate' the brewers urged Parliament to live up to the spirit of its expressed solicitude for the industry. The brewers proposed the removal of the excise from beer and ale, and an additional duty on malt to replace it; the active discouragement of distilling and additional duties on imported malt liquors; drawbacks for beer exports; the removal of bounties paid on malt brought to Dublin, which they said had encouraged frauds and lessened quality.

Grattan presented the petition to the House of Commons. He recalled that he and others had previously urged Parliament to adopt legislation to restrain the consumption of spirits and to encourage 'the substitution of an wholesome and nourishing beverage for a liquid poison'. As the measures already adopted had not been successful he hoped that more vigorous ones would be proposed. This time Beresford, the Chancellor of the Exchequer, agreed with the principle stated by Grattan, and promised to move the following day for lower duties. His proposals might reduce revenue but 'they would be beneficial to health and morals'. The Chancellor moved his new duty on 24 February 1795 and the legislation was passed.

Beresford, by this time, may have been an ally of the brewers. His son, John Claudius, certainly was so seven years later. After Grattan's decline in political influence the Guild, notwithstanding his claim on their gratitude, decided in January 1802 to take no further risks and resolved to support John Claudius Beresford at the next election, since 'it is essential to the commercial interests of Dublin that its representatives in Parliament should be men engaged in trade and thereby personally concerned with the extension thereof'.

The lowering of the duty was a temporary palliative because on 4 March 1795 the House resolved 'that for the encouragement of the brewery all regulations heretofore made for collecting the duties thereon should no longer be continued, and that all restrictions affecting the brewer in the free exercise of his trade should be repealed'. This resolution was read a second time and the House ordered Grattan, the Chancellor of the Exchequer, Vandeleur and George Ponsonby to prepare a Bill which was soon passed. The excise duty on beer was abolished and the tax on malt which had first been imposed in 1785 was increased.

The brewers did not escape completely from state regulation after this. With the replacement of the beer tax by the malt tax it was necessary to ensure that the brewers made correct returns of the malt they used and that there was no adulteration with unmalted (and therefore untaxed) barley. In 1809, for example, new regulations were introduced to improve the quality of Irish beer by forbidding the use of unmalted corn and deleterious ingredients. The brewers protested—not against the principle of the Bill, but its form. The regulations were revised in 1827. But, essentially, the interference of the state in this trade was very minor.

The repeal of the beer tax in 1795 was the culmination of the campaign which the Dublin brewers had waged for more than twenty years. They had made articulate the grievances of their industry, and their petitions to Parliament directed public attention to their problems. The outcome of their efforts in 1795 was the radical alteration in the tax code, the replacement of the old beer tax by a tax on malt, and a simplification in the great web of regulations which over the years the Commissioners for Revenue had designed to protect the public from the brewers. In the seventeen-sixties and seventeen-seventies the demands of the brewers were modest and tentative, but when minor concessions failed to stop the decline of their trade they demanded more and more. Grattan powerfully supported their case and a number of well-informed pamphleteers were able to relate the obsolete apparatus of state regulation to the wider background of contemporary economic thought.[1] The shift in tax from beer to malt improved the competitive position of the brewers against the distillers because whiskey was double-taxed. The simplification of the restrictions on brewers was part of a flood of opinion against the older complexity of the regulated economic

[1] See especially Agricola, *Letters to the Rt Hon. the Chancellor of the Exchequer,* (Dublin, 1791).

system in favour of simplicity. The new thought favoured simple taxes and no regulations to protect consumers from producers or producers from each other. The market would solve all the problems. Economic freedom would wash away corruption and adulteration. The legislation adopted in 1795 was a decisive step towards freeing the Dublin brewing industry from the residue of an earlier age of mercantilist regulations. The Act was the most decisive and important single event in the whole history of Irish brewing. Its essential features were retained after the Union of 1801, giving Irish brewers an advantage over their British competitors who were still subject to the beer tax until 1830. Possibly the reforms introduced in 1795 were the main reason for the emergence of the Irish brewing industry from local obscurity to the status of a national industry in the next thirty-five years.

[4]

The First Arthur Guinness and James's Gate Brewery

Being neither demigods nor heroes,
But ingenious, hard-working descendants of *homo sapiens*,
Who had the luck to plant their seedlings in fine weather,
Not in the frost or storm, but when the slow ripening of time, the
    felicitous crossing of circumstance
Presented unimagined opportunities,
Which they seized. . . .

> (*Godfrey Armitage, a master cotton-spinner, quoted in T. S. Ashton,*
> '*The Industrial Revolution 1760–1830*' (*London, 1948*).)

THE FIRST ARTHUR GUINNESS

ARTHUR GUINNESS, born in 1725, was the eldest son of Richard Guinness of Celbridge, County Kildare, agent and receiver for Dr Arthur Price, Archbishop of Cashel. When Dr Price died in 1752 he left Richard and his son Arthur £100 each in his will. This legacy probably helped to start Arthur on his career; before the end of 1755 he was already being described as 'Arthur Guinness of Leixlip, County Dublin, brewer'.[1] His lease of a small brewery at Leixlip dated from 29 September 1756 when he was 31 years of age. Three years later he obtained the lease of a brewery at James's Gate in Dublin, and left his brother Richard to carry on the Leixlip business.[2]

The premises in James's Gate were owned in 1670 by Alderman Giles Mee, later Lord Mayor of Dublin. Mee died in 1691 and James's Gate passed to his son-in-law, Alderman Sir Mark Rainsford who also inherited certain water rights in the district. Rainsford manufactured 'beer and fine ales' and was succeeded in 1709 by his son,

---

[1] Leixlip is in County Kildare, but the boundary separating it from County Dublin is nearby.

[2] The earliest recorded public reference to the first Arthur Guinness in Dublin is contained in a notice published in *Faulkner's Dublin Journal* on 22–5 March 1760, less than three months after he had settled at James's Gate. This was an advertisement offering a thirty-one year lease of seventy acres of meadowland at Oldtown near Celbridge in which Guinness was named as one of the two persons to whom applications might be sent.

another Mark. In 1715 the property was leased to Paul Espinasse for a term of ninety-nine years. He carried on the business until 1750 when the Rainsford family resumed possession.

Arthur Guinness's brother, Benjamin, became a merchant in Dublin where he died unmarried in 1778. One brother, Samuel, was a successful and prosperous goldbeater, and another, Richard, worked the brewery at Leixlip in County Kildare.

By the standards of Dublin in 1759 the property which Arthur Guinness acquired on 'the ground called the Pipes' at James's Gate in December of that year was quite considerable, but the brewery was small and poorly equipped. The dwelling house was commodious; the garden was spacious and contained a fish pond. The brewery, such as it was, 'ready for business', had a copper kieve and a mill, two malthouses, stables for twelve horses with a loft to hold '200 loads of hay'. A frontage of eighty-nine feet faced north on James's Street; the rear extended southwards almost four hundred feet to Rainsford Street. On the eastern or city side there was the property of Mr Joyce, another brewer; and to the west lay 'the pipe wall or city watercourse', which was the main attraction in James's Gate for brewers. Besides the dwelling-house and gardens, the property consisted of a brewhouse, storehouse, out-houses, stables and a summer-house. The lease recited, in addition to the water rights, rights of entry and exit at Rainsford Street, and open land 'together with the use and privilege and all and every other brewing utensils, vessells and particulars...in as ample manner as Paul Espinasse held and enjoyed the said premises'.

The brewery, house property and land were leased for a term of 9000 years at a rent of £45 a year. The brewery may not have been the most substantial one then in James's Gate but it was certainly larger than many of its nearer rivals. When Guinness bought it the brewery had been out of use for some years. An account of the excise paid by forty Dublin brewers some seven years later shows that almost half of them then had higher outputs than Guinness. Three of them— Taylor, Thwaites and Phepoe—paid over £4000 each in 1766; Guinness paid only £1498. The capacity of his brewery in 1759 would probably have enabled Guinness to produce an annual output of about 200 hogsheads. For the first fifteen or sixteen years he seems to have brewed only ale and table beer. It is not known when he first produced porter, but according to records dating from 1796

THE FIRST ARTHUR GUINNESS, FOUNDER OF THE BREWERY,
1725–1803
Copy of portrait. Artist and date unknown: Guinness Collection

BEAUMONT, COUNTY DUBLIN

The first country house of the Guinnesses. Artist and date unknown:
Guinness Collection

he was then brewing porter and a weaker beer (with less malt and hops) which he called ale.

In June 1761 Arthur Guinness married Olivia Whitmore, a ward of William Lunell of Dublin, who inherited over £1000 from her father.[1] Two years later he was elected Warden of the Dublin Corporation of Brewers, and—as further testimony to his rapid success—took part in the annual civic ceremony of Riding the Franchise with representatives of the other Guilds and Corporations of the city in August 1764. In the same year he bought a country house at Beaumont, County Dublin. After only six years in business he could afford to live in the style of a gentleman. In the same short time he became sufficiently well known in Dublin to warrant a report in the *Freeman's Journal* of 12 March 1765 that the 'eminent brewer' who had recently died in James's Street had been a Mr Ennis, not Arthur Guinness, as had been stated in some papers. The report was indeed premature; Guinness had half a lifetime ahead of him.

He had not been long in James's Gate before he was participating actively in public life. He expressed his views with vigour and firmness and took a responsible part in political and civic affairs. His practical side was reflected in his belief that trade should be adequately represented in Parliament, and he was one of a group of Dublin merchants selected to petition their parliamentary representatives in 1766. His humanity expressed itself in his support of charities and the cause of penal reform. He became an administrator of the Meath Hospital, first as Treasurer and later Governor. He was Secretary of the principal Knot in County Kildare of the Friendly Brothers of St Patrick, one of the original aims of which was said to be the discouraging of duelling. He was initiated a member of the Order before he settled in Dublin. By 1767 he was Master of his Guild, the Corporation of Brewers, to which he had been admitted in April 1759, and after twenty years in business he became brewer to Dublin Castle, the Whitehall of Ireland. He began the long association of his family with St Patrick's Cathedral, Dublin, by advancing the Dean and Chapter 250 guineas to cover the cost of

---

[1] The Guinnesses were well-connected through their womenfolk. Olivia Whitmore, for instance, was a Grattan on her mother's side, and through the Grattans, related to the Smyths (ecclesiastics, merchants and architects), the La Touches (Huguenot bankers) and the Darleys (speculative builders). The importance of the families is confirmed by M. J. Craig, *Dublin 1660–1860, A Social and Architectural History* (London, 1952), pp. 118, 178–9, 211, 212 (see below, ch. 8).

71

alterations and repairs to the Chapel schools; instead of accepting repayment he gave the money for distribution in premiums to the pupils. In 1786 he founded Ireland's first Sunday School.

All these aspects of Guinness's part in public life reflected the growth of his business and his influence in the city. His main business interest was brewing, but his good sense and practical intelligence were also applied to any form of commercial activity that might be useful or profitable. During 1789 and 1790, for instance, apart from extending his brewery, he was able to spend between £4000 and £5000 in building flour-mills, and he provided initial working capital of about £3000 for them. He was grateful to God for his material success, which he regarded as a token of divine favour, and grateful, too, for his son Arthur, now 'grown up to be able to assist me in the business, or I would not have attempted it, though prompted by a demand of providing for ten children now living, out of one and twenty born to us, and more yet to come'.

He took a prominent part in public affairs. His principal public office was as representative of the Brewers' Corporation on the Common Council of the city of Dublin. He would have wished the conduct of public affairs to be more sternly guided by the virtues which had served to promote his private fortunes. He once proposed the discontinuance of the Dublin tradition that newly elected Aldermen on the City Council should give a dinner to the whole City Corporation. Guinness suggested that the money be used for charitable purposes by the Blue Coat Hospital. The city fathers, however, were in no mood for abridging municipal conviviality in accordance with the Guinness standards of civic conduct. His proposal was 'universally scouted'. 'Good eating, and above all, good drinking, were strong bonds of good fellowship and unity', the City Council declared, and then added more emphatically, 'the vital principle, and the very essence of their Charter, was blended with hospitality and good living, and they must stand or fall together'.

As a member of the Brewers' Corporation Guinness was able to work most energetically and fruitfully for the development of the Dublin brewing industry and to direct attention to its grievances. In spite of many adverse influences on the brewing industry, Guinness's business made steady progress. His prestige and influence continued to grow. His increased opportunities enabled him to display his high sense of public duty, informed by principles of upright conduct and by the propensities towards thrift and industry which characterized the foundation and enlargement of his own commercial interests. His views were forcibly and sometimes magisterially expressed to the Parliament in College Green, when he appeared there as a witness to testify to the grievances of the brewers.

Guinness believed that the maintenance of law, order and seemly restraint in public life could best be achieved by liberal and enlightened methods. He was opposed to political or social revolution, as it threatened the rights of property and undermined the constitution but he supported reforms which combined the demands of justice with proposals of practical advantage. Unlike some Protestants in Irish commercial life, he consistently supported in the Dublin City Council and elsewhere the claims of the Irish religious majority for equality before the law. When a report was circulated in 1793 that he had opposed the election to the Freedom of the City of Dublin of a man named Valentine O'Connor, Guinness published a denial, stating that in conformity with his unvarying support of their claim to equality he had in fact voted for O'Connor, and solicited votes on his behalf.[1]

Arthur Guinness's religious views were probably influenced by John Wesley. In politics, however, he had the sceptical tolerance of the rising merchant class whose capacity for adaptation and flexibility left them free of doctrinal commitments to adjust themselves to changing situations. Success demanded more than mere business acumen. A successful manufacturer had to navigate the shoals of religious faction, of civil disturbance and political corruption. In the proceedings of the Dublin Guild of Brewers, Arthur Guinness's ability to do this was particularly useful, for the Guild and the Dublin Society were the two most persistent and successful organizations in informing public opinion and making practical proposals for improving the fortunes of the Irish brewing industry in the eighteenth century.

In 1798, at the age of 73, he was still in good health, still conducting his business with his customary vigour and vigilance. He came to the brewery for an hour or two every day and rode out afterwards to his mills in Kilmainham. His son Benjamin was helping him to

---

[1] This was the year of enfranchisement of the religious majority in Ireland. At that time they were still subject to legal disabilities: although they were not denied the right to vote, they were unable to stand for Parliament and were formally unable to hold land except in trust for members of the established Church.

look after his affairs. Arthur, and two other sons, Edward and William Lunell, joined the Yeomanry which was raised to defend Dublin against the revolutionaries. This was the year of the first Irish republican rising, and in some parts of the country the insurgents were rallying popular support. Inspired by the democratic doctrines of the French Revolution, Presbyterians in the north and Catholics in the south had joined forces. The French reinforcements which the republicans had expected failed to land in any strength and the insurrection was effectively crushed. Even in Dublin, which was securely held by the authorities, there was economic dislocation for a time and communications with the surrounding country districts were affected. Supplies of beer from James's Gate to Athy in County Kildare were temporarily interrupted.

By 1798 Guinness had established a country trade with Athy, a town which lay over forty miles from the capital along the Grand Canal. The brewery was by then amongst the biggest employers in Dublin. In 1797 nearly 12,000 barrels of beer were sold, at a profit of £6000. Profits from the flour-mill were about £2000. By any standards the Guinnesses were already prosperous.

Arthur Guinness died in 1803 at the age of 78, and was buried in the family vault in the churchyard at Oughterard, County Kildare. The last years of his life were spent at Beaumont. His estate was valued for probate at between £20,000 and £25,000 and divided between his children. The eldest son, Hosea, had taken orders, after Winchester and Oxford, and the brewery passed to the second surviving son, Arthur, and to the younger sons Benjamin and William Lunell.

JAMES'S GATE BREWERY

James's Gate, where the Guinness brewery is situated, was the ancient entrance to the city of Dublin from the south-west and is shown on the earliest maps of the city. The district, called after the parish church and well of St James, has had long associations with brewing.[1]

---

[1] In the Middle Ages the saint's feast was celebrated at the well on 25 July. Religious exercises and tasting the waters was a prelude to merriment and refreshment at a fair nearby. Richard Stanihurst gave an account of the festivities in his 'Description of Dublin', *History of Ireland* (London, 1577). Over thirty years later Barnaby Rich, another traveller, was astonished to find nothing but ale on sale at the fair. He was shocked by the 'multitude of rascal people', who installed themselves in some booth to sit and drink ale for the rest of the day. As Rich, however, had been easily disedified during his Irish travels, his reflexions need not be taken too seriously.

James's Gate Brewery

James's Gate, on the south-western outskirts of old Dublin, was approached up-hill from Dublin Castle, through High Street and Thomas Street. The focal point of the medieval city was the hill at Christ Church, a short distance from the Castle. Down-hill to the north, and roughly parallel to this line of streets, was the River Liffey. To the south from Christ Church, the ridge sloped towards the valley of the Coombe, St Patrick's Cathedral, Harold's Cross, Kimmage and away to the Dublin mountains, about ten miles from the city. From these hills the medieval city drew its water supply. The Poddle river has its source near Tallaght in County Dublin; it flows in an easterly direction to Kimmage, then north through Harold's Cross towards St Patrick's Cathedral near the Coombe, where it is deflected round the base of Christ Church hill to the Liffey, north-east of the Castle. This river was the main source of fresh water for the medieval city, for the Liffey was tidal as far as Island Bridge, well outside the city's bounds. The narrow ridge from the top of Christ Church hill, through Thomas Street to James's Gate, did not have a continuous supply of fresh water until the thirteenth century, when the municipal authorities took action to meet the needs of the expanding city and provided the area around James's Gate with this first requisite for its industrial development.

James's Gate has given its name to the Guinness brewery in Dublin. According to legend the character of the brewery's products derived from the miraculous properties of the holy well, but the popularity of brewing in the district for centuries and the reputation of its beverages owe a more mundane debt to the plentiful supply of suitable water drawn from the hills outside Dublin and from the plains of Kildare. Water rights were a specific and prominent feature of the lease which Arthur Guinness secured when he first bought the brewery. The vigour with which he subsequently defended these rights against the importunities of the city authorities testified to the significance that both parties attached to them. Water supply had a vital role in the development of Dublin and in the localization of the brewing industry in James's Gate.

In 1773 Arthur Guinness began a protracted dispute with the Corporation about the nature and extent of his water rights. He and two other industrial users, Foster and Greene, were alleged by an investigating committee of the city Corporation to have tapped the conduit leading to the old cistern, 'all of which conveys of said water are very injurious and unjust in the opinion of your committee as the persons receiving said water do not pay for it nor have not for several years past'. The committee referred to the agreement of 1705, under which tenants on the property of the Earl of Limerick were entitled to water 'out of that part of the watercourse' leading from Guinness's concerns to the basin; but they found that many pipes leading from the watercourse were larger than the regulations permitted and that there were many unauthorized breaches in its walls used presumably for the purpose of serving Guinness, and his neighbours, Foster and Greene, with water.

In April 1775 the Corporation decided that the Back Course should be filled up and that tenants entitled to a water supply on the property should be served by a wooden main pipe. The terms of the Guinness lease were examined and Mr Guinness and his landlord Mr Rainsford gave evidence. The committee observed that the watercourse beside the Guinness property had been described in the lease as belonging to the city. They decided that neither Mr Rainsford nor his tenant had any claim to the ground in question, and that the Corporation should recover these rights from Mr Guinness for the city—a task which in practice meant filling up the channel from which Mr Guinness drew his water supply.

The Corporation's emissaries advanced on James's Gate on 10 May 1775. 'Desirous of treating every citizen with all possible respect and lenity and considering that by a sudden privation of water, Mr Guinness, as a brewer, must be considerably injured', the committee of the Corporation 'thought it consistent with that dignity and forgetfulness of injuries, which this honourable city has ever manifested, to inform Mr Guinness of the business the committee were sent about, to allow him a reasonable time for the accomplishment thereof'. But Mr Guinness was not intimidated by these courtesies. He 'gave for answer that the water was his and he would defend it by force of arms'. When the committee asserted their determination to execute their duty he 'invited them to try how far their strength would prevail'. Attended by the city sheriff, the committee set to work closing up the watercourse. After a preliminary encounter with one of the brewer's servants, who desisted in his efforts to obstruct only under threats of committal to Newgate prison, the committee was confronted by the formidable Mr Guinness himself. He wrenched a pick-axe from a workman and 'declaring

76

James's Gate Brewery

with very much improper language, that they should not proceed...
declared that if they filled it up from end to end, he would immediately
re-open it'. He refused to yield his position in the face of rebukes
and expostulations, and eventually the sheriff decided to exercise
diplomacy since his display of force had so far proved unrewarding.
The committee, he said, had asserted the city's claim to the watercourse; but 'it would be wrong to proceed further'. A 'proposal
of accommodation was made when Mr Guinness promised on his
word of honour that...he would submit his title to the water to the
examination of the pipe water committee'. In the event, however,
'all the right he offered was ancient custom'. He filed a bill against
the Corporation and obtained an injunction in respect of the ground,
pipes and watercourse.

The inevitable delays of the law suited Mr Guinness. In 1779
a new complaint was made against him: he had further encroached
on the disputed territory 'by erecting a stone and brick wall on the
city's ground at the narrow passage' adjoining his 'concern'; as a
result, the Corporation's officers were now prevented from examining
the state of the Back Course. Two years later, to the relief, no doubt,
of the Corporation he proposed that a settlement be reached 'in
order to avoid expense'; the pipe-water committee immediately
assented. The matter was referred to arbitration, and in May 1785
the Corporation's honour and Mr Guinness's interests were, apparently, reconciled. 'To put an end to the suit between him and the
city, he proposed to become tenant [to the Corporation] for the
ground contained in the watercourse and pipes from James's Gate
to Echlin's Lane and for a sufficient supply of water by a two-inch
bore to his concerns adjoining thereto during the term of his lease
from Mark Rainsford, Esquire at the annual rent of £10.'

The Corporation speedily agreed to this proposal. The water
rights reserved a quarter of a century earlier in the lease from Mark
Rainsford were successfully protected, and the future supply of water
for the brewery was satisfactorily assured.

77

[5]

The Irish Brewing Industry
in 1797 and After

. . . the immense importations of Irish porter, which, during the past few years, has been sold at such extreme low prices, that no English brewer can compete with it. (*A Witness before the House of Commons in 1835.*)

INTRODUCTION

THE STRUCTURE of the Irish brewing industry changed radically during the nineteenth century. After 1830 the output of beer rose; whiskey was becoming the victim of the excise and public opinion; and after 1850 the money incomes of the population were growing. The number of commercial breweries fell, and their average size increased. Private brewing, which had never existed to any extent in Ireland, contracted rapidly. Although there were many causes for the fall in the number of breweries, the economies of large scale, heavy capitalization and improved efficiency were the decisive factors in winning the expanding market for the bigger breweries.

The small breweries became redundant when their local markets contracted or vanished, and obsolete because the costs of their product were considerably higher than those of their bigger rivals, but the course of rationalization did not become really apparent until after the Great Famine. At the end of the nineteenth century forty breweries were producing four times the quantity of beer of five times that number at the beginning. The character of the markets for beer changed. In rural Ireland people took to drinking beer once money had got into their hands, and the activities of the excise men, together with the concentration of the population in villages and better communications, tended to make illicit distillation too dangerous and too expensive.

After a decline in the post-1815 depression brewing was re-established by 1830 as a thriving and expanding industry. It received a slight setback from 1838 to the Great Famine during Father Mathew's

Introduction

temperance campaign, though beer production was much less affected than distilling and benefited in the long run from a switch from spirits to beer.[1]

BREWING OUTPUT

The number of businesses in brewing was large, relative to the total output. It is unlikely that any firm brewed more than 5000 barrels a year before 1760, and the majority brewed far less.

A little light is thrown on conditions in Dublin in 1811 by a petition of the brewers of Dublin, Cork and Waterford, which was presented by the Hon. John Leeson 'during the illness of Mr Guinness'.[2] The affidavit for Arthur, Benjamin and W. Lunell Guinness was sworn by John Purser, book-keeper. Trade fell very seriously between 1810 and 1811, according to the brewers because of an increase in spirit-drinking; the only concrete evidence appears to have been that of Leeson, who, when asked 'did these gentlemen sell any beer for exportation during these years?' replied, 'a little in 1810, but much more in 1811'.

A hint, a mere hint, is given of the rivalry between firms in 1829 in a letter to the director of the Grand Canal from Guinness's brewery.

16 May 1829
To Francis Berry, Esq.

Dear Sir,

For some time past the subject of our trade on the Grand Canal has been frequently before us and we wish to call your attention to the subject and (with you) to consider what course would best benefit our mutual interests.

It appears to us that the expected increase of trade from the recent extensions of the line and the evident advantage of having *two* stores has not been realized and we fear that it is to be accounted for by the interferences of other brewers and boatmen. Now we think that the best check on the encroachments of this nature is by keeping the prices so low as to deter speculators from entering on an unproductive competition or to render it unavailing if they should have done so.

---

[1] The amount of malt on which duty was paid during the years 1838–47 was a third lower than during the previous decade, and this fall may in part be attributed to Father Mathew's efforts (Morewood, *A Philosophical and Statistical History of the Inventions and Customs of Ancient and Modern Nations in the Manufacture and Use of Inebriating Liquors*, p. 624).

[2] P.P. 1810–11 (222), vol. v, p. 17. Petition of Dublin, Cork and Waterford Brewers.

In 1810 and 1811 Guinness produced almost exactly one-quarter (by volume) of the beer brewed by the common brewers of Dublin. It is probable that by 1815 this proportion had risen, and possible that in the eighteen-twenties the proportion fell. The nearest rivals of the firm in 1810 were Connolly and Somers, who produced about one-sixth of the total. They were followed by Twining and Keogh, with about one-tenth. The other brewers were all rather smaller. The totals are not available for every year, nor by value. By 1810, however, Guinness was the leading brewer in Dublin. Moreover, the bulk of the firm's sales were in Dublin itself.

In a letter to John G. Guinness in 1825 Arthur Guinness appeared to say that his firm was the eighth in the Irish trade in Liverpool, while the Bristol Port Records show that Guinness was very small fry in Bristol compared with the Cork porter brewers and, perhaps, some Dublin firms. Certainly by 1855 Guinness was exporting over half the total of Dublin beer, and Manders was second with about a quarter. The exports of the other firms were insignificant. This suggests what the Liverpool Port Records confirm, that Irish exports to England fell off very seriously from 1815 to about 1830, and that only Guinness and Manders were able to revive their English connexion.

In 1832 there were 216 breweries in Ireland producing over 771,632 barrels of beer. Five years later the number of breweries had increased to 247, and their total production to 1,017,278 barrels. The decline in the number of breweries began after 1838. There were 191 breweries in 1840, of which nineteen were in Dublin; in 1852 in the whole country there were only ninety-six and this number was halved before the end of the century. In 1838 there were over 21,000 retailers of beer in Ireland; in 1842 only 13,000. Between 1837 and 1840 production of beer fell from 1,017,230 barrels to 639,733 barrels; in 1843 production fell to just over 500,000 barrels, the lowest recorded output for forty-three years. The decline after 1837 coincided with the great temperance campaign conducted by Father Mathew, a famous friar.

Exports of Irish beer also grew. In 1823 the amount sent to Great Britain was 1686 barrels and to other destinations 3326 barrels. In 1827 7141 barrels went to Great Britain, and 8035 barrels the following year. Dublin was the chief source of Irish beer exports. From Waterford and Cork supplies were sent to Wales and southern

Brewing Output

England throughout the century, and from these ports and Dublin exports were also going to the Mediterranean, to the West Indies and Newfoundland.[1]

It is possible to attribute the growth of exports to a number of causes, but not to say which was the most important. Contemporary commentators were certain that it was the quality of Irish beer. Before the middle of the century the excellence of Irish porter was recognized in the London market. Its quality was said to be better than that of a good deal of London porter, and greatly surpassed the products of most English provincial brewers. In *The Theory and Practice of Brewing*, published in 1846, Tizard gave special praise to the merits of Dublin porter and remarked on its distinctive flavour. In contrasting it with beers made in the English provinces he observed that:[2]

a more striking difference still is discernable among some of the Dublin houses, none of which yield a flavour like country brewed porters, many of which are shockingly bad, being sometimes blunted, often tasting of empyreum, some black, some musty, some muddy, some barmy, and some having the predominant taste of Spanish juice, which is not an uncommon ingredient, and generally speaks for itself when taken upon a delicate stomach.[3]

He complained elsewhere that in many British breweries the porter was a black, sulky beverage, on the taste of which the stranger experienced a shake, as sudden and electrical as that which seized a spaniel when quitting the water. 'The most respectable of the Irish brewers', he added, 'are deservedly noted for the genuine qualities and peculiarly pleasant flavour of their porter.' It was, he said, 'a mild, soft, and agreeable potation of established soundness and permanently good quality'.

Another explanation for the success of Irish beer was the evasion of excise duty.[4] The English brewers were well aware that the competitive capacity of many of their Irish rivals was due to excise evasion. As the London brewers turned from porter- to ale-brewing they raised little complaint of the extent or nature of Irish

[1] P.P. 1828 (440), vol. xviii, *Exports of Beer 1809–1828*, p. 471.
[2] W. L. Tizard, *The Theory and Practice of Brewing*, illustrated 2nd ed. (London, 1846), p. 484.
[3] Spanish juice was the extract of liquorice root.
[4] The duty on malt averaged 2s. a bushel for the ten years after 1795; it subsequently settled at 2s. 7d. after several fluctuations.

competition, but the English country brewers were not silent. A petition to Parliament from the brewers of ale and porter in Chester in 1835 alleged that:

It is now a notorious fact that a very great quantity of malt is made in Ireland upon which no duty is paid on account of obstacles in the way of its collection: and thereby not only has the respectable maltster in Ireland, who does pay the duty, to sustain an almost ruinous competition in the market against those individuals who evade the duty, but also the Irish malt revenue is considerably reduced; that it is chiefly owing to non-payment of duty that malt can be purchased in Ireland at a much lower rate than in England, the difference being frequently not less than 20s. per quarter of malt, and thereby (notwithstanding the expense of importation) the brewers of ale and porter are enabled to undersell the English brewers even in their own market; that the unequal competition which the petitioners have thus to sustain has of late years so much increased and extended as to threaten ere long to drive the English porter out of the market; the petitioners further represent to the House that indirect injury is done to the *English* malt revenue (which is efficiently collected), by the demand which the extensive consumption of Irish porter creates for malt upon which no duty has been paid.[1]

The evasion of the malt duty appeared to contemporaries to have played an important part in the growth of Irish brewing. In the evidence before the Commission of Excise Inquiry (held in 1833–4 and published in 1835) there are numerous complaints that the Irish evaded the malt duty and consequently their beer was unduly cheap.[2]

Thus Patrick Stead, a maltster from Yarmouth, said:

The Irish porter comes over in very large quantities from Ireland into England, without being subject to the duty of malt; it is, therefore, cutting out the English porter from Liverpool and Manchester; nay, even it comes into London in large quantities and increasing daily. Mr Bass, the eminent brewer at Burton, tells me that it is selling next door to him at Burton cheaper than he can make it.[3]

This view is confirmed by another East Anglian maltster, John Young:

the immense importations of Irish porter, which, during the past few years, has been sold at such extreme low prices, that no English brewer can compete with it. It is also a fact, that a commission of 20 per cent is

[1] *House of Commons Journal*, 20 July 1835.
[2] P.P. 1835 (17), vol. xxxi—*15th Report of the Commission of Excise Inquiry*.
[3] *Ibid.* p. 499—Patrick Stead, App. 61.

paid on this porter to the salesmen and agents; there is also the heavy charge of freight and land carriage to all parts of the north of England which makes it obvious to every thinking person that the Irish malt, from which it is made, cannot possibly pay anything like a fair proportion of the duty.[1]

From Ireland itself Beamish & Crawford's agent, Henry Feath, said that his proprietors were badly hit.

Messrs Beamish & Crawford [intend] to discontinue working in several of their malthouses, which they have actually been compelled to do, as they have this season worked only *three* houses out of *six*...nothing else will enable them to carry on their brewery, or to compete with the country brewers who cannot, from the price they charge for their liquor, have paid duty on one fourth of the malt they consume.

The amount of malt on which duty had been paid fell in the early decades of the century because of tax evasion, not because output was falling. The amount of licensed production in 1816 was below 2,000,000 bushels for the first time since records were kept. This was a sign of successful evasion. In the decade after 1830, however, when licensed production fell below an average of 1,500,000 bushels annually it indicated the result of a vigorous and successful anti-spirits crusade.[2]

Irish brewing was undoubtedly stimulated by the opportunities for tax evasion. In course of time the enforcement machinery became more efficient. The difficulties, however, of effective administrative control were well recognized except perhaps by some of the officials responsible for enforcement. Their published comments on the industry often show a reluctance to accept tax evasion as an explanation of the discrepancy between the declining returns of the malt tax and the increasing output of the breweries. There is, indeed, little doubt that the difficulties of collecting the malt tax in Ireland helped to postpone until 1830 the repeal of the beer duty in Britain. The returns for exports of Irish beer and the virtual disappearance of imports of British beer in the first three decades of the century are sufficient proof that, notwithstanding the fall in the production of licensed malt, there was a rapid expansion in Irish brewing in the early nineteenth century interrupted by the post-1815 depression,

[1] *Ibid.* p. 508—John Young, App. 64.
[2] Soon after the mid-point of the century licensed output recovered to over 2,000,000 bushels annually and continued to increase afterwards.

83

and resumed in the late eighteen-twenties. Since 1793 imports had fallen from 125,000 barrels to a few hundred barrels in 1830, and a steadily expanding export trade had begun.

SPIRITS

The great rival to beer was spirits, of which there were two kinds— poteen, made from grains partly fermented, and whiskey. The latter was sanctioned by law while the former was drunk. In 1808 the production of spirits was forbidden in the United Kingdom, initially for several months and then for nearly three years. This had a profound influence on the beer trade.

The grain harvest of 1808 was not good, and the restriction of imports of grain from Europe had led to great increases in the price of bread. At first the suspension was only for a few months, but as Spencer Perceval, the First Lord of the Treasury, wrote to John Foster on 11 November 1808 it was necessary to prolong the restriction:[1]

Downing Street
11 November 1808

The Rt Hon. John Foster

My dear Sir,

I did not answer your last letter, because I was unable at that time to state to you what would be the determination of the Government with respect to the Distillation of your Grain; the prohibition of which would expire at the end of December if not prolonged by Proclamation before that time...the only Circumstances which caused any doubt in my mind, is the effect it may have upon your Revenue in Ireland. But notwithstanding all the weight which is due to that consideration, yet seeing from the Prices of Grain in our Markets, that the harvest of this year was not such as would at all justify the expectation of its superior abundance counteracting the inconvenience which would be felt from the want of importation from foreign countries, and therefore that the same state of things seemed to exist, which in the judgement of Parliament made it necessary to suspend the Distilleries, the Government has felt itself obliged to adopt the resolution of continuing the suspension for the period allowed by the Act.

I am
My Dr Sir
Yrs very truly
SP. PERCEVAL

---

[1] Foster Papers, Northern Ireland P.R.O., Belfast, D.o.D., 562/2121.

Spirits

To this letter John Foster replied as follows, emphasizing the effects on Irish agriculture:[1]

Collon, 18 November 1808

Mr Spen. Perceval.

My Dear Sir,

I am much obliged by your kind attention in communicating the Determination of Government to continue the Prohibition of Distilleries— you must allow me to lament sincerely the existence of Circumstances to require such a measure. Its injurious effects on Agriculture will be more particularly felt in this Island where the unexampled state of our Potato Crop, greater in Extent of Ground planted, more productive by the Acre and entirely saved from frost by being already dug out earlier than any Man living remembers a similar instance of promises a most abundant supply for the People, and of course a much smaller Demand for Oats and Barley as food, than in preceding years.

Foster then comments on 'the strange phenomenon' that the production of whiskey was forbidden because of the allegedly high price of barley, yet the import of barley into England, and its export from Ireland, was encouraged because of its low price. He continued.

You are aware it [the prohibition] will affect the Revenue. In truth an Interruption to a Revenue that would produce £1,500,000 in a Country not abundant in Money resources is a matter of most serious Tendency, and I cannot but express my fears, that the great advances we have made towards suppressing private Distilleries will receive a fatal check, and then we can hardly hope to continue, much less to complete the full co-operation of the Country Gentlemen and Farmers, which was visibly encreasing, and that the Effects of this measure will continue to our Prejudice long after the Measure itself shall cease.

My Belief is that no Corn will be turned into Food by it, but that the illegal and nut Sugar Distillation will be likely to supply the Consumption in spite of all the Efforts which the Comrs. of Excise can make.

However, since it has been thought necessary, I must conclude it to be so and it is our Duty to make the best of it. I will mean time indulge a hope that it may end with the 40 days [after the resumption of Parliament].

I have the Honour to remain with sincere regards,

My Dr Sir
Your very faithful & Obed. servant
JOHN FOSTER

To this letter Spencer Perceval replied that he felt the exigencies of the situation required him to prolong the prohibition:[2]

[1] *Ibid.* 562/2122.　　　　[2] *Ibid.* 562/2119.

The Irish Brewing Industry in 1797 and After

The Rt Hon. John Foster

Downing Street
27 November 1808

My dear Sir,

I need not state to you, in answer to your letter of the 18 instant, (because it would only be to repeat what I have said before) how sincerely I regret the necessity of prolonging the prohibition of the distilleries, and more especially as far as regards the Irish Revenue. The apprehension of the mischief which it will do to the agriculture of Ireland, I trust, very confidently, will prove to be unfounded; as I cannot conceive that a measure adopted because of the insufficiency of the supply, and of the high price of grain in England can, so long as the market of England continues so advantageously open to the Irish Farmer, check him by any dread of loss or disappointment of expected profit, from pursuing the cultivation of it with the same spirit which has lately prevailed with such good effect in Ireland. . . .

I am, my Dear Sir,
Yours very truly,
Sp. Perceval

The prohibition, which continued until 1811, benefited the breweries immensely. In 1811, when distilling began again, Arthur Guinness (on behalf of the Dublin brewers) wrote as follows to John Foster, the Chancellor of the Irish Exchequer:[1]

Dublin, 25 February 1811

Dear Sir,

. . . The Committee is entrusted with a painful duty; to announce to every Friend of the Irish Brewery that all the evil which we expected to result from the Distillery measures of the last Session have taken place to an extent beyond what our fears had foreboded, insomuch that the Brewery which for some years previous to the suspension of the Distillery in 1808, had been prospering under the encouragement afforded by the Legislature, has, in the short period since the Distilleries re-commenced, not only lost all the advantages derived from the sober habits acquired during the suspension, but so alarming is the falling off of the consumption of Malt Liquor [i.e. beer], that We are threatened with utter ruin to those extensive Establishments which We had erected, on the pledge of the progressive protection which Parliament had continued to extend to the Breweries as connected with the prosperity of the Country. . . it is manifest that no *small* increase of the Duties on Spirits will be adopted as nothing short of a Duty so high as to raise the price of Whiskey beyond the reach of the poorer Classes (for the purposes of intoxication) will ever effect the desired object. The experience of England has fully proved this, and has also fully proved that this object is attainable in connexion with the other

[1] Foster Papers, Northern Ireland P.R.O., Belfast, D.o.D., 562/342.

Spirits

namely Revenue: and surely Sir present circumstances in Ireland are highly favourable to such a measure. The enormous price of Wines and the prohibitory duties on foreign Spirits have secured a most extensive *legitimate* consumption of Whiskey and this is a species of consumption that will not be endangered by such a duty as would destroy the deplorable habits of intoxication which are so widely extended by the present low Duties.

The Committee humbly suggests that it is now plainly proved that a low duty will not destroy illicit Distillation. The Measure of licencing small Stills has as yet proved also ineffectual. We know Sir that this Measure never met your hearty concurrance and if it should be persevered in, We are led to hope that by your influence it will at least be so modified as that small Stills will not be encouraged except in Districts where illicit distillation is deeply rooted.

The Committee is further constrained to remark that as smuggling in the Public Distillery is well known to be carried on to a great extent, so such an amendment in the regulations as would correct this evil would afford protection to the fair Trade and likewise improve the Revenue. . . .

> I have the honor to be Dear Sir,
> with the greatest respect
> Your very humble
> and most obliged Servant
> ARTH. GUINNESS.

The Right Honourable John Foster.

The brewers were unsuccessful in gaining Foster's support, though they sent Benjamin Guinness to seek it. In August 1811 they tried again, by correspondence:[1]

Dublin, 31 August 1811

Dear Sir,

Although the Brewers have lately had the Misfortune of failing to obtain your approbation of the time chosen for urging our complaints against the overwhelming weight of the Distillery, yet We fondly and confidently hope that We may venture still to look up to You as our Patron and our Friend, for We remember that You were the powerful Advocate of the Irish Brewery when she was low and despised, and as we are sure that the principle which then actuated your exertions is unimpaired, so We cannot doubt of a continuance of your desire to serve us. . . .

I have the honor to remain with the greatest Respect and esteem,

> Dr Sir,
> Your most obedient and most
> obliged humble Servant,
> ARTH. GUINNESS

The Right Honourable John Foster,
Collon.

[1] *Ibid.* 562/342.

Thereafter, the brewing trade revived from the impact of this competition, but competition continued to remain serious. Drunkenness was still a problem, and so, too, was the evasion of the duty on spirits by illegal distillation of poteen. The legislature tried constantly to encourage legal malt spirit consumption. Drawback on malt for distillation was first allowed in 1823 to make malt spirits nearly as cheap as illicitly distilled grain spirits. This was a result of the widespread evasion of the duty both in Scotland and Ireland.[1] The drawback was unsuccessful in its object in Ireland, and by 1842 there were only four legal malt distillers while the distillation of poteen was widespread.

The evidence appears strong that the consumption of grain liquor, whether illicitly distilled or not, was high in Ireland. The officially recorded consumption of spirits of all kinds rose from 8·7 million gallons in 1831 to 12·2 million in 1836, then after 1838 fell to 6·5 million in 1841. The fall after 1838 coincides with Father Mathew's temperance campaign and is more likely to be evidence of an actual decline than the earlier rise is likely to be evidence of anything more than more efficient excise officers.

In Belfast, particularly, the consumption of imported Scotch whisky was an important trade.[2] In 1841 6½ million gallons of taxed spirits were consumed of which about 430,000 gallons came from Scotland. The position was broadly that the good liquor was being imported while the country people were making their own.

The direct results of Father Mathew, who was then preaching his remarkably successful temperance campaign, were dramatic but not long-lived, though the effect of tightening the excise law on spirits was permanent. This boosted the brewing industry, which was probably unaffected, even helped perhaps, by Father Mathew. The temperance movement had no defined attitude towards brewing. At first temperance campaigners favoured what was commonly called 'wholesome malt liquor'. The famous 'J.K.L.', Dr Doyle, bishop of Kildare and Leighlin, urged the government to encourage brewing in order to get rid of drunkenness. The attitude of the Hibernian Temperance Society was that the rich might have their wine and the poor their beer, but that spirits were the enemy. Father

---

[1] P.P. 1842 (338), vol. xiv, p. 423, *Report from the Select Committee on the Spirit Trade (Ireland)*. Evidence of James Jameson, the Dublin distiller.
[2] *Ibid.* vol. xiv, Q. 84–6.

Mathew, however, advocated total abstinence, though at first he was concerned almost exclusively with spirits. When his crusade became successful he condemned alcohol of all kinds, as he seems to have decided that the earlier temperance movement had failed because it had condemned spirits alone. But the effects of his efforts were not enduring, least of all on the brewing industry. Heavy increases in the spirit duty, however, especially in 1858 when the English and Irish rates were equalized at 8*s.* a gallon, treble the rates of five years previously, helped, no doubt, to increase the consumption of beer.

GUINNESS'S RIVALS

Who were the other Irish brewers? Early in the nineteenth century Beamish & Crawford, owners of the Cork Porter Brewery, were the most important brewers in Ireland. They acquired the brewery in 1792, managed it capably and prudently, and quickly expanded the business.[1] They soon established for Cork brewing a reputation which contrasted vividly with an earlier tradition.

There had been an earlier brewery on the site they selected but little is known of it except that it seems to have made bad beer. In 1785, for instance, the English traveller, William Dyott, who tasted a good deal of beer in his time, found Cork beer 'the very worst' he had ever tasted.[2] But the standards of Cork brewing were raised soon afterwards. After only four years in trade, Beamish & Crawford were producing nearly 44,000 barrels in 1796, and they doubled this within a decade. At the beginning of the nineteenth century their reputation as porter brewers was very high, and until 1833 they were the leading Irish brewery.[3] Between 1806 and 1815 their output averaged well over 100,000 barrels a year; their scale of production had approached that which the great London brewers had reached in the previous century. It dropped by more than a

---

[1] The evidence for Beamish & Crawford comes from the firm's private papers.

[2] Wm. Dyott, *Diary* (London, 1907), vol. I, pp. 4–5. A typical extract is: 'Friday: We all dined with 32nd Regiment who were in Cork. Got very drunk. Saturday: We dined with the 11th Regiment who were also in the garrison of Cork; and also got very drunk.'

[3] Edward Wakefield in his *An Account of Ireland, Statistical and Political* (London, 1812), vol. I, p. 744 (footnote), stated that in 1809 Beamish & Crawford were brewing 2000 barrels of 46 gallons each per week, which they sold at 10*d.* per gallon. Guinness's was the second largest output at that time and were using, he said, '1200 barrels of malt per week. ...A barrel of malt...makes one and a half barrels of porter; 3½ lb. of hops are allowed to the barrel....'

quarter in 1816, however, as a result of the post-war depression and continued to decline until 1824 when it recovered slightly, and then settled at an annual average of about 61,000 barrels for the next fifteen years. In 1833 Beamish & Crawford produced 65,570 barrels, but were exceeded by Guinness with an output of 69,177 barrels. The Dublin brewery then took the lead and probably never again lost it.

The recession of 1839 was especially a setback for Beamish & Crawford because it coincided with the introduction of Father Mathew's temperance crusade of which Cork was centre. The output of the Cork Porter Brewery fell by nearly 40 per cent between 1839 and 1845 and did not regain its original level until 1856, whereas Guinness's production fell slightly after 1839 but had recovered by 1843.

The market for Beamish & Crawford stout was mainly a local one. The firm eventually owned a large number of tied houses in Cork and elsewhere in the south of Ireland, though in its early years instead of acquiring houses it advanced money for licences.[1] Its trade was not harmed by the Great Famine, but its rate of growth was slow, and the firm seems to have been relatively unsuccessful in extending its sales in the Irish market or in England in the eighteen-sixties and eighteen-seventies when Guinness's home and export trade was rapidly expanding.

Guinness's other rivals were in Dublin. One was a close neighbour in James's Gate: on the north side of the street opposite Guinness's brewery, at the corner of Watling Street, the Phoenix Brewery had an extensive frontage and premises stretching back towards the River Liffey.[2] It had been founded in 1778 by an Englishman named Samuel Madder. He bought the equipment of a bankrupt brewer and set up a business which soon prospered. Madder was important in the history of Irish brewing. He had originally come from London as a working brewer and served as an instructor in various breweries in Dublin and the provinces, where he had popularized the thermometer, the use of which had previously been largely unknown. He has been described as the best porter brewer of his time in Dublin, and even his rivals regarded him as amongst the very first in Ireland

[1] Wakefield, *An Account of Ireland, Statistical and Political*, vol. 1, p. 745 (footnote).
[2] The evidence for this brewery is from the memorandum book of the brewery in the possession of Mr Garret FitzGerald.

to brew porter which compared favourably with London porter. As a business man, however, he was a disastrous failure. He undertook expansions of his premises which he could not afford and starved his business of working capital by mortgaging it to buy out his partners. The story of his imprudent ventures pointed a moral for other Dublin brewers.

In 1788 Madder, in partnership with John and Paul Patrick, began to brew in James's Street. Spurred on by success he leased in his own name adjoining properties between 1796 and 1804 and embarked on an ambitious building programme, which, at the inflated war-time prices, cost him £40,000. With his property heavily mortgaged he recklessly dissolved the partnership without having the means to pay his partners. After his death the business was continued by his widow, but the burden of debt was too heavy, and the brewery changed hands a number of times until 1831 when Daniel O'Connell, fourth son of the Liberator, and his partners acquired it and temporarily changed the name to O'Connell's Brewery. None of the new proprietors knew anything of business or indeed of brewing, and their porter, despite the Liberator's high testimony to its quality, was usually unsaleable.[1] The paid-up capital of £6500 was becoming exhausted when in 1832 a benefactor came to the rescue. He was John Brenan, a qualified brewer, and a partner in a brewery in Kilkenny.[2] He invested £5000 in O'Connell's brewery, and advanced credit to the extent of a further £5000. But all of this money was soon lost and in spite of Brenan's efforts the weight of debt and the drag of inefficient colleagues proved too much and the brewery foundered in 1840. The temperance campaign was blamed for its failure, but it would probably have failed even if Father Mathew had been a brewers' advocate. The capital was entirely lost and no profits had been made since 1831.

The premises were assigned to John Brenan who paid the debts totalling £4000. From June 1841 until 1843 he remained sole owner. In 1843 he formed a partnership with Robert Cassidy of Monasterevan, but they ran into difficulties owing to high prices during the famine years. In 1847 Brenan formed a new partnership, and in 1855 assigned his interest to his son Charles. Under the proprietorship of Charles Brenan the Phoenix Brewery was considerably enlarged and managed with competence. It acquired the adjacent

[1] See below, p. 144.   [2] See below, p. 94.

property of Manders' brewery which occupied six acres. A very extensive trade in home and export markets was built up. The Brenans were good business men and the capacity of their brewery, but of course not their output, was among the biggest in Ireland at the end of the nineteenth century. They and perhaps their rivals in James's Gate had learned a useful lesson from the experience of the unfortunate Madder who had founded the brewery. John Brenan left a record of his reflexions on Madder's lack of business prudence:

> Here let me repeat that it is neither wise nor safe for any man or firm especially a manufacturing one to abstract the capital of the firm for any purpose to any extent without absolute necessity. I have known several most successful men ruined by it. Michael Brenan, a clever man and most successful, crippled himself purchasing an annuity for his children. His former partner in the Kilkenny Bank, James Loughman, failed with 20s. in the £ and an estate. Denis Cormick took £600 out of a most successful business and failed probably for want of this money. Mr Robert Cassidy [his partner] told me that his father John Cassidy, a most prudent and successful man paid between £30,000 and £40,000 for an estate and was inconvenienced by it ever afterwards. In fact commercial history is full of examples of ruin brought on wealthy houses from the same cause.

The Anchor Brewery in Usher Street, Dublin, was established in 1740.[1] In the latter part of the eighteenth century the owners were Kavanagh and Brett, who in 1798 employed the London expert Charles Page to make porter for them. This porter, in the words of a contemporary advertisement, was 'of a very superior quality, which will be found on trial to equal any imported from England'. From Kavanagh and Brett the brewery passed to John Byrne. He worked it so successfully that he was able to sell it in 1818 to John D'Arcy for £35,000—an indication that at that time the Anchor brewery must have been a valuable one. The new owner made further additions to the property in land, buildings and machinery until the brewery became one of the largest in Ireland.

The Ardee Street Brewery was situated on land which in 1536 had become the property of the Earl of Meath on the suppression of the monasteries. This was probably the oldest firm in Dublin, and brewing is believed to have been continuously conducted there from the middle of the sixteenth century. At the end of the eighteenth century Sir James Taylor, its owner, headed the list of brewers

---

[1] The remainder of this section relies in part on W. P. Coyne (ed.), *Ireland, Industrial and Agricultural* (Dublin, 1902).

paying excise in Dublin. To judge from the excise returns the Ardee Street Brewery was then over four times the size of James's Gate Brewery.

Another Dublin brewery of consequence in the middle of the nineteenth century was that of Manders and Powell, later Robert Manders and Company. Like the Phoenix Brewery it was a neighbour of Guinness in James's Gate. It was later absorbed in the North Anne Street Brewery, the proprietors of which were Jameson, Pim & Co. This brewery also acquired the business of Thunder & Co. and Ally & Co. It had a large local trade and a considerable English trade.

Sweetman's Brewery was a leading competitor which survived until the end of the nineteenth century. As early as 1780, Sweetman was advertising 'Irish Porter', at two guineas a hogshead and describing it as 'Equal if not superior to any English'. This brewery was first established in St Stephen's Green, Dublin, but it later moved to Francis Street.

The Mountjoy Brewery from its foundation in 1850 manufactured only porter and stout. In addition to a local market it had a considerable trade to Britain, Gibraltar, Malta and Cyprus. At one time its export business from Dublin was in volume second only to that of Guinness.

The Lady's Well Brewery, established in 1856 by the Murphy family, was second in importance among Cork breweries. It quickly took advantage of the increase in incomes and the growing demand for stout in the later eighteen-fifties and throughout the eighteen-sixties. Like the firm of Beamish & Crawford it acquired tied houses in the south of Ireland, and its product soon added to the reputation which Cork had already obtained as a noted brewing centre. An export trade, which was quickly established, carried the name of Murphy's Brewery to the English market, especially to the midlands. The firm did much to promote the growth of Irish barley. It played an important role in the banking history of Ireland in the nineteenth century when its proprietor, James J. Murphy, helping to alleviate the difficulties that might have followed the failure of the Munster Bank, took the initiative in forming the Munster and Leinster Bank.[1]

The growing strength of the breweries in Cork and the extension of their markets to the surrounding countryside aggravated the

---

[1] Hall, *History of the Bank of Ireland*, pp. 285–94.

difficulties which economic conditions created for small breweries in adjoining rural areas. As a result there were many failures and amalgamations in County Cork in the second part of the century. The Deasy Brewery in Clonakilty, however, survived and extended its business when rivals in Bandon and Skibbereen succumbed. The Bandon Brewery itself built up a steady local trade largely on the prevailing Cork pattern of the tied house, and became known as a manufacturer of a high-class product.

In Kilkenny the St Francis Abbey Brewery owned by Smithwicks was founded in 1710, and the St James's Street Brewery in 1702. Their local markets were severely curtailed by the emigration after the Great Famine, and Smithwick's Brewery also suffered the loss of some custom abroad as a result of the extension of the tied-house system in England. The James's Street Brewery had a considerable trade in Belfast as well as a large local trade in stout and ale. The spread of the sales of Dublin and Cork beer after the coming of the railways gave them severe competition. John Brenan (who became associated with O'Connell's brewery in Dublin) managed another brewery in Kilkenny with his partner, Thomas Cormick, until the business was discontinued in 1841.

Waterford was linked to Dublin by the Barrow navigation system which joined the canal at Athy. After the Great Famine increasing traffic from James's Gate passed along this waterway to towns in the forlorn and depopulated countryside. The traffic, however, has since been diverted to road and rail, and water flows silently past trees drooping with age, derelict houses and the flaking paint on signs that formerly proclaimed the property of 'The Grand Canal Company'.

In 1806 there were two breweries in Waterford, owned by the Cherry Brothers. Thomas Cherry set up the Creywell Brewery in New Ross in 1828, and another brother moved to Dublin in 1849. Very early in the nineteenth century Waterford had a name for ale of high quality, which rapidly replaced the imports from London and Bristol on which it had formerly depended. An export trade was also developed, first to Newfoundland, with which Waterford fishermen had established trading connexions, and later with Bristol. The brewery acquired in 1792 by William Strangman and later known as Davis, Strangman & Co. produced ale and beer for home consumption and for export. Exports were sent mainly to southern

England and Wales. Another Waterford brewery, St Stephen's, had a large local market, used barley grown in Kilkenny and Wexford, and sold part of its output in southern England, particularly in Plymouth, and in Belfast.

The Creywell Brewery which was established in New Ross in 1828 had an unusual ancestry. The premises had originally been occupied by a distillery which failed in the opening years of the nineteenth century. They were then converted into a bank operated by Colclough and Company, but the results of the new venture were as unsuccessful as those of the old, and more fatal. One of the partners, John Colclough of Tintern Abbey, who sat as Member of Parliament for Wexford, fought a duel in 1807 and was killed. Presumably because he was the banking expert the bereft partners decided to liquidate the bank. They were forestalled, however, by their creditors, and a run on their inadequate resources compelled them to close their doors early in 1808. The gross liabilities of the bank were fifty times the amount of the capital invested. The property was later bought by Thomas Cherry of Waterford who re-established his brewery there.

The St Bridget's Well Brewery in Dungarvan suffered seriously from the economic vicissitudes of rural Ireland in the nineteenth century. It was once a flourishing firm and the chief local industrial concern of an outstanding barley-growing district; but this part of the country was severely depopulated by emigration after the Great Famine, and the brewery adapted itself only with difficulty to the new economic climate.

The Monasterevan Brewery was founded after the Great Famine when porter was replacing whiskey as a popular drink; its owner, the prudent Mr Cassidy, insured, however, against a time-lag in the change in drinking habits by engaging in distilling as well. The brewery was well placed. At Monasterevan the Grand Canal divides, and ruined houses and abandoned distilleries now lie beside a straight and clear stretch of water. The former Grand Canal hotel stands by the shell of a noble warehouse. Great walls enclose an empty yard. An aura of vanished grandeur survives. Mr Cassidy chose his site by the harbour, a few hundred yards above the division of the canal. Like the Tullamore Brewery nearby, the Monasterevan Brewery used local barley. Its trade also was local, but the Tullamore concern sent supplies to the west and south of Ireland along the canal. The brewing industry in this area was greatly reduced in the later decades of the century when seven breweries within a twenty-mile radius of Tullamore were closed. They were in Mullingar, Athlone, Birr, Mountmellick, Kilbeggan, Rosenalis and in Tullamore itself. There had also been small breweries in the nineteenth century in Clonmel, Limerick, Tralee and Carrick-on-Suir. Rathdowney Brewery, owned by Robert Perry and Son Ltd, manufactured malt which was widely noted for its excellence. The brewery had an admirable water supply, brewed a non-deposit ale, held the royal warrant as brewers to Queen Victoria, and survived the trials which defeated most of its rivals in that part of the country.

At the end of the nineteenth century there were five breweries in the Louth corn-growing district. The Drogheda Brewery was founded in 1825 by William Cairnes, and produced an ale which quickly became well known throughout Ireland. After 1850, however, when popular taste for porter was growing, the Cairnes firm began to brew porter. The Castlebellingham Brewery established a reputation for its ale in Dublin before the end of the eighteenth century, and in the nineteenth century its business continued to increase. The Dundalk Brewery at Cambrickville, after many variations in its fortunes in the later eighteenth century, allegedly fell a victim to the temperance crusade, but another brewery survived in the town and eventually acquired the property at Cambrickville.

Two other County Louth breweries at the end of the nineteenth century were the Great Northern Brewery in Dundalk and Casey's Brewery in Drogheda. At that time these breweries were amongst the most successful outside Dublin and Cork. They owed their position largely to a traditionally established trade with the north of Ireland where the brewing industry had never acquired firm roots.[1] Dundalk was also fortunate in being close to a regular supply of good malting-barley, and its geographical situation offered particular attractions to commerce, since it was the pivot of the Great Northern Railway system and had a regular steamer service with England and Scotland.

The decline of local brewing in the west of Ireland is reflected in the report of thirteen brewers in Foxford in 1830 and their disappearance from subsequent records.[2] The conditions in the west

---

[1] Possibly this was because of imports of Scottish beer.
[2] P.P. 1831 (60), vol. xvii, p. 67.

were the least favourable for brewing. The failure of brewing to become established in Ulster is more surprising because, while brewing failed to develop, the distilling industry was conducted with outstanding success.[1] When the population of Belfast in 1850 was only a third of what it became fifty years later, there were nine breweries working to full capacity in the city and more than a dozen elsewhere in the province. Whether the lack of success of the industry was due to the initial absence of barley in Ulster, to the difficulty of finding a water supply suitable for brewing or to the competition from Scottish brewers, it is not possible to say, but by the end of the nineteenth century there were only three small breweries in Belfast and the surrounding district.

THE BREWERS' ASSOCIATIONS AND COMPETITION

The associations of brewers—the descendants of the eighteenth-century Brewers' Corporation—continued throughout the nineteenth century. There was a Dublin Brewers' Society that controlled prices and conditions of sale in Dublin and of sales by them outside Dublin, in the countryside and in Great Britain. The following resolution of 1831 indicates how detailed was the control exercised over all its members, and in chapter 7 reasons are given for believing that this control helped to maintain Guinness's rivals in Dublin. Possibly the control in other areas was less strict.

COPY OF BREWERS' RESOLUTION AT MEETING HELD
8 December 1831

At a Meeting of the Porter Brewers of Dublin, held this day at the Chamber of Commerce, the following resolutions were adopted:
Resolved:
    That finding with regret that an individual house in our trade still perseveres in a reduction of its prices to £1. 16. 6. a hhd. and £1. 3. 2. a barrel, a reduction in our opinion not warranted by the present price of Malt and Hops, nor by the average of those articles for many years past, and feeling it indispensable that our respective customers should be supplied on as moderate terms as those of the house in question, we have determined to reduce our prices to the same rate to commence from 1st December instant.
    That in making this sacrifice, which we trust will only be temporary, we pledge ourselves to the Public, that be the loss incurred what it may,

[1] It was in this part of Ireland that cash was most abundant, and so spirits—such as Scotch whisky—could be bought.

we are determined that the present improved quality of our liquor shall be maintained.

The arrangement of prices to be as follows:

Town porter					Country porter				
Gross price per hhd.	.	£1	18	3	Gross price per hhd.	.	£1	18	6
Discount and Xmas					Carriage and Xmas				
Allowance.	.	.	1	9	Allowance	.	.	3	0
Net price	.	.	£1 16	6	Net	.	.	£1 15	6
Gross price per brl.	.	£1	4	4	Gross price per brl.	.	£1	4	6
Discount and Xmas					Carriage and Xmas				
Allowance	.	.	1	2	Allowance	.	.	1	11
Net price	.	.	£1 3	2	Net	.	.	£1 2	7

(Signed) A. Guinness Son & Co.
John D'Arcy & Co.
Maunders & Powell
Laurence Finn
W. E. & J. Conlan
R. & J. Watkins
John Jameson

Competition in Ireland was limited by these agreements. It was also restricted by the tied-house system. A correspondent writing in the *Dublin Evening Post* on 2 August 1810 urged legislation to prohibit brewers from 'paying directly or indirectly for a licence or part of a licence from any retailer, for to this practice is owing the present degraded state of malt liquor'. As against this, reputable brewers were anxious to make such arrangements as they could to prevent unscrupulous publicans from adulterating their porter or mixing good beer with bad.

That was the period, however, during which the brewing industry was facing a temporary recession mainly as a result of the revival of distilling. The suspension of distilling in the preceding years had accorded all brewers an advantage which the less viable amongst them were unable to retain when competition from distilling increased. Those brewers who were not able to hold their markets bought or acquired tied houses as a method of keeping down retail margins. The devices which they adopted were probably more conspicuous than effective, and the comments which they evoked suggest that attempts by brewers directly to create retail outlets for their porter were the exception rather than the rule. The populace misinterpreted this process as an attempt by the brewers to raise retail prices; rather was it an attempt to raise wholesale prices while keeping retail prices constant. At no time did these expedients have the official sanction of the Brewers' Corporation; the available evidence suggests that when trade improved they disappeared. Occasionally there were allusions to these practices in advertisements. In May 1810, for instance, there was an offer of an 'Hotel, Tavern and Porter House—For Sale—The interest in the Lease of the Above'. The establishment was stated to possess 'many advantages that other houses in this city have not, which will be more fully explained by applying to Michael Lowry's Windsor Ale Brewery, Crane St, Thomas Street'. On 4 October 1814 an advertisement in the *Freeman's Journal* offered a public house for letting 'to brewers, publicans, etc.', and there were some other advertisements of the same kind.

The existence of covenants binding publicans to sell exclusively a particular brand of beer led to a court action in 1815. The plaintiff was a brewer named William Conlon, and the defendant Walter Mulligan—his tenant—a publican in Bride Street, Dublin. There had been a covenant in the lease requiring the defendant to purchase all his porter from the plaintiff. Mulligan complained of the penalties which had been awarded against him as a result of his default. He had found the porter of another Dublin brewery (that of Byrne and McNulty) better than his landlord's brew, and his Counsel argued that the penal clauses in the lease were improper, 'preventing fair competition, an encouragement to the manufacture of bad porter, and operating as a monopoly'. One of the Judges criticized severely the practice of enforcing these covenants; 'after much private consideration', however, the court decided in favour of the brewer.

Some brewers may well have fortuitously acquired an interest in public houses in part discharge of publicans' debts to them. The system of exclusive dealing was probably more prevalent than the public references made to it, for the essence of a successful compact was that its operation should be kept secret. There would certainly have been greater publicity if retailers or consumers suffered much inconvenience, as was happening in England during this period.

Guinness had singularly few tied houses for a firm of its size in 1815, and the falling off in Guinness sales after 1815 may have been a sign of a brewer handicapped by a lack of tied publicans. There are, however, other reasons why the trade of the firm could have fallen after 1815. There was a general slump and the number of brewers undoubtedly fell from 1815 to 1820, and there is, too, the evidence that in 1819 there was what Arthur Guinness called an 'obstinate refusal of the Dublin brewers to raise prices' in the face of rising costs, and this must be attributed to difficulties in selling the beer. There is no sign, however, that the brewing trade was especially hard hit, and its fortunes were at that time fairly closely linked to those of the economy as a whole.

Apart from the general fortunes of the industry the house of Guinness might have suffered an especial blow directed more at it than at the other brewers. An analogy from London suggests itself. Before 1818 the rise in the number of tied houses was especially noticeable there and caused much public outcry. In 1818 the House of Commons examined the situation in London and a report was produced that was eminently reasonable. Its conclusion, also applicable to Dublin, was as follows:[1]

Your Committee...feel themselves called upon to revert to the investment of very large capitals in the purchase of licensed houses by brewers, and the consequent continued decrease of free houses, both in the Metropolis and in the country....When at most the only competitors in the trade will be the proprietors of these houses...the meetings of brewers to fix and lower prices, (and which is not disguised by them, but declared to be necessary,) will no longer be as unprejudicial as it now is stated to be, but may be and probably will be used as a means of demanding such an unfair price from the Public as they may be compelled to submit to. It is true, that price and not quality is the subject of their present determinations and meetings, and that a competition in quality is more effectual than any competition in reasonableness of price....

What of the brewers in Ireland who were behind in the race for tied houses? Two conditions have to be examined before it can be surmised that this was Arthur Guinness's position. First, why was this a period of increasing connexions between brewers and publicans? In a period of falling trade it seems clear that the publicans would fall behind in their accounts. Indebtedness was the origin of the tie in most instances, and therefore its increase would tend to be associated with the years of extremely bad trade from 1815 onwards. This would be particularly the case in Dublin where the depression was severe. The second condition that has to be examined is ability of the brewer to advance money. In general this would be a difficult

[1] P.P. 1818 (399), vol. III, p. 299, *Report from the Select Committee on Public Breweries.*

The Irish Brewing Industry in 1797 and After

task for him at a time when money was scarce, and for some years after 1815 it was especially difficult for the firm of Arthur Guinness because his capital was employed elsewhere.[1] It may easily be, therefore, that Guinness suffered after 1815 because he was unable to advance capital to his customers. The commercial brewers were important sources of capital for their publican customers and the costs of holding a licence and storing beer were often borne by them in return for an exclusive contract.

In the early eighteen-thirties the costs of keeping a public house fell because in 1830 the Beerhouse Act enabled any householder assessed to the poor-rate to sell beer free from control of the justices on payment of a sum of £2. 2s. to the excise; as far as the licensing laws were concerned there was now free trade in beer, and a new era had begun, in which the impulse to the tied house was less strong than before. The licence duties were less and the turnover was greater. Consequently the impulse towards the tied house was greatly reduced.

A further check occurred in 1833 when brewers were prohibited by legislation from holding a retailer's licence. This prevented them from directly controlling public houses, but indirect influence was of course still possible. As late as 1836 a witness before a Parliamentary Committee alleged that brewers still owned a 'great many' public houses in Dublin, but as he was Secretary of the Grocers' Trade Association he was possibly biased. Guinness owned a few public houses until 1875 at least. The tied-house system, however, was probably less developed in Dublin at this period than it was in London.

CONCLUSIONS

The most important factor in the growth of the industry was the availability of capital and skill. The process of industrialization led to the elimination of many firms in the industry. Efficiency varied from brewery to brewery and those which were less adequately endowed than their rivals with technical skill, capital or business talent were compelled to close when poor trading conditions or competition confronted them. The reduction in the number of breweries was most striking in Belfast and in the provinces, but failures or amalgamations were also common in Dublin and Cork. It was in this environment that Guinness's brewery eventually prospered.

[1] See below, p. 124 and pages following.

[6]

The Second Arthur Guinness

He was what is untruly called 'a liberal'. (*The Reverend John Alcock, A.M., in a funeral sermon on the death of Arthur Guinness, preached in Bethesda Chapel, Dublin, 17 June 1855.*)

THE SECOND ARTHUR GUINNESS

THE SECOND Arthur Guinness was born on 12 March 1768 at James's Gate. He was his parents' third child, born in his father's forty-third year and his mother's twenty-sixth. His elder sister Elizabeth was five, and his elder brother Hosea was nearly three years older than he. Elizabeth married Frederick Darley, who became Lord Mayor of Dublin in 1809 and was the father of a son who worked in the brewery and of the second Arthur's solicitor. Hosea took orders after being at Winchester, and he became rector of St Werburgh's (where Dr Price, later archbishop of Cashel and employer of Richard Guinness, had been curate) in 1811, a living held until his death in 1841. He had thirteen children, and some of his grandchildren (the Wallers) worked in the brewery. In 1772, four years after the second Arthur, his brother Edward was born. He became a solicitor, an iron-master, and a bankrupt. His eight children included some of the second Arthur's favourite nieces— one of whom, Bessie, married Arthur's third son. After Edward came Olivia, in 1775, and Benjamin in 1777. This brother was the second Arthur's partner in the brewery and the father of Susan, who married Arthur's eldest son.[1] The next son, William Lunell, was born in 1779, became a partner in the brewery, and died in 1842. When the second Arthur was thirteen his sister Louisa was born, who married the Vicar-General of Limerick, William Hoare. She died at the age of twenty-eight. In 1783 his brother John Grattan was born; he went into the Indian Army and then returned to Dublin, where he led a life of pecuniary embarrass- ment—and put his son in the brewery from which he was ejected.

---

[1] Benjamin died in 1826, aged forty-nine, having been extremely active in the business.

103

The Second Arthur Guinness

In 1787, when Arthur was nineteen, his sister Mary Anne was born. She married a clergyman called John Burke, of Galway, and was the mother of the Burkes who built up the export trade.

The second Arthur was thus one of ten children who survived infancy, and the uncle of probably over forty nephews and nieces, three of whom married his own children. In 1793, when he was twenty-five, he married Anne Lee, daughter of Benjamin Lee of Merrion; they had nine children. His wife, to whom he was devoted, died in 1817 when he was forty-eight. Four years later he married again, Maria Barker, a friend of his wife.

Of Arthur's character a great deal is known. In business he was shrewd, forthright and immensely able. He became his father's partner when he was thirty, and five years later, in 1803, he was his father's main successor.

The first Arthur Guinness in his will made in 1799 left his wife £200 a year (she died in 1814) together with the £200 from her marriage jointure, and the use of his house in Gardiner Street and his coach and coach horses. His daughter Elizabeth Darley was left £1000 in trust, and his unmarried daughters Louisa and Mary Anne were left £2000 each in trust. Hosea, Arthur and Edward were provided for by earlier arrangements; Hosea inherited Beaumont and the residuary, 'not being in any line of life whereby he is likely by Industry to enlarge his Property'. He also gave a small bequest to his nieces Jane, Matilda, Anne and Olivia, daughters of Richard Guinness of Leixlip. His sons Benjamin, William Lunell and John Grattan were given £1500 each. Arthur was made the brewer by being left 'the Silver Salver presented...to me by the Corporation of Brewers of the City of Dublin...to go to the Eldest Male Branch of my Family...who shall be in the Brewing Trade'.[1] The flour mill, called the Hibernian Mills, was to go to the son best able to manage it. This was Arthur, helped by Benjamin. Thus, the second Arthur became in fact if not in name the head of the family. He was known to be successful in business, and some of his relations, friends and acquaintances, especially the unlucky, the unfortunate and the feckless, often acted in the belief that because he was wealthier than they he had more money than he needed. These aspects of the man, the demands on his forbearance, the importuning of his generosity, are all vividly and strikingly shown in his correspondence. As head

[1] This salver is in the possession of the present Lord Iveagh.

of the family business and of a growing and scattered family, he accepted as a matter of course responsibilities for people and decisions which a less conscientious and less wealthy man might have avoided.

In 1808 the second Arthur Guinness's long association with banking began when he was elected a director of the Bank of Ireland. Ten years later he became Deputy Governor, and he was made Governor in 1820. He was a figure in Irish banking at one of the critical periods of its history when decisions taken on currency had far-reaching effects on the Irish economy. His colleagues in the Bank were pleased with the outcome of the negotiations which their Governor conducted with the government, and in 1821 they voted him a special sum of £300 in recognition of his services. That year during King George IV's state visit to Ireland it was Guinness who received the King when he inspected the Bank of Ireland. Some of his banking colleagues were not so pleased with Guinness in 1826, when he opposed a proposal for an increase in the salaries of the Governor and the directors. His opposition was based on the belief that public opinion might construe a salary increase to be a con sequence of the recent currency reform. Three years later he again successfully resisted that proposal. For bank directors, apparently, virtue was its own reward.

After brewing, banking was the second Arthur Guinness's principal business interest, but the range of his activities was extensive. It reflected the esteem felt for him as an energetic organizer, a trustworthy representative of his fellow citizens and a skilful negotiator. As a leading merchant in Dublin it was inevitable that he should become a public figure and he acquitted himself in that role with the same distinction as marked his performance in business. And so, one after another the titles accumulated of the offices he held. Some of the offices were honorary; many were not; all made heavy demands on his time. He served in the Farming Society of Ireland, the Dublin Ballast Board which managed the port and docks, the Ouzel Galley Society—an exclusive business club, the Dublin Society, the Meath Hospital, the Dublin Chamber of Commerce (of which he was for many years President) and in other bodies.

The two great political issues in Ireland during the first thirty years of the nineteenth century were Catholic emancipation and parliamentary reform. The second Arthur Guinness had been an advocate of both before the century opened. In 1819 he organized the members of St Catherine's parish in Dublin to support the claims of the religious majority in Ireland. He sought as early as 1825 to have its members eligible for admission to the Court of the Bank of Ireland. In 1826 he supported Daniel O'Connell and Henry Grattan's son in their campaign for emancipation. When emancipation was conceded in 1829 he went to a public meeting to celebrate it. He was equally fervent as an advocate of the Reform Bill. In spite of illness he attended a meeting in Dublin in May 1831 after the dissolution of Parliament 'lest his absence might be construed into an indifference on the great question in which they were all so vitally interested'. Later in the month, seconding the adoption of a Reform candidate for the county of Dublin he said:

A great change was taking place all over the world. Men were awakening. Reason and intelligence were upon their majestic way, and everywhere the grand principle was beginning to be asserted that Governments were instituted only for the benefit of the people. Even in empires where despotic sway had been long exercised, the principle of liberty had begun to be extended, the struggle of popular power had loosened the iron hold of tyranny, and prostrated the oppression that would seek to build itself on the oppression of the human race.

Notwithstanding his eloquent expression of liberal sentiments, which was greatly applauded, the opponents of reform were successful in the Dublin elections.

Six years later, in 1835, Guinness found himself opposing the extreme liberals and O'Connell on the repeal of the Union. 'I think', he was reported as saying, 'the time has come when it is the bounden duty of every man to speak his sentiments, and to declare whether he is for the destruction or preservation of the constitution.' The Irish Church measure had profoundly shaken many members of the Church of Ireland, when the reformed Parliament laid its hands on the distribution of the Church's income.

In the election O'Connell sought to form all the liberals into an 'anti-Tory association'. Peel, in the Tamworth Manifesto, had accepted the 1832 settlement, and so O'Connell's attitude was now in effect much more radical than it had formerly been. The moderate liberals ran their own campaign, against both the Tories and O'Connell.[1] The second Arthur Guinness was a moderate liberal and denied that he had changed his political allegiance by opposing O'Connell.

---

[1] McDowell, *Public Opinion and Government Policy in Ireland, 1801–1846*, p. 161 and pages following.

The Second Arthur Guinness

O'Connell's paper *The Pilot* was more bewildered than angered by Guinness's vote against the 'Liberator'. It paid tribute to the liberal views that Guinness had expressed throughout his life and described him as a man 'who never committed but this one public error, and whose motives for committing this one are unquestioned'. Guinness wrote to the editor to explain his vote and repudiated the suggestion that he had associated with the 'Orange system'. *The Pilot* accepted his disavowal and condemned efforts which were being made to victimize Guinness for his part in the election by damaging his business. O'Connell himself condemned attacks on Guinness's property on the grounds that unlawful conduct brought political causes into disrepute. He added that Guinness would lose little as his property was insured, but that the citizens of Dublin would feel the pinch when the grand jury imposed its levy for malicious damage. He deplored Guinness's vote because Guinness had belonged 'to the liberal party when in the full strength of his intellect, and in the youthful vigour of his mind he was on our side'. 'Some clerical relations of his, however, got about him' and persuaded him into giving 'the first bad vote he ever gave'.

His role in his family is central to an understanding of his character —he was adviser, friend and above all the banker. This is a term explicitly used by Arthur Guinness in a letter to his elder brother Hosea in 1821.[1] The family were united by a deep and close affection and an unaffected religious faith. They were evangelical in their persuasion and their second birth in Christ was to them an event of unique importance, by the side of which nothing else could be said to matter. Their loyalty to their Church was profound and exemplary.

The second Arthur wrote a long letter to his son Benjamin Lee on 12 March 1847. In it he discussed business matters, malt and hop supplies, and the Irish Famine—('How awful do the accounts from Ireland continue and how evident is it that the exertions of the Government need to be aided by those of [private] individuals.') But the letter opened on the religious note which was characteristic of his personal correspondence:

Torquay

My dear Ben,

Your kind letter of the 8th is before me and the continued good account of our Business calls for much thankfulness to Almighty God while we

---

[1] Cited below, in ch. 7.

107

humbly ask for the infinitely higher blessings of His Grace in the Lord Jesus Christ. I have entered this day upon my 80th year. Surely it becomes me to speak of the Lord's patience and longsuffering towards one so utterly evil and sinful and to pray that I might be enabled through Grace to live every hour under the teaching of the Holy Spirit patiently abiding His time for calling me to that Place [of] Everlasting Rest, the purchase of the precious blood of the Lamb of God for saved sinners. Amen....

It would be difficult to exaggerate the place of religion in Arthur Guinness's life. This religious faith, drawn from the Bible, the Book of Common Prayer, and from Bunyan, refreshed by the Wesleys and George Whitefield, was the central fact of the second Arthur Guinness's life. 'The Bible', said the preacher at his funeral,

was his constant companion in his study and I rarely entered it and met him there that the book was not open; and invariably, when alone, he would conclude the interview by saying, 'Let us pray'. He was what is untruly called 'a liberal'. But while he developed those views, partly, it might have been from his associations, partly from his circumstances, and with a judgement not yet fully enlightened in divine truth, and, therefore, without the perception of their error and evil tendencies, he yet manifested much of his natural character in the firmness with which he carried out his convictions. But more marked still was the decision, the fearless and undaunted resolution, with which, when once convinced of his error, he passed over, and took his stand on the opposite side—on that side which shall ultimately be pronounced true liberality by the voice of God.

Later generations have seen members of this persuasion as narrow-minded bigots, killing joy and generous instincts wherever they were to be found. Fortunately, the evidence given by the letters written at a time of crisis in all their lives enables us to refute this. The Guinnesses' faith was a generous broadening one, it comforted and it strengthened them.

SOME FAMILY BUSINESS MATTERS

Arthur's ability in business was considerably greater than that of the rest of his family. His brother Edward, in particular, went bankrupt in 1811, taking with him his brother John Grattan Guinness. About Edward Guinness's early career a Dublin newspaper had this to say:

This Gentleman is well known as the former proprietor of the great ironworks at Palmerstown and Lucan; he was the first trader who could claim

Some Family Business Matters

the merit of rendering his native country not only independent of, but superior to, her neighbours in this branch of manufactures. He gave bread to several hundred fellow creatures, who prospered under his auspices; his establishment turned out annually more than £170,000; he was candid and honourable in his dealings; highly esteemed and respected not only as a merchant but as a private gentleman; he was enterprising and successful in his speculations; yet even this man is now made a bankrupt.[1]

Edward's business as an ironfounder and merchant collapsed; he was being pressed by 'the Major', a creditor, and Alderman Redford (a connexion by marriage), and Arthur's guarantees were called upon. Arthur's cousin, the barrister Samuel Guinness (son of the goldbeater), and his cousin Dick, another barrister, were involved in this. The following letter, typical of many, from Samuel Guinness to Richard Guinness shows that Samuel Guinness thought highly of Arthur's opinion on business matters, and that he trusted him to pay up for his brothers ('their brother Arthur is my mark for full reparation').

8 November 1811

Richard Guinness, Esq.

Dear Dick,

The moment I quitted you today I went to the Major; I have no influence in prevailing with him to adopt *my* opinion when it differs from his own, and can now only answer for myself. Whatever Arthur G. approves of...I not only sanction, but will save him harmless from any objections the Major can by possibility make on that head. I think (but subject to Arthur's better judgment) all the raw material that can, ought to be forthwith manufactured, and the rest held over if there be any rational hope of its meeting a better market....

As to our friend Redford's Suit I refer to my letters of 7th ulto. disclaiming all concern with it; if by any act of E. & J. G.'s[2] *my* property is unjustly trenched-upon, their Brother Arthur is my mark for full reparation...let him [Edward] learn that Partners tho' Anonymous are not mere Cyphers, and that he can't bind them by a Lease or Deed, tho' he certainly could by a Bill of Exchange[—], however improperly, during the existence of their joint firm, tho' thank God, not before or after the existence of said joint firm, as ascertained by the clear Evidence of their Deed, and not by rigmarole talk or foolish ungrammatical construction of a plain instrument....

Ever Dear Dick truly yours

S. GUINNESS

[1] *Saunders' News-Letter*, 12 September 1812 (reprinted from *Freeman's Journal*).
[2] Edward and John Guinness.

The Second Arthur Guinness

Edward Guinness not only presumed upon his relatives, as Samuel Guinness expressly stated, but he was overcome by a maudlin and sanctimonious self-pity when he was faced with imprisonment for debt. His expertise was bankruptcy—he knew perfectly the law on the subject in Ireland, England, the Isle of Man, Scotland and France. At the time he wrote the Isle of Man was about to close its doors to debtors—for many years it had been their haven and refuge. He wrote to Arthur Guinness from Cambrickville, near Dundalk, where he had fled from his creditors, in 1813, to state his circumstances, his hopes—and fears:

Cambrickville—Sunday
1 August 1813

Arthur Guinness, Esqr.

My dear Arthur,

. . . I feel that the present situation of my affairs are not likely soon to grow much better. I must wait for the Lord's good time, & use reasonable means to save my person. Now as to the Insolvent Bill, I am aware it does not, it could not affect the Isle of Man. That Island has a Parliament distinct of its own & Mr Smyth[1] told me the day before I came away but one, that, the Court of Keys, there, (its Parliament) has passed the Bill to exclude all strangers from protection as heretofore enjoyed from arrest for debts contracted else where, & that it has gone to receive the Royal assent, & that as it was immediately to be had, he was obliged to sail the next day with several persons for the last time before the Bill returned finally passed. Thus it is that ends the former protection held there, & not the Insolvent Act, so I believe it is now at an end, however I should suppose Mr Smyth is returned to Dublin and may now be seen on the subject, at all events that place, from its present class of Inhabitants is not very desirable, & I fear would injure Character not a little, as few but of the worst description go there, & particularly after Bankruptcy—in Scotland as I mentioned in my letter to Margaret,[2] there is a Law called Cessio Bonorum by which in 31 days after an arrest I would be free, having given up all recently by Bankruptcy, & then an arrest cannot take place for a debt not contracted there without previous notice, so that I would have full opportunity of returning, it is therefore that I proposed to go there, indeed the question is whether I should not take the benefit of the new Insolvent Act here, & whether it would relieve one from the Rent, for tho' future acquired Property is liable, yet if I cannot obtain release from the parties opposed to me, I will be driven to a foreign Country, so after being freed in person here under the new Act, I might go & come to &

---

[1] This man, a cousin, was the owner of the packet vessel that sailed to Bristol via the Isle of Man and Liverpool.
[2] His wife.

Some Family Business Matters

from a foreign Country, possessing property there, free from any attempt,
& it would be a serious matter indeed if after having acquired property
abroad I could not have personal freedom to come here occasionally....
Believe me my Dear Arthur ever to be your truly & sincerely affectionate
Brother

EDWD. GUINNESS

By the next letter Edward had fled to the Isle of Man, despite
his earlier hopes, and it fulfilled his worst expectations.

Douglas, Isle of Man
14 August 1813

Arthur Guinness, Esqr.,
Dublin.

My dear Arthur,

...I shall now state what I have heard of Scotland. There education
can be obtained of all sorts, & I wish much to have the whole family &
myself taught French, to prepare for a foreign Country, this then decides
me in being anxious to go there, & if I was arrested there, it matters little
for I must be released finally in 30 days, & I had rather be a close prisoner
for many months with a certainty of enlargement, than to be in the prison
which Douglas or any part of this Island is. Now I have met a Gentln.
here Major Lyle a Scotch man of considerable Estate there who is now
on the point of returning having sold a part of his Estate & paid all his
Creditors, he is a settled Married Man of nearly fifty, Mr Smyth introduced me to him, & I find he is much and justly I believe respected here.
He tells me that Musselborough within six miles of Edinburgh, possesses
all the advantages of education & is a most desirable place of residence,
on the Sea Shore too, possessing several local advantages for cheapness
and beauty of situation, having good houses well circumstanced....

A year later Edward and his whole family were still in the Isle of
Man. He wrote again about family troubles. Their brother Hosea's
eldest daughter, Olivia Archer, was mentally ill, and his brother-
in-law, Frederick Darley (the former Lord Mayor), was going bankrupt. This roused Edward to a passion of spiritual exhortation.
Immediately after all this he settled down to business. He presented
his accounts, which are a masterpiece of blinding statistical manipula-
tion. They show a high standard of living for his wife and himself
and five children. They had two servants and had only reluctantly
given up the horse for their carriage (which they kept). Many gifts
had come from his brewing brothers. He had rented an expensive
house, his reason for moving from his more modest one being given
with disarming ease: 'From the very confined space we have had in

The Second Arthur Guinness

the House we are in, having so many children within so few square feet & no yard or garden, & a tanner's yard immediately under our back windows, the offence of which by this hot weather & his increase of business daily becoming greater.' He excused himself for his extravagance, and hinted that his wife's health was suffering from the constant anxiety about money—almost a straight demand for more. Then, to crown it all, he found that he had made an error in putting the credits in Irish money and the expenditure in British money. This made a difference of some £70 (Irish), putting him firmly in the red. He explained it away with masterly and, perhaps, confusing irrelevance in a footnote to a letter which even for him was uncommonly long, apart from the detailed 'statement' of his accounts that accompanied it.

P.S. Since I closed this letter I recollected that the sums I put at the debit of my statement are in Irish money & that the Credits are in English, this makes so much the more expended than recd. taking both as Eng.[1] But on talking to Mrgt. I find that she had nearly £30 of savings of her allowance in former times, which she paid away for general purposes this year. This then shows how the matter was....

Edward then fades out of the story. In 1826 his brother Benjamin died and left him £1865, and he received an annuity. For some time he worked as a clerk in the brewery and, later, his brother Hosea was reproved for interceding on his behalf. His daughter Bessie married Sir Benjamin Lee Guinness. There are wastrels in every generation, and Arthur was plagued with them more than most men. One can sympathize with his reply to another importunate correspondent, John W. Topp, in February 1844:

It appears from your letter [he wrote] to be your opinion that I am extremely wealthy and my children so independent that on making my will I shall have much property to spare for others. Now you have formed a very mistaken estimate on both points. I have from various casualties, which have in the act of the Lord's Providence fallen out, chiefly affecting the property of my many dear Relations, had several individuals and families depending on me solely or partially for support...so that although the Lord has been pleased to prosper mine and my sons' industry, I have not been accumulating as you suppose, and indeed, I think I could not have done so acting as a Christian man....

[1] In fact, of course, his recollection was at fault.

ARTHUR LEE GUINNESS, 1797–1863
Artist and date unknown: Guinness Collection

ARTHUR LEE GUINNESS

The reconstruction of a man's character, its evocation and its delineation, is an exceedingly difficult, perhaps an impossible task. A great family crisis reveals the people in it more nakedly than any other happening. Nerves are torn, and the jagged edges of early childhood memories stand above the alluvium of later life. Rarely, however, does a crisis take place by correspondence. The angry scene, the violence, the tears and the conciliatory embrace are remembered, and perhaps recorded. They are not often entrusted at the time to the mails.

In 1839 such a crisis occurred in the Guinness family; it took place to a great extent through letters sent to each other though the participants were often in the same building, and it reveals the characters of the leading actors more clearly than any other incident.

In June 1839 Arthur Guinness was 71. His second wife, Maria Barker, had died two years before, and he was living at Beaumont with his unmarried daughters. Arthur Lee was 42 and unmarried: he lived as a bachelor in James's Gate. Benjamin Lee was 41 and lived at St Anne's with his wife Elizabeth—or 'Bessie'—his cousin whom he had married two years before. Suddenly Arthur Lee wrote a letter to his father. Arthur Lee was a partner, and his advice appears to have been as frequently asked and followed as that of his brother. In this crisis his father and his brother dealt with him gently and considerately. John Purser, junior (of whom more later), was also a partner, and William Smythe-Lee-Grattan-Guinness, another brother, was in orders. John Purser, junior, was an old and valued friend of the Guinness family and his son, John Tertius Purser, was a brewer in the firm and had been tutored with the Guinness boys in the same schoolroom.

Arthur Lee fell into great difficulties and he sought help from his father and brother:

James's Gate
13 June 1839

(Forgive such a Note—I *can not now write* letters. A. L. G.)

My dear Father,

I well know it is impossible to justify to you my conduct if you will for-give me, it is much to ask, but I already feel you have & I will ever be sincerely grateful. . . . I know not what I should say, but do my dear Father believe me I feel deeply. . . the extreem & undeserved kindness you have ever, and *now*, *More than ever* shown me.

Believe me above all that 'for worlds' I would not hurt your mind, if I could avoid it—of all the living. Your feelings are most sacred to me, this situation, in which I have placed myself, has long caused me the acutest pain & your wishes on the subject must be *religiously* obeyed by me. I *only implore you* to *allow me* to hope and forbear a little longer, I *feel it* but *just* to do so. . . .

Your dutiful, grateful but distressed son,
A. L. G.

In some way this crisis was overcome. What is important to us is the way that it was resolved. Arthur and Benjamin Lee did not reproach Arthur Lee but helped him sensibly and effectively. It was at his own wish that he withdrew from the partnership, and in so doing he resisted all their generous offers. With his £12,000 from his brewery partnership, and his other shares, he was satisfied. He moved, eventually, to Stillorgan Park. First, in 1839, he had to agree not to issue any more notes without the consent of the firm. Then he requested the conclusion of the partnership. In order to avoid his getting further into debt the partners signed a common declaration that they would not advance money without mutual consultation.

The reconsideration of the partnership evidently led to a proposal that the business might be wound up. In November Arthur Lee wrote to his brother a letter which indicates that Benjamin Lee was already the managing partner, in fact if not in name, while the second Arthur Guinness was already withdrawing from active management. This letter is one of the most important surviving in the Guinness records, for it shows clearly that Arthur Guinness before 1839 was the dominant partner, and that after 1839 he was succeeded by Benjamin Lee.

James's Gate
7 November 1839

My dear Ben,

I trust I am not mistaken in considering you inclined to carry-on the important Manufactory here into a new Partnership for though I would have no right to influence you so to do yet I can not but feel it a pity that so well-established & prosperous a Business should be given up when one in

Arthur Lee Guinness

every way suited to conduct it is already so much at the Helm; it would be indelicate for me to contemplate my Father's either withdrawing or otherwise, I would only say I trust God may long grant him health & strength to *preside* over its interests, as he has ever done, not only NOMINALLY (which I recollect was *your expressed* wish should ever be the case—at the formation of the present Partnership & in which we all so heartily joined) but so far as may be desirable with his own superior and most important presence. Now connected with these feelings is the situation in which I am myself placed and this it is creates the occasion for my Letter. I wished to have conversed with you on the subject but really fear I could not express myself as I would desire and think I ought not longer to delay removing any possible misapprehension from yr. mind by opening my own more fully to you than I have had an opportunity of doing. *Decidedly* then my Dear Brother I would decline entering into another Partnership of even the shortest duration for I feel that even if my Father & you wished me to do so; I ought not, I ought not to be in receipt of profits which I honestly confess I feel myself uninstrumental in realizing, and as for the pecuniary advantage, I would with equal truth say that I would *prefer* my present moderate expenditure to an increased one—such being my *long* confirmed sentiments is not the time arrived to act on them?—by leaving perfectly at liberty, as far as feelings are concerned, other Parties, to make those arrangements which may even now be urgent considering the uncertainty of Life and the difficulties that *may* arise, which however *I* need not anticipate; having thus endeavoured to put you in possession of my *real* sentiments as far perhaps as is necessary to trouble you with in this shape, and requesting you to lay this communication before my Father as early as you may think it judicious, I conclude assuring you as ever, of my being yr. gratefully affect. Brother

A. L. GUINNESS

In May 1840 the new arrangement was projected which left the capital in the firm, though it allowed Arthur Lee to draw a considerable sum to buy and rebuild a house at Stillorgan, where he lived until his death in 1863. Here he collected pictures, composed verses in praise of nature, and sealed his letters with designs of a young Greek god. But his withdrawal to this rural retreat did not prevent a recurrence of financial troubles, and he further embarrassed his brothers by his political sympathies and associations, especially in 1848. In the end his family forgave him all and paid his debts. He lacked the temperament necessary for success in business, and the stability of character to find happiness in life. But he had a kind heart, and his memory is preserved by a simple testimonial to his exertions during the Great Famine. These are recorded by the

The Second Arthur Guinness

inscription on a small commemorative obelisk of Connemara marble, which reads:

1847
TO ARTHUR LEE GUINNESS ESQ.
STILORGAN PARK

To mark the veneration of his faithfull labourers who in a period of dire distress were protected by his generous liberality from the prevailing destitution.

This humble testimonial is respectfully dedicated consisting of home material.

Its colour serves to remind that the memory of benefits will ever remain green in Irish hearts.

JOHN PURSER, JUNIOR

Where, in all this, were the Pursers? John Purser, junior, was also a partner, and his son was high up in the brewery hierarchy. John Purser, junior, knew about the crisis; it broke at James's Gate (where he lived) and not at St Anne's or Beaumont. Evidently at the end of 1840 he attempted to put pressure on the family to raise his share in the partnership, for there exists a much damaged copy of a letter written in reply by Arthur Guinness. It took John Purser, junior, firmly to task:

Dublin
7 January 1841

My dear John,

I have received your letter and shall endeavour to reply to each point in order. You assign as a reason for communication 'as of late it has occasionally happened that the expression of your sentiments has given me pain', I confess that on one or two occasions there was a coldness and dissatisfaction manifested in your manner towards me which I felt I did not deserve at your hands and this naturally [led to] some reaction on my part which was momentary as I am not in the habit of retaining in my mind feelings of the kind. You [say] 'I feel the present occasion to be not only important but as likely to be the last of the series of earthly engagements with you, which [have] happily continued in one form or another since I first came under your kind notice nearly 42 years ago'. I can surely have similar feelings seeing that upwards of 54 years have elapsed since [my family first had] communication with [yours], and never can memories of that period passed in conversation with your late excellent father and yourself have been more [agreeable] and have afforded me a rich satisfaction.

JOHN PURSER, JUNIOR, 1783–1858

Thought to be a copy by Sir Frederick Burton of a portrait
painted by him, date unknown: Guinness Collection

John Purser, Junior

Your letter presents two points for consideration. The first relates to the distribution of the shares vacated by my son Arthur's retirement. You say that his brother and myself being the original partners and myself now becoming a dormant partner...

[he expresses his withdrawal from active business]

...involving, it is true, less bodily labour (and rightly so) but possibly somewhat more of mental care and exertion and not a little of time also. And I cannot for a moment admit your claim of more than your due proportion of any difference of amount which shall arise from the vacated shares after deducting the annuity [being paid to my son Arthur. You say that for you 'more] self-denial as to domestic comfort' will be incurred. I would reply to this in a great degree...to be made by proper clerical assistance which should be provided out of savings from the vacated shares ...as more reasonable both as regarding the health of the partners and in every way than a surrender of my proportion of this part of the profits under [an arrangement] that any junior partner would by the retirement of the other have an additional burden of 50 % on time, labour and self-denial of domestic comfort.

As to your second point 'the present existing Sinking Fund' I cannot give my consent to the principle involved in your proposition, namely the right on the part of any partner in the firm to give to himself the taking out his full capital and also his share in an apparent balance on the 'Sinking Fund' after deducting merely the debts ascertained to be due by making no reserve to meet any possible loss on this which might afterwards prove so, and especially in our case where the amount of debts due is so very large, besides the certain loss and extensive costs which must arise when the casks come to be disposed of....You say 'the winding up the concern is an affair with which I have nothing to do, I could neither cause nor prevent it'. I reply that by the partnership deed each partner virtually consents and agrees to a winding up, a determining the debt of the partnership and certain stated contingencies and these are consequently bound to be attendant upon such determination. I do not say that some modification of the objection made to the proportion of any approved existent Sinking Fund may not be considered (please God). You in the conclusion of your letter say, 'in these remarks on the subject as one man to another' and again, 'I should be undeserving of a family did I not regard their interests'. I feel constrained to say that the evident implication conveyed in the first remark is not borne out by the conduct towards you during the past 42 years, and as to the second, I do not think you have any cause for fearing that the interests of your family will be overlooked or endangered in the event of our winding up the concern.

[...] partnership in which you [over the] period of seven years (through the goodness of Providence towards our firm) realised a sum of £28,809.

I hope, my dear John, you will see cause to alter the judgments you have formed on the subject in question and that we shall, by God's blessing, maintain the harmony and peace which has so long prevailed amongst us.

I trust that you will agree with me that our future communication had better be oral and I shall do everything on my part towards a kindly ...and feeling and manner between us.

> I remain, my dear John,
> Yours most truly,
> ARTHUR GUINNESS

In no other letter, perhaps, does the second Arthur Guinness's character appear more clearly. It expresses his clarity of thought and his firmness. He was also forgiving once his position was established beyond doubt. Seven years later, on his eightieth birthday, he ended a letter to his son Benjamin Lee with a request to be remembered 'affectionately to dear Mr Purser...'.

[7]

The Development of Guinness's Trade

...we are especially bound to notice our highly esteemed and valued
friend Mr Waring.... (*Letter from the partners of Guinness's brewery to
Henry Tuckett, 10 March 1832.*)

INTRODUCTION

THE STORY of Guinness's trade falls into several well-defined periods.
Before 1806 the firm was predominantly a Dublin porter brewery
and it shared with the other Dublin porter breweries in the fight
against English competition. Then it shared in the rise of the Dublin
trade after the English brewers had been driven out. By the eighteen-
twenties Guinness's had a strong English connexion, but were
fighting bitterly to defend their Dublin trade. This they did successfully, and in the eighteen-forties there was a resurgence of demand in
Dublin, followed in the eighteen-fifties by the beginning of an enormous growth in demand in the rest of Ireland. From 1870 (until
much later on) the major part of Guinness's trade by volume was
in Ireland, although the value of the English trade was still very
important.

But at the end of the eighteenth century the greater part of Guinness's trade was still in Dublin. A number of other Irish centres
were being supplied, of which the principal ones were Athy, Athlone,
Derry and Shannon Harbour, with a very small trade to Liverpool
and Bristol. The figures suggest that the pattern remained the same
from 1806 until about 1824. It was in that year that the main
Liverpool agency of Bewley and Nevill was established, followed
shortly by the Bristol agency of Samuel Waring, and in 1825 the
Bristol agent established the London agency of Henry Tuckett.

In 1806 most of the firm's trade was in Dublin and the remainder
in the country. The bulk of this trade was in porter sold at 55*s*.
a hogshead. Of the 1550 hogsheads sold in the country, 450 hogsheads were of Double Stout at 58*s*. a hogshead, and of 2600 hogsheads sold in Dublin, 1000 were of Double Stout. The market in
Dublin was therefore for the stronger and more expensive beer, and

these figures are confirmed by a similar brewery estimate in February 1807.

The sales of beer from Guinness rose from 6704 hogsheads in 1800–1 to 44,981 hogsheads in 1816. Thereafter they fell to 18,468 hogsheads in 1820. Gradually they crept up to 54,637 hogsheads in 1834. By 1840 the sales were 53,922 hogsheads, and in 1850 they were 65,541 hogsheads. Thus from the end of the Napoleonic Wars to the end of the Great Famine the output of Guinness rose by 50 per cent. By this time the market was chiefly in England. In 1855, for instance, 40,000 hogsheads of Double Stout were sold in England, and 16,000 in Ireland (6000 in Dublin), while a further 15,000 hogsheads of Single Stout (or porter) were sold in Ireland (8000 in Dublin and 7000 elsewhere).

The Proprietors Memorandum Book and the brewing books of the period throw light on Guinness's trading conditions during and after the Napoleonic Wars. In 1803 the fire insurance was raised on the brewery by £5000 and on the mills by £3500. The main business, therefore, was brewing, but it was only just the biggest part of the occupations of the firm unless the mills had earlier been grossly under-insured. In many respects the two businesses were operated jointly: in 1803 certainly the wages of the out-clerk (or traveller in Dublin) for the flour-mills appears in the brewery's accounts. The relationship between the two businesses was, no doubt, more than incidental. The knowledge acquired by the miller in buying corn and flour may have provided valuable experience for the brewer. After 1815 Arthur Guinness's main interest seems to have been in banking, so that the brewery was only one concern of the family, and the absence of the accounts of the mill and the Bank of Ireland may tend to exaggerate both the importance and the independence of the brewery.

THE HIBERNIAN MILLS

The Hibernian flour-mills at Kilmainham were extremely important from 1800 to 1815, and perhaps later.[1] The mills were established by

[1] The firm was known as 'Arthur Guinness, brewer and flour dealer'. In the *Dublin Directory* for 1793 there is an entry 'Guinness, Arthur and Co., brewers and flour factors'. In 1794 this entry reappears, with a 'corrigendum: Guinness, Arthur and Son, brewers'. From 1795 to 1807 the entry is 'Guinness, Arthur and Son, brewer and flour merchant', and then in 1808 the entry becomes 'Guinness (A., Ben., and W. L.) brewer'.

SHANNON HARBOUR, NEAR BANAGHER, OFFALY
Photograph by D. F. Strachan

The Hibernian Mills

the first Arthur Guinness in 1782[1] and left by him to his sons when he died in 1803. The second Arthur appears to have managed them, and they were not finally leased to another miller until 1828.[2] In calculations relating to the half-year 1 November 1805 to 22 May 1806 the total purchases of wheat during this time were 5809 barrels, while a 'proffit' of £1322. 10s. 0½d. was made on a turnover of £14,950: this was about one-half of the turnover of the brewery in a half-year. The flour-mills therefore contributed about a quarter of the Guinness manufacturing turnover and profits during this period. What is especially interesting is that the calculations are in the second Arthur's handwriting and show that he was in control.

The wheat for the mill was bought at Ballinderry in County Tipperary in 1804 for 42s. a bushel. The twining, weighing and filling came to 6d., the expenses of the Ballinderry store (managed by one Champion) to 1s. 1d., the cost of bank charges at Birr to 6d., carriage from Ballinderry to the Shannon at 3½d., freight to Shannon Harbour from Lough Derg 1s. 6d., from Shannon Harbour to Dublin via the Grand Canal 2s. 9½d., from the canal to the mills, 2½d., and sacks 3d. The total cost of wheat was therefore £2. 9s. 1½d., transport costs being equal to one-sixth of the original cost of the wheat. Thereafter charges for manufacturing were 6s. The overheads of milling were far less than for brewing.

There was a temporary setback in 1806 when a fire destroyed the mill. A large quantity of flour and malt was lost and although Guinness got £4750 in compensation from the underwriters there was a report that the property had been insufficiently insured. The insurance was carried by the Hibernian Insurance Company, the first fire-insurance company to be established in Dublin. The first Arthur Guinness and Samuel Guinness had been founder-members

[1] This date is significant, because it is three years before Foster's Act that allegedly led to a great deal of the increase in tillage that took place in this decade. The digging of the canals was probably more important than has been assumed.

[2] The first document is dated 1758 and refers to the watermill at Kilmainham 'called the Boarded mill and heretofore called the tucking mill situate between the old convent or Priory of Kilmainham and the river Cammock', which is about a mile to the west of James's Gate. A contemporary map shows it to be between Bow Bridge and Golden Bridge. In 1803 the mill passed to the second Arthur Guinness's management and was called 'the Hibernia Mill', and by 1838 it was in the hands of John Birkby; in 1854 the lease was sold to Arthur Guinness of Beaumont and Arthur Lee Guinness of Stillorgan, as trustees of the Reverend William Smythe Guinness and R. S. Guinness, subject to a life-interest of John Wilmot, the freeholder, who died in 1881, having broken the entail, so that it passed to Edward Cecil Guinness. The freehold, therefore, became Guinness property only many years after the operation of the mill had passed from their hands.

of the company. The loss of the mill, however, does not seem to have interrupted Guinness's business progress or caused even transient financial embarrassment.

THE SALES OF BEER

The Dublin brewers' agreements fixed the prices and trading conditions of the brewery, and the price pattern of the period can be reconstructed from a list in the Proprietors Book. From 1796 to 1799 the price of porter was 50s. per hogshead. In the later years it rose to 55s. In 1800 the price rose first to 60s. and then to 70s., and in 1802 it fell first to 60s. and then to 50s. In 1808 it rose to 52s. 8d., and in 1809 to 55s. It remained at about this until 1812 when it became 58s. 4d., and then in 1813 and 1814 it was 60s. Various allowances were made on these prices, usually of 5 per cent to regular or possibly tied customers.

Most of the beer was sold in Dublin. In the season of 1807–8 nearly six-sevenths of total output was sold there. A few years earlier a few hogsheads are recorded as having been sold at Derry, and some porter was shipped to Leith. Some years later Athlone and Limerick are mentioned. It is reasonable to assume that there were accounts at these towns all through the period, and that there are others now untraceable, so that it becomes clear that most porter was sold in Dublin, and that the rest went mainly along the canal to Athy and Shannon Harbour, with a few shiploads going to ports like Derry and Leith.

Some beer was brewed for the West Indies (the first reference is in 1802) at £3 a hogshead, which was 5s. more than ordinary porter, 'to pay for the Encreased quantity of Malt and Hops'. West Indies Porter was fairly regularly brewed after this.

The selling was done by regular private accounts, presumably to private customers, and by 'out-clerks' in Dublin who were paid mainly on commission of 6d. or 4d. or 2d. a hogshead, depending upon the turnover of their accounts. They were in regular communication with the agents at the ports to which they shipped. Some of them appear to have had special arrangements. Some of them, like Pim's, were shipping companies on the canals or the Irish Sea.

Two main kinds of beer were sold which were called Town Porter and Country Porter. A third kind, known as Keeping Beer, was brewed and there were two other beers—Superior and West Indies Porter. There is some confusion in the nomenclature and, indeed, in the varieties sold. Almost all the beers were a mixture and there was no great consistency in strength or colour from season to season. In 1826 the Bristol Port records show a cargo of ale from Guinness's to the Bristol agent. Later Guinness's regularly sent 'Alloa ale' to Bristol until 1839, but this may have been ale bought in Alloa, sent to Dublin via the Clyde and Forth Canal, and transhipped at Dublin. There are no entries in the Dublin port books to show this, but the absence of entries is not evidence that ale was not transhipped because cargoes were entered only when they paid duty, and Guinness's were wholesale merchants exempt from customs duty on goods held in bond. There is no record of ale brewing in the available brewing books of that period.

By 1820 the beer sold in the British Isles became regularly defined as weaker dark beer, called Single Stout, and a stronger dark beer called Double Stout. A stronger brew, West Indies Porter, had an added hop content. This is a simplification, but only a small one, because the beers themselves altered slightly from year to year under the press of changes of price for raw materials and sporadic manufacturing difficulties. Nevertheless the simplification is permissible for the purpose of explaining the changes in the output of Guinness's beer and the marketing conditions in which it was sold.[1]

THE COURSE OF TRADE

In the first decades of the nineteenth century the sales of Guinness's beer were mainly in Dublin; about one-third of the sales were elsewhere in Ireland and in England. In 1807, out of a total production of 20,000 hogsheads about 5000 were being sent to Shannon Harbour, on the Grand Canal. Other sales were made at Boyle, Athy, Loughrea, Athlone and Limerick. All these places were on the canals or waterways from Dublin. Two names of agents are preserved—Pim's Stores at Shannon Harbour and John Tinsley at Limerick. On 2 March 1810 twenty hogsheads of beer were shipped to Derry to Thomas and David Ramsay, and in August of the same year fifteen barrels were sent to Douglas in the Isle of Man. In 1812 agents at Liverpool are identifiable for the first time, and the same year agents

[1] See below, ch. 8.

123

appear in Athy, Carlow, Longford and Granard. Between 1800 and 1815, then, when trade expanded six times, the market for Guinness's beers spread first into Ireland and then across the Irish Sea to the Isle of Man and to England. In March 1811, indeed, it reached Lisbon because that city was one of the few not affected by the Berlin decrees forbidding English trade in Napoleonic Europe.[1]

After 1815 the output of beer fell rapidly from 66,000 bulk barrels to 27,000 in 1820.[2] This fall of sales to three-sevenths of their former total in a period of only five years appears to have occurred mainly in Dublin because there is evidence of spreading trade in Ireland and in England. In 1817 there is a reference to some twenty or more towns in Ireland that were being supplied with Guinness's beer. In 1816 the first steam-packets began to operate from Dublin to Holyhead, and the ties with England probably became even stronger than they had formerly been. Certainly by 1824, when output was only slightly higher than in 1820, it was in certain circumstances cheaper to use the paddle-steamers than to use sailing ships to send stout to Liverpool.[3] In 1819 stout was being supplied to Whitehaven, and in 1821 to Belfast, going to both places by sea. If there was a fall in consumption mainly in Dublin it is hard to assign reasons for it. There is no documentary evidence remaining in the brewery. There are references to distress in Dublin itself, and there are references to the inordinately high price of raw materials. Hops and barley reached their highest prices of the nineteenth century in 1816. The period from 1815 to 1824 was a bad one in the whole of the British Isles, with only a small revival from 1821 to 1822, years in which the sales of Guinness's beer rose by about one-ninth.

A possible further reason for the falling off of the brewery's trade after 1815 is a shortage of capital to finance it.[4] In the correspondence concerned with the Liverpool agency in 1824 there are several references to the need to avoid the tying up of capital in the trade,

---

[1] It may have been a gift to the Peninsular Army from the partners because there is no entry of payment. The Duke of Wellington was born in Ireland and lived there at some stages of his life.

[2] The total sales figures were not quite as seriously affected because the strength of the beer was reduced slightly.

[3] The first steamer service between Dublin and Liverpool was established in 1824. The journey took fourteen hours: the average time for a sailing vessel on the same journey was a week.

[4] In 1815 the firm had to pay over £5900 as the result of a final settlement on behalf of Edward Guinness, Arthur's bankrupt brother.

The Course of Trade

and in 1829 Arthur Guinness wrote to his niece at Bristol, of whose father's affairs he was sole executor, to exhort her to sell her government stock. The family held large quantities of stock. There were at least three trusts established by the Guinness brothers for their children, or by the first Arthur Guinness for his daughters, which had claims on the brewery profits, and which in a number of cases appear to have been converted to government stock. The second Arthur Guinness wrote: 'We wished to employ our money in a profitable way, but in this we have I think been disappointed and our great difficulty in the way has been that owing to the low prices of government funds compared with the prices at the period of investment a great loss would have been incurred had we sold out. That difficulty is now removed in as much as prices would nearly bring £100 for ea. £100 stock.' It may very well be that the urge for security which the family situation of the brothers gave them at the end of the Napoleonic Wars was a potent factor in starving the business of capital at that time. Certainly the expansion after 1826 was accompanied by a 'heavy' investment, and this may have included outlay made necessary by the postponement of investment in earlier years. There were also the other demands: Arthur Guinness once complained, with justice, of the burdens of 'many, so many relations', most of whom appear to have been fecund and many, especially the clergy, feckless. 'May I recommend, my dear Olivia, that you keep a systematic account of all your expenditures for in that way you may more easily judge...'—this is a recurring theme in the family letters.

A letter to his eldest brother Hosea, the rector of St Werburgh's, deals with Arthur Guinness's position as the 'Family Banker'.

Dr G.

Rathdrum,[1] *17 May 1821*

My dear Hosea,

I feel myself placed in a painful & delicate situation when called upon to address my Elder Brother, and a Brother who I so sincerely love and respect upon the subject of his pecuniary concerns but my situation by which I am unavoidably obliged to act as the Family Banker forces me to speak plainly. Your Letter recd. this day mentions that Brother William says 'that it was understood at the time that Edward's allowance might be considered as much a charge upon the Trade as any of the Clerks' Salaries as it was given in consideration of Edward's having acted in that capacity for 6 years previously to the commencement of the annuity and

---

[1] The house of Arthur Guinness's son, William Smythe-Lee-Grattan-Guinness.

The Development of Guinness's Trade

having given up all expectation of further advantage from a continuance in the House, in that he [—] thought that our late dear Brother Ben was of that opinion'. Now in the first place I would ask Brother William how it was, that [—] feelings that led our late dear Brother to acquiesce in charging the annuity at the end of each year not to the Trade but to the Family fund? But I would ask again what claim had Edward upon the Trade? Had he rendered any service to the Trade to entitle him to an annuity, and was it for a given period of years? Certainly not; upon what could He have founded 'expectation of future advantage from continuance in the House'. Surely upon nothing. . . .

The second Arthur, as Governor of the Bank of Ireland, went frequently to London and to Limerick on bank business, and appears to have worked very hard for the bank.[1] He held at least £15,000 of bank stock (either in his own or his family's names).

Arthur's preoccupation with bank business is shown by his appearance before the House of Lords Select Committee on Promissory Notes in 1826 as one of the two Dublin directors of the Bank of Ireland called upon to give evidence.[2] He gave a series of careful and informative answers to the Committee, revealing himself to be a carefully coached member of the currency school, believing firmly that prosperity depended upon a sound currency, and that the currency should be a funded one, not based upon bank credit. This point of view might seem to some observers to have been a dogma unrelated to his own business experience: his colleague, Lunell, said in evidence that he was not in trade himself, 'but my friends and connections have been engaged in trade. I have been in the Bank of Ireland some years'.[3] Arthur Guinness was, presumably, an important friend and connexion whose experience was used to confirm his views on the relationship between trade and credit policy.

The period of Arthur Guinness's high office at the Bank coincides with a decline in the brewery's trade. The Bank of Ireland took up a great deal of his time and money, and it would have been against his own interests to sink more money into a declining trade like brewing. Secondly, the firm itself was short of capital as a result of the falling profit margins associated with reduced turnover, high raw-material prices and falling market prices. Lastly, it is possible that the family had made unwise investments in consols which had

[1] See above, pp. 105 and 120.
[2] P.P. 1826–7 (245), vol. VI, p. 377, *Report from the Select Committee of the House of Lords on Promissory Notes.*
[3] *Ibid.* p. 446.

slumped. Many thousands had been invested in government stock which they were unable to realize because of its low prices.

For these reasons therefore it is possible that Guinness's may have given harder terms to their customers than their competitors did, and they may have in consequence lost some of their share of the Dublin trade.

COSTS

The management of the brewery was very cost-conscious. The profitability of the firm was closely related to the quantity sold. In 1802 the average rate of profit was 8s. 3d. per barrel, or nearly £10,000. Overhead costs or 'charges' were about 12s. a barrel, so that 30s. to 35s. represented the cost of raw materials—about 25s. to 30s. for malt, and about 5s. for hops. The variation in the price of malt and hops was very significant for the building up of costs, but the quantity produced was almost as important. This last became clearest at a time of falling output, especially in the period 1813 to 1818. On a trade of 53,360 barrels the 'charges' were 8s. 4d. a barrel, while on a trade of 35,570 barrels they were 10s. 1d.

The 'charges' were divided in 1818 between, 'No. 1, those absolutely proportionate' (5s. 3d.) which included the 5 per cent allowance to agents (1s.), Christmas allowance (1s.), sinking fund (1s.), and another unidentifiable item of 3d. The second class of charges were 'partially proportionate'. These included 'coal, Brewery Labour, Clerks' Salaries, Cooperage, Forage, Horses, Bungs, Paper, Taps, Postage Stamps and several other articles of which there are less consumed when less business is done'. This Arthur Guinness put down as 2s. 11d. The third class of charge was 'fixed and permanent'. This 'includes Rent, Taxes, Brewery Concerns, Fire Insurances and Servants' Wages'. This class was 4s. 2d. in the higher year and 6s. 3d. in the lower year.

The relationship between prices, costs and profits was made more complicated by the long period of time that elapsed between the first purchase of a raw material, whether it was malt or hops, and the final receipt of the proceeds of the sale of porter. Barley from the harvest of the autumn of 1826 was bought and malted later in the year; some of it was used in the winter brewings, and the porter was sent to Bristol for the summer season of 1827; the Bristol agent was in the habit of remitting his summer receipts to Dublin in the late

The Development of Guinness's Trade

autumn. At the least, therefore, a year elapsed between the expenditure on some barley and the receipts from the sale of the porter made from it, and over a year the prices of barley, malt and porter could fluctuate a great deal. But a year was the shortest period that could elapse. Some of the malt bought in 1826 was not used in the winter of 1826–7, but in the winter of 1827–8, because if a harvest produced a malt of outstanding quality the brewer took advantage of this by buying it and storing it either as malt—or more usually as a Keeping Beer which he could make more successfully when the malt was excellent. Some of the porter in any case made from 1826 barley was not sold in the summer of 1828, but held over as Keeping Beer, and sold in a mixture in the summer of 1829. Three years might easily elapse, therefore, between expenditure on barley and receipt from the sale of beer. These complications are difficult to analyse but they are important because it was in the successful negotiation of this series of complicated hurdles that profit was to be made; a wrong guess might mean a loss. The possibility of loss and the length of the period in which the circulating capital was tied up explain, too, the width of the profit margin in the early nineteenth century.

The price of malt was the most important factor in costs. The brewery bought its malt as cheaply as it could during a period of great local and seasonal variations in price. At that time a 'prevailing market price' for any commodity is difficult to find; and Guinness's experience with malt shows how important local differences could be in determining the margin between profit and loss. The average price of malt paid by the brewery differs from that of the parliamentary papers, and there was a serious conflict of evidence before the Select Committee of 1818. Originally the malt appears to have been made from Irish barley on commission in Dublin, though there 'our maltings' were soon acquired and operated.

Buying barley or malt and hops was one of the main business activities of the firm. It is possible to trace each spring the beginning of the calculation of the likely annual requirements of raw materials in the light of prospective sales of beer, the stocks of beer, and the stocks of malt and hops. By the late autumn the main purchases were made, according to revised estimates of likely sales, and in the light of the prices and qualities of the new crops. In the winter and spring there were supplementary purchases. The calculation of the

128

Costs

amount needed was varied slightly by the strength of the beer—'In October 1801 exactly 10 stones of Malt to the Hhd. of Porter—in October 1802 exactly 9 stone 10⅔ lbs.' The calculation was possibly also varied by the estimated extract of the malt. The calculation of the amount of hops also varied according to the likely production of Keeping and Country Porter—the hop rate varied from 3 to 6 lb. per hogshead for beers sold in Europe, and was as high as 6½ lb. per barrel for the West Indies Porter.

In 1802 the malt that was bought was largely English: 'Saturday, 20th November—We calculate our Stock of Malt this day to be 2,200 Bls. including all that we have Bt. since 1st inst. some of which is not yet Delivered. This will be only enough to bring us up to the beginning of January, so that we think we should purchase 2,000 Bls. of prime old Malt out of the next Fleet that comes in.' Malt was sometimes bought in London and brought to Dublin on the ship *Esther* from London, but most of the English barley used by the firm was malted in Ireland. The Irish maltings were owned by Redmond at Athy and by Stewart at Dungarvan. There was another at Charleston.[1] The firm's malt houses were in Dublin, one actually at the brewery. Mountmellick, at the terminus of a branch of the Grand Canal, is first mentioned in 1800, but the Grand Canal records show that malt was being brought from there to Dublin much earlier.

The barley from England came from Norwich, via Yarmouth,[2] the freight costing per quarter (in 1812) 3s. 6d., shipping expenses 7d., insurance 1s. 3d. and interest and other charges at Norwich 5½d. This compared with a cost of barley at £2. 5s. 11d., malting charges at 6s. 6d., and duty at 4½d. In 1818 barley was bought in Southampton but this was an exception.

In 1816 malt was bought from McCabe and Taylor of Midleton. It appears that on the whole the barley was bought by Guinness and malted on commission—the Irish barley came mainly from Midleton, Drogheda, Limerick and Youghal, as well as from Waterford and Wexford, after 1818. Sometimes the barley came from other brewers —in 1816 there was a purchase from Beamish & Crawford in Cork.

The hops were almost all bought in London, on the samples offered by travellers for the hop merchants—usually Talver, Milburn &

---

[1] Near Midleton, County Cork.
[2] The barley came in the *Ruby*, the *Endeavour* and the *Liberty*, out of Yarmouth, and the *Enterprize* and the *Fortitude* out of London.

Prestwick, or Bush and Ware, all of the Borough. For the most part the hops were from Kent, but in 1801–2 and again in 1809 and 1811 there are records of Flemish hops having been bought—despite the war with France. The stocks were kept at the brewery and in London, and shipped in by the ordinary trading vessels.[1]

The sale of barm, or the surplus yeast from brewing, and grains to distillers and dairy farmers was a substantial trade in itself. According to some calculations the proceeds from some sales were as much as 15 per cent of the total receipts of the brewery in 1803 (20 October), when direct costs were £1. 14s. 2d., 'charges' 12s., and the receipts of barm and grains 5s. 10d. per hogshead of porter.

Waste was also extremely important; it was about 2 gallons 3⅛ quarts per hogshead in 1801–2, and later rose to 3 gallons—about 6–7 per cent of the total brewings. The precision of these calculations at such an early period is another sign of careful attention to the brewing process and to the importance of controlling costs as far as was technically possible.

BRISTOL

The original venue of Guinness's English expansion was the port of Bristol. The choice of Bristol for an important entrepôt of Irish beer is due, in Guinness's case at least, to the chance of a good connexion. There were, however, deeper factors at work. Before 1820 Bristol was the second city of England, though it was economically stagnant. In 1827 when the Gloucester and Berkeley Canal was first opened it carried 107,000 tons of trade,[2] showing that it was the centre of a prosperous region. The people drank beer, or malt liquor, as it was then often called—the southern agricultural labourers were renowned for this: 'Purchased liquor is an article of expenditure particularly prevalent in the South, and there is hardly a labouring man who does not think it necessary to indulge himself every day in a certain quantity of malt liquor', wrote Eden in 1797.[3] What was true of the labouring classes was certainly true of the prosperous bourgeois of Bristol.

The north of England was less propitious as a centre for commercial

[1] The *Jason* and the *Belinda* are ships mentioned. These ships called in at Bristol and Liverpool on their way to Dublin.
[2] *Victoria History of the County of Gloucester* (London, 1907), vol. II, p. 192.
[3] Sir F. M. Eden, *State of the Poor* (London, 1797; reprinted, abridged, London, 1928), p. 107.

brewing. The proportion of brewing-victuallers was high there, and domestic brewing existed on a large scale.[1] This was less true of Manchester than of most towns in the North,[2] and not at all true of Liverpool. Liverpool, like London and Norwich, was dominated by big brewers,[3] and probably, like London, had a large number of tied houses.

The origins of the Bristol connexion are obscure. The Guinnesses had many relations in and near the city, and G. and S. Lunell (a name that recurs in the family tree) were big import merchants, bringing oats, barley and wheat from Waterford and Galway to Bristol. Bristol and Ireland had strong trading connexions, and these were strengthened after the steam-packets began to operate in 1821 to Cork, and in·May 1822 to Dublin. It often took a fortnight to cross the Irish Sea by sailing-boat, so that the steam-packets were greatly welcomed.[4] Bristol merchants operated all over the British Isles, but especially in Gloucester, Dublin, Liverpool and London. The Kennet and Avon Canal linked the city with London, while the Dublin boats sailed via Liverpool. Bristol's trade with Ireland more than doubled between 1824 and 1834 mainly as a result of the steamships, and the removal of export dues to Ireland in 1826. It was mainly an export trade, so the return freights from Dublin were cheapened.[5]

The imports to Bristol were mainly oats, barley, wheat, flour, pigs, potatoes, butter and horses. Beer came only in small quantities and mainly from Cork and Waterford. The local trade of Bristol appears to have been relatively stagnant in the eighteen-twenties and eighteen-thirties judging from the volume of local criticism of the Dock Company and the City Corporation. There were a few porter breweries, but a great deal of the beer sold came from elsewhere. From 1820 to 1825 as well as the products of the Bath Pale Beer and Porter Brewery and Bristol breweries there were agents for Bradford Strong Beer and Porter, beer from Shepton Mallet, Whitbread's London Porter, Beamish & Crawford's Cork Porter, Greer & Murphy's Irish Porter and Scotch Ale,[6] Sweetman's Dublin Stout and Strong Ale, Barclay, Perkins' Extra Stout and other porters.

---

[1] Clapham, *The Economic History of Modern Britain*, vol. I, pp. 159 and 170.
[2] *Ibid.* p. 171.   [3] *Ibid.*
[4] John Latimer, *The Annals of Bristol* (Bristol, 1887), pp. 75–6.
[5] John Barnett Kington, *Trade of Bristol by a Burgess* (Bristol, 1834).
[6] See below, p. 132.

This indicates a vigorous import trade from the rest of the kingdom. Ale was the more expensive drink—Scotch Ale was 11s. a dozen quarts, Burton Ale 10s., Taunton Ale 9s. 6d., local ale 9s., while London, Bath and Dublin porter was 7s.

Ten barrels of porter were sent by Guinness to one N. James in 1819, and odd quantities later, but there was no agent. The first reference to Guinness occurs in the 1825 *Bristol Trade Directory*, published on 14 January, when William Smith of 5 Grove (*sic*) is put down as 'sole agent' for Guinness and Co's. Dublin Porter. A year later, 14 January 1826, he is replaced by S. Waring, 25 King Street. Samuel Waring is first mentioned in the *Bristol Mercury* of 25 September 1825, as importing 10 hogsheads of Guinness's porter from Dublin. He had opened an account on 8 August 1825 with the brewery. At the same time two other merchants, James and Roche, were importing from Dublin. By the autumn of 1826 cargoes went to Waring monthly, usually in the *Ann*, and they went in substantial quantities —for instance on 25 November 75 hogsheads, 25 barrels and 50 half-barrels came in to Waring from Guinness. The trade by this time was about half that of Beamish & Crawford. About a third of the Guinness trade was in ale, and by 1836 this was referred to regularly as Guinness's Alloa ale.[1] By 1836 Samuel Waring, now of 13 King Street, 'residence Stoke Bishop', a prosperous suburb near the houses of the local Guinness family, was importing 50 hogsheads and as many barrels and half-barrels a week, and twice as much in the weeks before Christmas and in the summer. Ships were coming two or three times a week. About half the Bristol imports from Ireland at this time were of Guinness's stout and ale, the remainder coming mainly from Cork and Waterford.

The establishment of the connexion in Bristol was a fortunate stroke. Samuel Waring, the agent, was a man of enterprise and ability. There are frequent and grateful references to his enthusiasm and efficiency in the firm's letter-books, as early as 1825. In 1832, in a letter to the London correspondent, Henry Tuckett, the second Arthur Guinness wrote as follows:

---

[1] This ale cannot be traced in the brewing books, and was presumably bought for resale from another brewery. There is no evidence surviving in Alloa, Edinburgh, Glasgow or Dublin that Guinness's bought the ale in Scotland; it may have been bought from another Dublin brewer and sold by Waring as Scotch ale because Scotch ale commanded a premium in Bristol. It is significant (see p. 133) that when Waring's son took over the Guinness agency the references to ale cease.

Bristol

Dublin. 10 March 1832

Henry Tuckett, Esq.

In replying to your letter of the 7 inst. we shall in the first place confine our observations to the existing connections with our British trade. A progressive increase of demand has (under Providence) been for several years past arising from the approved quality of the article aided by the zeal of our agents amongst whom we are specially bound to notice our highly esteemed and valued friend Mr Waring to whose enterprising spirit only equaled by his judgment and discretion we are chiefly indebted for having not only opened various channels from Bristol for the sale of our Porter in the West and South of England but into London itself until at last he succeeded in planting a principal agency in the Metropolis.

Samuel Waring had placed the London agency in the hands of Henry Tuckett (about whom he heard 'from a gentleman in Bath') and rapidly increased the brewery's sales in Bristol. The Guinness family were frequent visitors there. The second Arthur Guinness's sister lived there, and his nieces as well, so that Bristol was the English town with which they were most familiar.

The Bristol trade suffered a setback in 1837. Samuel Waring invested a large sum in 'railroad stock', and in the September of that year Guinness's heard from a third party[1] that he was being forced into bankruptcy. So great had been their trust that they had no record of his outstanding debt, no exact knowledge of his customers and their obligations, no precise estimate of his stocks, nor how far the London trade was in his hands. A flurry of correspondence took place and Benjamin Lee was sent to Bristol. By November, after the ship taking Benjamin Lee to Bristol had almost foundered, and after many protestations of faith in Samuel Waring (while at the same time accompanying them with searching examinations of his estate), the crisis passed. The brewery appears to have advanced him money on a mortgage of his house at Stoke Bishop (28 November 1837), and there was help, too, from his 'good friend Mr Fry'.

His son Edward assumed the agency with his father, and the accounts were put on a businesslike footing. At the same time the London agency was separated entirely from Bristol.

The first mention of Edward Waring as the agent is on 4 August

---

[1] Louisa Guinness's son-in-law, the Reverend Dr Samuel Day, whose son later married William Smythe-Lee-Grattan-Guinness's daughter.

1838; on 21 July the beer was still sent to Samuel Waring. Evidently the change-over took place between those two dates. No cargo of ale is ever attributed to Edward Waring.[1]

LONDON

The London agency was a success from the start although relationships with the agent, Henry Tuckett, were often strained.[2] He was irascible and prone to complain in immoderate terms if anything went wrong. In 1832 Arthur Guinness wrote to Henry Tuckett:

You are aware that the sudden increase of demand in the last two years, but more especially in the last, notwithstanding a prompt and extensive outlay on our part to prepare a proportionate supply drained our stock so low that altho' we last summer curtail'd our deliveries far within the requirements of our agents for the purpose of retaining a sufficiency for the spring demand before our new stock should be ripe for use, yet we have been obliged to come upon our beers brew'd last autumn sooner than was desirable. New beer under such circumstances could not arrive at the same degree of mellowness which winter brewed beer, permitted to ripen by time would naturally acquire and hence arises the apparent deficiency of fullness, which however from the excellence of the materials and the great care and skill exercised in the manufacture will now [?] daily disappear. And here we declare that the strength of our D.S.[3] *in itself* as well as its proportionate strength with our S.S.[4] this year equals with the year 1828 and with every other year has become fully and '*conscientiously*' manufactured according to the prices of both.

We now proceed to the painful part of our subject, namely to notice the terms in which your letter is couched, a style of address which we had hoped after what had passed on a late occasion would not have been repeated....

No earthly consideration would induce us to subject ourselves to revivals of similar feelings with those which at present distressingly impress our minds.

A violent riposte must have been sent because six days later Arthur Guinness wrote:

[1] The local bottlers of Guinness's beers were M. A. Wetherman & Co., 5 St Michael's Crescent. Wetherman became Bristol agent in 1850; he had been accountant to Waring, and was not apparently a bottler himself.

[2] Waring, Tuckett and Foster, Consignees for Guinness's Dublin Stout, 79 Lower Thames Street, appear in the *London Directory* in 1831 and 1833. According to the *London Directory*, Waring and Moline were the sole consignees for Guinness's Dublin Stout after 1834; their address from 1834 to 1836 was 79 Lower Thames Street, and in 1837 and 1838, 5 Adelaide Place, King William Street, City. Sparkes Moline (alone) appears as warehouse keeper in 1834 and 1835 at 8 Billiter Street.

[3] Double Stout.   [4] Single Stout.

London

Dublin 16 March 1832

Henry Tuckett, Esq.

We have first to say that we see no cause for changing our view of the subject referred to in our letter of the 10th instant which contained the *united* opinion of our Firm and not of an individual as you have ventured to insinuate. Your guess at the writer is equally without foundation. . . .

If your opinion of the estimation in which our porter is held in London be correct it would independently of these important considerations be inexpedient to make any further consignments at present. In the interim it will remain with our valued friend Mr Waring to whom this whole subject is referred to recommend some arrangement which may satisfy us.

This and other letters suggest that Tuckett tried to make trouble between the Guinnesses and John Purser, junior. In the spring of the next year it was Purser who terminated the agency personally while on a visit to London. Before this, however, there was a reconciliation:

Dublin 12 April 1832

Henry Tuckett, Esq.

The receipt of your letter from Bristol dated the 9th inst. has afforded us heartfelt gratification and we must cordially unite in your expression of a hope that our future correspondence will be maintained in a manner calculated to secure that friendship and the kindly feeling which we trust now does and will continue to exist between us.

The end of the affair in the next spring is worth quoting in full for the light it throws on the character of the second Arthur Guinness, and on the business habits of the time. In it Tuckett is firmly and fairly dismissed, with much dignity and no ill-will. The first letter asks him to state his case:

Private   *Dublin 27 February 1833*
H. Tuckett, Esq.

Dr Sir,

My anxiety to preserve that good understanding and kindly feeling between you and my firm which are vitally essential to our mutual comfort and advantage alone induces me to call yr attention to two of yr late letters, viz., those of the 7th and 14th Inst. in which the following expressions are used, 'I don't admire yr remark', 'gross neglect', 'doing me great injustice', etc. Now my Dr Sir I do not by any means wish to imply the idea that you should not freely and candidly state every complaint which may at any time exist, on the contrary I feel this to be the bounden duty of an Agent to do, but I would only suggest yr avoiding as much as possible attributing to us motives or charging us with intentions and according to the usual mercantile mode present statements of the circumstances

135

The Development of Guinness's Trade

themselves without any severe comments, one other expression I must allude to, in yr letter of the 14th 'at time you are suspicious that I charged you with more ullage than actually belonged to you'. This is indeed a severe charge and one we do not deserve as we are incapable of harbouring such a suspicion or expressing such a sentiment and this we before assured you of in a former correspondence on a similar painful occasion. I do hope my Dr Sir that you will receive this confidential communication with kindness for truly it is offered in friendship and with a sincere desire to promote and perpetuate a good feeling between you and my Firm and render our correspondence free from any thing which could for a moment interrupt the flow of mutual friendship and regard.

> Believe me to be
> My Dr Sir,
> Very sincerely yrs,
> A. G.

The reply was unsatisfactory. In the next letter Arthur Guinness dismissed him—regretfully because his work in promoting trade had been admirable.[1]

London *Dublin 4 April 1833*
Henry Tuckett, Esq.

Dear Sir,

We have rec'd yours of the 26 Ultimo in which you express your trust that upon the late interview with Mr Waring and Mr Purser you had proved your innocence of every charge except the state of your correspondence and your having declined to try the experiment we had requested you to make on some beer. You add that you had been unconscious of any defect in your mode of expression but would adopt measures in future to prevent a recurrence and that as to the latter objection you had acted for the best as you thought but that you equally regretted having incurred our displeasure thereby and you conclude with an assurance of your not having entertained any unfriendly or disrespectful feelings towards us. Your letter is silent regarding the main result of the interview at Bristol namely your having resigned the agency and expressed previously to Mr Waring that it had been your determination so to do for one or two months prior to the present complaint and added your wish that Mr Waring would undertake the business. Of this result we had been informed by our partner Mr Purser and by Mr Waring, who had in consequence proceeded to Bath and held a preliminary conversation with a gentleman who Mr Waring proposed to unite with him in the London agency. Mr Warings proposal had met our fullest approbation and came to us strongly recommended by Mr Purser. Under the circumstances the change of mind

---

[1] The letter quoted is a first draft and a slightly different version was actually sent; this is too damaged to be reproduced.

implied in your letter has come upon us by surprize. It has however engaged our deliberate attention and notwithstanding that we attach the fullest credit to your declaration that you were unconscious of having given offence and had no intention so to do and to your being now desirous in future to avoid such a recurrence, and although we can declare that we entertain for you the most sincere esteem and friendship and further that we appreciate very highly your exertion during the period you have been connected with us. Yet on a full review of all that has passed on the occasions which have given rise to Three solemn remonstrances on our part, we are with sincere regret obliged to say that we could not venture to look forward to any permanent continuance of a commercial correspondence upon a footing of mutual comfort and advantage and therefore we would suggest the expediency for your sake and ours that your resignation should not be withdrawn.

We cannot conclude without a fresh assurance of our personal regard for you and of the happiness it will give to hear at all times of your future success in any undertaking in which you shall engage. We omitted to say that one day after receipt of your letter a letter arrived from Mr Purser mentioning that you intended to write to us to the effect expressed in yours, and stating that He had declined acting on the subject having already committed it fully to the consideration of the Firm.

We remain Dear Sir
Yours truly
ARTH. GUINNESS SONS & CO.

The London agency was then put into the hands of Samuel Waring and Sparkes Moline, about whom Waring had heard 'from a gentleman in Bath'—as he had heard of Tuckett.

LIVERPOOL

In the Proprietors Memorandum Book for 3 July 1821 a note appears:

It is this day agreed to allow Henry Antisell to go to Liverpool, he being particularly desirous to do so and quite confident of being able to establish a considerable sale of porter there. We therefore consent to his taking 50 hhds. of porter on trial, on Commission. He to be allowed a Commission of 7s. 6d. British per hhd. and finding storage and making no charge whatever for cartage or otherwise, and from the regard we have for him we agree that provided the Commission on porter sold and other Profit and Commission in any other business he shall transact in the first six months shall not amount to £50 British clear of charges we will make up the deficiency of that sum—A. G.

Henry Antisell had come into the firm in 1814, or earlier, as an office apprentice. He had a Christmas bonus of £5. 13s. 9d. in that year, 25*s*. 6*d*. more the year after, £11. 7*s*. 6*d*. in 1817 and 1818 (by which time he was an office clerk) and £15 in 1819. In the middle of that year he became cashier. Then he sailed, solitarily, to Liverpool, and established the agency.

Liverpool was a considerable town by 1821, and *Gore's General Advertiser* carries notices of London Porter, Burton Ale, London Brown and Dublin Brown Stout, Edinburgh and Liverpool Ales, London Pale Ales and Welsh Ale. Barclay was the only brewer mentioned by name until in 1822 appears:

Brown Stout

Henry Antisell is constantly supplied with Porter from the Brewery of A. B. & W. L. Guinness & Co. of Dublin brewed in the winter of 1821–2 and which is of such quality as will stand the East and West India Climates.

Price £3. 15*s*. per hogshead and the casks 17*s*. Terms ready money and a discount of four months allowed.

29 Manesty Lane (26 September)

Thereafter Goodwyn's London Porter is advertised, as well as Bibby's Dublin Porter, Cork Brown Stout Porter, Belfast Porter and Strong Ale, and Nicholson's Superior Dublin Porter.

Henry Antisell set up as a commission agent at 29 Manesty Lane, Liverpool. He was one of ten porter dealers in 1821–2, and remained as Guinness agent until 1824. In that year Guinness, Bewley and Nevill, of 14 Manesty Lane, took his place, and in the following year, 1825, their address was 29 Manesty Lane—Antisell's address. John Guinness[1] left the business in 1826, and Bewley and Nevill kept on the agency until 1833–4, when Nevill and Frankland (of Hanover Street, where the agent had moved in 1829) took over. In 1837, with increasing business, they removed to Duke Street.

Guinness, Bewley and Nevill, in 1825, stepped up the advertising of Guinness's beer, as the following advertisement suggests:

Guinness & Co's. Dublin Porter

A constant supply of the above superior porter suitable for the East and West Indies and American markets. This article is well worthy of the attention of exporters from its moderate price and well known character in these markets. Apply to

Guinness, Bewley and Nevill, 29 Manesty Lane (23 September)

---

[1] See below, p. 139.

Liverpool

Possibly this effort was because Manders had opened an agency in Liverpool for their porter, and a number of other Dublin brewers followed suit, as well as Beamish & Crawford and the Cork brewers. The growth of the Liverpool trade appears to have been in two phases. First, there was a growth of trade before the end of the Napoleonic War. This appears to have died off after Waterloo. The total Irish exports of porter to Liverpool had been very small in 1817, when 12 hogsheads were sent from Dublin; by 1821 when Guinness sent 5 barrels, this was about one-fortieth of the total trade of about 100 hogsheads. In 1822, however, Antisell (the Guinness agent) imported nearly nine-tenths of the Irish porter; and this remained the same until 1823. When in February 1824 the Antisell agency was replaced by Bewley and Nevill, their share of a rapidly growing trade was rather smaller than Antisell's, but by 1826 Bewley and Nevill had returned to a bigger proportion. From 1827 the trade grew absolutely, but it fell as a proportion of the total Dublin trade to Liverpool, until by 1832 it was about a quarter. The Guinness trade was particularly strong in the smaller casks, suggesting that at that time the porter was not going much into bottle but was being sold in cask by publicans to ordinary customers. The decline in their share of the trade occurred mainly because the trade in the bigger casks grew and Guinness apparently took little part in it. Possibly, therefore, the other Dublin brewers had links with Liverpool bottlers, or even with the bigger Liverpool publicans, while Guinness exploited the market opened by the many new beer-houses in the industrial North.

John Grattan Guinness, sixth son of the first Arthur, became a partner of Bewley and Nevill. In a letter of 18 June 1825 the second Arthur Guinness told John that he was 'instrumental in forming your partnership', though the business was to be 'entirely separate—not directly connected with our agency'. In other words, Bewley and Nevill had been agents on behalf of the Dublin firm, while the new partnership was to be an independent business. This arrangement soon broke down. The division was too arbitrary, perhaps, and certainly the Liverpool trade was not a model to be followed. By about 1826 John Grattan Guinness appears to have withdrawn from the partnership. Unfortunately the letters of the period are almost all illegible, but it appears that his 'ideas' (unspecified) were not successful. Possibly these ideas were of selling porter with another

139

The Development of Guinness's Trade

commodity through a general dealer because the business at Liverpool was mainly one of importing Irish whiskey with porter as a side-line. On 26 July 1825 Benjamin Guinness wrote to his brother to say that the firm was eighth in the total Irish trade in Liverpool.

REASONS FOR THE TREND OF TRADE

The reasons for the growth of the English trade are hard to assign. The advantage of the Irish devaluation had finished in 1815. There had been an elimination of customs duty but the costs of freight had not fallen: in 1831 steamer freights were 6 per cent higher than freights on sailing-vessels for hogsheads, and a fifth to a quarter higher for barrels and kilderkins. Freight was a considerable charge. The cost was 7s. to London, 3s. 6d. to Liverpool and 5s. 8d. to Bristol[1]— on a cost ex-brewery of 58s. 6d. Guinness's stout was therefore an expensive beer in England selling at 7d. a bottle (presumably a quart) to private customers in London. The London bottled porter sold at 4½d., and stout at 5d. while Edinburgh and Burton ales were 8½d. and ordinary ales 6½d. a bottle. It seems probable, therefore, that the growth in Guinness's trade was connected with the rising incomes of the middle class, and the recruitment of efficient agents at Bristol, London and other British towns.

By 1840 53 per cent of Guinness's sales in bulk barrels were in England and Scotland and about 60 per cent by value. The remaining 40 per cent or so was probably equally divided between consumption in Dublin and consumption in the rest of Ireland. In the years immediately before this the London agent had changed to Sparkes Moline, and in Bristol to Edward Waring.[2] About a sixth of Guinness's English sales were in London; the midlands had been opened to trade, and a substantial trade went to Macclesfield and Bolton. There was a small trade, too, at Newcastle upon Tyne. These were the years that railways were beginning to be built in Britain. In 1841 the railway reached Bristol. Nevertheless, it is clear that the expansion of English trade took place before the railways were an important means of communication, and indeed in the calculations of cost in England there are items for canal charges. The canals in

[1] Including returned empty casks.
[2] The son of Samuel Waring. This was in 1838 in both cases.

Reasons for the Trend of Trade

England and Ireland were the basis of Guinness's second great expansion.

From 1839 to 1843 Guinness's sales fell by nearly one-fifth. The explanation for this fall has traditionally been that Father Mathew's temperance campaign affected the brewery. Unfortunately for this explanation the fall in sales was almost wholly in England. These were years of trade depression in England. In 1840, as well, the malt tax and hop duty rose by 5 per cent. Beer did not fall in price until 1842 (when the income tax was reintroduced). From 1844 to 1846 there was another increase in sales and in the latter year the sales of Guinness reached 100,000 barrels for the first time. Then they fell again in 1848. Once more the fall was in English and not in Irish trade. Throughout the Great Famine sales of beer in Ireland rose, striking evidence that the market for beer did not lie among the people outside the maritime economy.

The trade in tied houses, that is in public houses owned by the brewery, may have been as much as nearly a tenth of the Dublin trade in 1831, certainly in that year these houses sold at least 1000 hogsheads, and there may well have been more because the figures available are for only eleven houses, and not for the total number. How much else of the trade was restricted by loans or agreements there is no evidence to enable a conclusion to be reached. The proportion of beer sold in Dublin in tied houses fell throughout the eighteen-thirties.

Only one tied-house agreement survives. It dates from 1821, and concerns a public house in Trinity Street.

Messrs A. B. & W. L. Guinness & Co.

GENTLEMEN,

I hereby agree to take your House in Trinity St (No. 14) at the rate of Four Pounds per week to be paid weekly on every Monday the first payment to be made on Monday next the 13th inst. and I will sell your Porter in said House and no other I will pay the taxes of said House and keep it in good order & repair.

I am Gents.
Your most Obed. Servt.
MATHEW CROSBIE

Trinity St
6 August 1821

The Development of Guinness's Trade

The course of trade was twice interrupted by sectarian troubles, first in 1812–13, and then from 1835 to 1842.

During the winter of 1812–13 a Protestant petition against concessions to the religious persuasion of the Irish majority was organized in Dublin. The petition emanated from the most extreme anti-Papist element and was probably inspired by a reckless journalist named John Giffard. Among the signatures, many of which were forgeries, appeared the name of Guinness, and a rumour was promptly circulated that this was Guinness the brewer.[1]

Several insertions were published of an advertisement from James's Gate, signed by Arthur, Benjamin and William L. Guinness, offering £500 reward to any person who within three months would discover and prosecute to conviction those who had invented and were circulating a report that they had signed the petition to Parliament 'against the claims of our Catholic brethren'. The petition, they declared, was in opposition to their principles. The signatures contained only one purporting to be of their name—Richard Guinness of Nicholas Street. But no Richard Guinness lived in Nicholas Street, and neither of the two Richard Guinnesses known in Ireland had signed the petition. They, on the contrary, had signed the petition to Parliament for complete emancipation—following in the footsteps of their late father who in 1795 had advocated the cause of his countrymen of persuasions other than his own in the Dublin Common Council. But interested parties had been going round to their friends and customers and spreading slanders about them 'and exciting the public by threats and persuasions against dealing in our brewery'.[2]

At a meeting of the Catholic Board on 22 May 1813 a Mr O'Gorman, referring to the attack on the Guinnesses, said he was sorry to find that Protestants who had striven on behalf of Catholics should now find themselves the victims of calumny. He suggested that the petition—a bogus one in any case—might have been spread by the enemies of the Catholic cause to split it. He suggested that the Board should clear the well-known brewers of the slur cast on their name

---

[1] *Dublin Evening Post*, 17 April 1813, p. 3, col. 1, published almost one hundred names subscribed to the petition which could not be traced in Dublin.
[2] *Dublin Evening Post*, 20 May–8 June 1813.

Religious Difficulties

by passing a resolution to the effect that the Guinnesses had not signed the petition and were entitled 'to the confidence, gratitude and thanks of the Catholics of Ireland'. A brewer of this persuasion, John Byrne, supported the resolution in a eulogy of the Guinnesses. The resolution was carried.

This was followed in June 1813 by an editorial comment in *Cox's Irish Magazine*, which hated the Guinnesses. Under the heading 'The Catholic Board and the Brewers' the Board was criticized for being cold to inferiors and fawning to superiors, cowardly and treacherous. The article continued:[1]

The catholic board exhibits not only acts of treason, but acts of folly, that tend to affect the entire community. Mr O'Gorman, who has always displayed sound sense and invariable good principles, has submitted the case of Guinness's brewery to the solemn consideration of the catholic board. We hope that Mr O'Gorman does not mean to interweave brewing into the catholic bill, nor make it one of the terms of our emancipation that we do give security to drink Guinness's porter: if these terms are imposed upon us, we must set up a board of our own, and insist upon drinking what we please when we pay for it. If Counsellor Guinness will get us porter for nothing, as he gave us a character for nothing, when he called us a *felonious rabble*, we may deal with his porter, but until some *domestic arrangement* is agreed on, we will drink what we like, and whenever we can.

A few months later the 'Protestant Porter' campaign was revived when the bizarre Dr Brennan weighed in with charges in his *Milesian Magazine* that 'poisonous doctrines were propagated through the medium of porter (principles totally subversive of the Catholic faith)'. An analysis had shown, he said, that brewers of anti-Popery porter had mashed up Protestant Bibles and Methodist hymn books in the brew, thus impregnating, in the fermentation, the volatile parts of the porter with the pure ethereal essence of heresy. Over the years, he said, Guinness's had consumed 136,000 tons of Bibles and 501,000 cartloads of hymn books and Protestant catechisms. The analyst went on to say that, happily, Pim's ale was an antidote to the heresy porter.

The charges were indignantly denied by the Guinnesses and solemnly repudiated by the religious authorities. The papers that carried them were small and unimportant, but they were cleverly designed to inflame the prejudices of the ignorant and susceptible who knew of

[1] *Cox's Irish Magazine* (June 1813), vol. VI, pp. 263–4.

them by hearsay. It may be assumed that many of the porter drinkers who heard the story of the mashed-up Bibles did not read, even if they could, the Guinness denials or the statements made by the Catholic Board. Thomas Moore in his memoirs refers to the case of a Dublin brewer in 1830 who 'lost all his customers by taking the side of the Veto'—a controversy concerning the role of the government in the appointment of bishops by Rome.[1] This may have been a reference to the affair of the 'Protestant Porter' as the Veto controversy was going on at the same time. But Guinness's certainly did not lose all their customers.

The second outburst of religious trouble took place about twenty years later. Daniel O'Connell's son had a brewery of his own, in Watling Street, next James's Gate, and it is reasonable to suppose that his trade and his politics were made to serve each other. Daniel O'Connell was keenly interested in the fortunes of his son's brewery, in which he had sunk £2000. Writing to P. V. Fitzpatrick from London on 11 February 1832 O'Connell said: 'I cannot write to ask of the distillers respecting my son's brewery....I will not in any way interfere with the distillers, that is, while I am in Parliament. When I leave the House and return to my profession, I then will not hesitate to canvass for the interests of my darling child—but until then, not one word.'[2] Writing on 25 August 1834 from Derrynane, County Kerry, O'Connell said that a consignment of his son's porter had awaited his arrival there and that he found it 'the very best Irish porter I ever tasted...it is really superlative'.[3] The fate of the brewery under his son's proprietorship suggests that the Liberator must have liked the porter it produced better than the public did, though O'Connell was not a beer drinker and did not consider himself a reliable judge of its merits.[4]

O'Connell was friendly to the Guinnesses until 1836 when he contemplated the possibility of Guinness standing for Parliament in the event of a petition to unseat himself being successful. Soon after this, however, Guinness (notwithstanding his earlier support of the emancipation party) voted against O'Connell.[5] As a result an attempt

---

[1] Thomas Moore, *Memoirs, Journal and Correspondence*, ed. by Lord John Russell (London, 1853–6), vol. VI, pp. 147–8.

[2] W. J. Fitzpatrick (ed.), *Correspondence of Daniel O'Connell, the Liberator* (London, 1888), vol. I, p. 288.

[3] *Ibid.* p. 463.   [4] See above, ch. 5.

[5] See below, p. 106.

Religious Difficulties

was made by some zealots to boycott Guinness's stout, even though they were reproved by O'Connell himself. But O'Connell felt bitter about Guinness's political conversion, and later referred to him as 'that miserable old apostate Arthur Guinness'.[1] There was an attempt to limit Guinness's Dublin sales during the time of the O'Connell repeal movement about the years 1835 to 1842. In the *Bristol Journal* for September 1837 occurs a hair-raising story of Papist persecution:[2]

> *The Guinness Persecution. (Private Correspondent of the 'Morning Post')*
> *Dublin, 15 September*
>
> The conspirators are still at work against the Messrs Guinness, with a view to destroy their trade in Ireland, or murder those who dare to neutralize their attempt—A man named Noonan, a carrier from the town of Longford, was commissioned yesterday to bring down two hogsheads of barm from the brewery of Messrs Guinness. On arriving in town yesterday he repaired with his horse and cart to the brewery. On going in at the gate he was accosted by a stranger, who cautioned him on his peril not to bring any drink out of that concern. Noonan did not heed the threat, but got his loading, and proceeded homewards on his journey. He had not got three miles out of the town, when six ruffians, armed, jumped from behind a wall, blindfolded him, and assaulted him grievously, and then knocked in the heads of the barm hogsheads, and spilled the liquor about the road. There can be no question but that this man was followed and waylaid until a lonesome place occurred, where they might commit the outrage without fear of apprehension.

It is only fair to say that there is no discoverable reference to this or any other episode in the surviving brewery records, and that the *Bristol Journal* was keenly alive to the dangers of the Papists in Ireland. In 1841, however, at least fifteen of the brewery's customers gave up dealing with it during the 'Repeal' election in which O'Connell was victorious. But they resumed trade within three months.

PRICES AND FREIGHT CHARGES

From 1846 or thereabouts there was an increasing concern with prices and with freight charges. This is a sign that both underlay Guinness's tremendous expansion. By 1851 the rates for transporting a hogshead from Dublin to Liverpool and bringing it back empty had fallen

---

[1] Fitzpatrick (ed.), *op. cit.* vol. II, p. 199. Letter to P. V. Fitzpatrick, 16 August 1839, concerning the Bank of Ireland Bill.
[2] *Felix Farley's Bristol Journal*, Saturday, 23 September 1837.

to 2*s.* 9*d.* from 5*s.* or more, and throughout the next decade there was continual bargaining with the City of Dublin Steam Packet Company. The British and Irish Steam Packet Company charged 5*s.* 6*d.* to London, and 5*s.* 9*d.* to towns on the south coast of England. In 1851 the railway reached Galway. In 1854 the towns along the coast to Bray were linked to Dublin. By the eighteen-sixties the main agencies were in railway, not canal, towns.

Other costs tended to fall. The price of raw materials and especially malt were tending downwards from 1850 onward. The corn duties ended finally in 1849. In 1860 the hop duty was reduced and in 1862 it was abolished. Only one cost was opposite to the general trend, labourers' wages were 12*s.* a week in 1849 and in 1854 they rose to 13*s.* where they stayed until 1871. The years of the Great Famine and the Crimean War were years of high prices. So high indeed that in 1847, and again in 1854, 'in consequence of the extremely high price of provisions for the past few months, and the prospect of this continuing for some time, a "small gift" was made to the gentlemen on the staff'. In the Clerks' Pay Book in John Purser, junior's, handwriting we note on 22 February 1847: 'The above was arranged prior to Mr Guinness's leaving home, but in the hurry consequent on his departure there was not an opportunity of making this communication earlier.' Later, on 24 September 1847, Purser writes: 'Referring to the grant made to our clerks on the 22nd February and taking into consideration the importance of effectively relieving them from any remaining pressure which may have arisen out of the late awful famine we have determined to make a further grant on the same principle as before but on an extended scale, viz., instead of 10, 8 and 5 per cent it will be 15, 12 and 7 given upon the similar period say (nine months) as before.' Eighteen months later, in March 1849, the firm gave a further gratuity of 10 per cent as an 'expression of the thankfulness we feel for the many mercies we have (as a firm) enjoyed for some years past, amidst so much general mercantile distress. Dublin, 8th March 1849. B. L. G., J.P.' When the price of raw materials went up prices were raised by agreement between the brewers. This led to a fall in sales during periods of bad trade.[1]

By 1850 Guinness's relied mainly on the English trade although

---

[1] See below, pp. 216 and 217, for a change in the nature of the market in the next twenty years.

the Irish country trade was becoming increasingly important. Steamer freights to England fell throughout the eighteen-forties. By 1842 the London trade had become so big and the number of direct accounts so difficult to manage that it was closed to bottlers; the agent appointed sub-agents, presumably in order to strengthen the Guinness ties with their forceful salesman, Sparkes Moline, as well as to delegate the management of the trade. Most of the English expansion appears to have been built on a vigorous sales policy by agents who were given exclusive rights in the towns in which they dealt and highly favourable discounts as well. There was an exception in Liverpool where a number of accounts were opened direct with the brewery independent of the agent, Thomas Blackburne. In the eighteen-forties, too, the evidence from Cork suggests that a large number of accounts were opened there without any stimulation from Guinness's. Guinness's policy of delegating authority and respon-sibility to employees was being rewarded. These men had been selected with care and then entrusted with considerable discretion. They earned the confidence and support of their employers by the sound ness of their judgement, and were given the flexibility of movement to be resourceful in their enterprise.

By 1842 Guinness's was becoming a substantial firm. They had twenty-four clerks; Mr Guinness had a confidential clerk (R. B. Ussher, later chief clerk); the profits were considerable. When Arthur Guinness died in 1855 probate was declared for £150,000. Much of this money was probably made during the previous fifteen years or so.

The rise in the brewery's Irish sales after 1840 is connected in part with the opening of the Irish railways. After 1850 Shannon Harbour and Ballinasloe began to decline in importance. In 1844 the railway from Dublin to Drogheda was opened, in 1846 that to Carlow, and in 1847 the Midland Great Western to Galway. By 1848 deliveries in the Dublin vicinity were being made by rail. Changes in the nature of the economy created great opportunities for expanding business. If Guinness's had failed to realize these potentialities their rate of growth might have been no greater than that of some rivals, or they might indeed have followed other Irish breweries towards extinction. Instead of being intimidated they extracted advantages from challenging situations. Aggressive sales campaigns were con-ducted by wisely chosen agents who proved their ability by their enterprise and decision. The increasing efficiency of production was reflected in the attitude of the brewery towards costs. The necessity for buying raw materials long in advance of selling the finished product demanded a high degree of accuracy in estimates and forecasts if losses were to be avoided. A system of cost control was evolved, that may have lacked refinement at first, but its adoption, even in an elementary form, reveals the qualities of mind and judgement which informed the policy of the brewery. Control of cost was an essential prerequisite of cutting profit margins—and of increasing output.

[8]

Brewing at James's Gate in the
Early Nineteenth Century

A porter brewer buys none but the best, as none else will answer.
(*The first Arthur Guinness in 1783.*)

INTRODUCTION

LITTLE is known with certainty of the technical story of Guinness before 1796, but thereafter, by piecing together material from a number of brewery records, it is possible to lift the curtain somewhat and examine the environment of the time. The history of technology is a difficult subject, mainly because in the days before scientific advance much work was done by rule of thumb and the results were not reduced to writing. Sometimes, indeed, the work included trade secrets only grudgingly passed on, and the people who operated a process had no real idea of the basic principles involved. This chapter tries to recreate the problems and actions of the brewer in the early nineteenth century, and to throw some light on the possibilities then available to the Guinnesses. They were good brewers, but technical failure was always round the corner.

THE ART OF BREWING

In its essentials, the art of brewing consists of the addition of hot water to ground malt so that the starch is dissolved and converted into malt sugar; the boiling of the wort (as this sugar solution is called) with hops to add the characteristic flavour of this plant; the fermentation of the hopped wort with yeast, a microscopic unicellular organism which has the power of converting the malt sugar into alcohol; and finally the cleansing process which removes the excess yeast which has grown during the fermentation.

The raw materials determine the main characteristics of a beer. Strength depends on the quality and quantity of the malt, and flavour on the quality and quantity of the hops. The distinctive dark colour of porter and stout is obtained by using roast malt or roast barley. Much depends, of course, on the technical competence of the brewer. He must ensure that the beer is stable in character, lest the flavour becomes impaired, as a result of action by organisms other than yeast, after the beer has left the brewery. The beer must be reasonably bright and free from suspended particles. It must foam when poured out, so as to produce the characteristic creamy head of porter and stout. There is also the contribution of the technical competence of the brewer to the economy of the brewery. Continual efforts were made to obtain more beer from the same amount of raw materials; and, where demand was increasing beyond all grounds of reasonable possibility, continual efforts were made to produce more beer from the same plant.

In the survey that follows of the different characteristics of the various beers made at James's Gate and how these beers were brewed, it will be convenient to use certain technical brewing terms, some peculiar to Guinness. These are explained in the Glossary.

GUINNESS'S BEERS

In 1796 Guinness's brewed two beers only, ale and porter.[1] They brewed no ale after 1799.[2] In 1801 they began to make a Keeping Beer and two years later a Country Porter (the original porter became Town Porter). For the next twenty years these were the three main qualities, although at various times porters of greater strength called West Indies Porter and Superior Porter were also brewed. Town Porter, brewed all the year round for a quick sale in Dublin and the vicinity, had the lowest hop rate. Keeping Beer, designed, as its name implies, to remain stable for some months, had a higher hop rate and was brewed only at the cooler time of the year. It was sold in the provinces and also used for reinforcing the Town Porter during the summer months. Country Porter was first brewed in 1803 due to a shortage of Keeping Beer, at a hop rate intermediate between Keeping Beer and Town Porter. Henceforth it was this beer which was sold in the provinces, but Keeping Beer continued to be brewed for summer mixing.

It seems that Superior Porter was brewed from 1806 as a stronger beer for sale in the home market, but the first direct statement of

---

[1] See above, p. 122.　　　[2] See above, p. 8.

policy seems to be that given in the Proprietors Memorandum Book in 1810—'to try whether the publicans will encourage a stouter kind of porter during the operation of the present Bounty on beer'.[1] An even stronger beer, Extra Superior Porter, was also brewed periodically, but neither was a regular feature of the trade until 1821. In that year regular brewings of Extra Superior Porter were made, and a definite brewing procedure laid down. It was this beer which was to become the spearhead of the attack on the English trade.

Extra Superior Porter, like Country Porter and Superior Porter brewed only from November to May, was about one-third as strong again as Country Porter and with a much higher hop rate. Its characteristics were 'great stability, softness, mildness and vinosity' and it was 'of so high a class that when Mr Waring was appointed the Bristol agent in 1825 he at once decided on bringing it to London (1828) and established with complete success the London agency Waring and Tuckett to supply the London vendors of Bottled Stout'. Extra Superior had a tremendous impact on Guinness's trade. In the year 1820–1 1200 barrels of it were brewed—4 per cent of the total trade. By 1828 brewings of Extra Superior represented 28 per cent of the trade, and this figure rose further to 59 per cent in 1835 and 82 per cent in 1840.

By this time the Extra Superior trade had increased so much that it had become inconvenient to brew it between November and May only. Henceforth it was brewed the whole year round. About this time too the Extra Superior became known as Double Stout, by which name it continued to be called until comparatively modern times.

West Indies Porter seems not to have been an important feature of the trade at this period. It was generally of the same strength as Extra Superior but with a rather higher hop rate and brewed only in the winter: but there were no regular brewings and in at least one year Keeping Beer was used for this trade. By 1840 it had become Triple Stout, even stronger than the Double Stout and with a still higher hop rate.

The balance of the trade had by now completely changed. The five beers of 1806 were still being brewed with roughly equivalent

[1] In 1810 a statute made provision for payment of a bounty to retailers of spirits who also retailed beer, provided they sold at least one barrel of beer for every four barrels of spirits. The bounty was withdrawn two years later because 'the provisions of the act have not proved beneficial'.

characters (although not necessarily under the same names), but whereas in 1806 the bulk of the trade consisted of Town and Country Porter, by 1840 it was very largely Double Stout. This was to remain so in future years although Town Porter was to recover some of its lost ground.

There were variations (sometimes considerable) in the strength of the different beers. It is not possible to say exactly how great these variations were. The strength of the Town Porter is not known before 1799, but a calculation from the amount of malt used and the amount of beer obtained (as given in the 1796–1815 Brewing Book) suggests that unless there was a big increase between 1796 and 1799 in the material extracted from the malt the strength of the porter was considerably greater in 1796 than subsequently. It seems probable, therefore, that the beer became weaker at the outset of the Napoleonic Wars, and although there was a temporary increase in strength at the end of the war, the Town Porter had by 1818 fallen again to the war level, at which it was to remain for the greater part of the century.

The hop rates also varied. There was a general fall during the Napoleonic Wars. Even the hop rate of the Keeping Beer was lowered in the years from 1812 to 1815. In the years immediately after the war there was an even greater fall; the price of hops that had begun to rise in 1812 'continued high up to the period of the extravagant rise in 1816 and 1817'. Trade began to slacken in 1817, and early in 1819 Guinness, recognizing that the low hop rates were harming the quality of the beer, restored the rate prevailing from 1812 to 1815.

After 1819 the hop rate of the Town Porter seems to have been less variable, and such fluctuations as occurred were probably due to the varying price of hops. There were, however, wide fluctuations in the other hop rates.

Apart from year-to-year variation in the hop rate there were often seasonal variations, more hops being used in the warmer months of the year and less in the cooler months, especially in the case of the Town Porter which was brewed throughout the summer months. But the fact that current beer needed to be brewed with a higher hop rate in the summer appears to have been a piece of knowledge which was discovered, discarded and rediscovered from time to time. In the period 1796–9 there is no evidence of summer hop rates for the

Town Porter. In 1800 higher summer hop rates were used and this procedure continued until 1814. It was dropped in 1815, perhaps due to the high price of hops. In 1824 there were again higher summer hop rates, but by 1840 this was no longer so.

The hops were mainly English, although foreign hops were used from time to time. Flemish hops appear in the 1801/2 Brewery Notes Book and accounted for as much as half the hops needed in a brewing. They even appear at the height of the war in 1811. It was a commonplace to brew with a certain proportion of hops three or four years old, possibly because of very big seasonal variations in price. It was desirable, therefore, to hold larger stocks when hops were cheap. But West Indies Porter seems always to have been brewed with the newest hops available.

Finally, with the strength and hop rate the colour of the beer must be considered. This was the third main characteristic depending on the raw materials. The dark colour of porter is produced by a caramelization of a part of the malt. Between 1796 and 1815 a large proportion of the malt was a lightly roasted brown malt. This must have been a highly variable substance giving, if used at a constant rate, wide variations in the colour of the beer, for the proportion used was sometimes as little as 25 per cent, while at other times it was as much as 47 per cent of the total malt used. For this reason alone it would have been unsatisfactory; but it was probably uneconomical as well, because a part of the extract of the malt was rendered insoluble and therefore useless by the roasting process. In 1815 there is a reference to an 'improved method of Browning Malt' allowing the brewer to get beer of the same colour but with less brown malt. A contemporary calculation shows that this Patent Brown Malt (as it came to be called), more highly roasted and more highly coloured than the ordinary brown malt, allowed a beer of the same strength and colour to be made more cheaply than with the brown malt. Thereafter Patent Brown Malt was used in increasing quantities and by 1828 had completely replaced brown malt. At first it was not mashed in the kieve with the pale malt but put straight into the copper, but by the time the use of brown malt had been discontinued the Patent Brown Malt was being extracted in the kieve together with the pale malt.

THE BREWING PROCESS

The first stage of the brewing process consists of the extraction of the soluble constituents of malt with hot liquor. The conditions under which this extraction takes place are of profound importance. Much of their importance may have escaped the brewer of the time, but one factor he can hardly have overlooked—the amount of extract to be obtained from a given quantity of malt. On this the whole economy of his brewery would have been based.

It is not possible to obtain any very exact record of changes in extract in the earlier years. There is a strong supposition that between 1796 and 1799 there was a considerable rise in extract. There was a further increase about 1824 and by 1840 it was still higher. The reason for the early increase is not known but it may have been due to improved methods of mashing. The 1824 increase was almost certainly due to the replacement of brown malt by Patent Brown Malt. The introduction of sparging accounted for the 1840 increase. There must have been a gradual improvement over the whole period in the quality of the malt used, although variations in extract from one season to another show that the malt was still very variable from season to season. This rise in extract over forty years (probably by about one-third) must have been an important factor in the economy of the brewery.

The technique of this part of the brewing process does not seem to have changed greatly during these years. In 1801 the malt, previously ground into the kieve,[1] was mashed with hot liquor and the wort run off after the mash had stood for some time. This process was then repeated at a rather higher temperature. Whether the mash was at this time stirred by hand or by mechanically-driven rakes is not known, but rakes were certainly in use by 1838. Following the mashes were a number of 'leakes' or 'dashes', that is additions of hot liquor made without the use of the rakes and at a rather lower temperature than the mashes—although as the contents of the kieve were already hot they were not lowered in temperature. The liquor for these operations was run from the 'dash box', a cylinder into which both hot and cold liquor could be run so as to produce

---

[1] The malt was ground by a horse-driven mill before 1809, when a steam-engine was introduced for this purpose. Later the steam-engine was used for most pumping operations in the brewery. The first engine, which was of the 'Independent Type' of 10 horse-power, was ordered from Boulton and Watt in 1808.

The Brewing Process

a mixture of the required temperature. Only one major change took place during these years, the introduction of 'sparging', in which the discontinuous additions provided by the dashes gave place to a continuous addition from a spray or sparge arm which rotated over the goods in the kieve. The temperature of the sparge liquor was much higher than it had been for the dashes and this increased the extract considerably.

The next stage consisted of boiling the wort with hops. There were at various times two and three boilings, the second and third being of successively weaker worts boiled longer than the first, thus to some extent raising the strength of the later worts. No important changes in this part of the process seem to have taken place.

The hopped wort, having been separated from the hops (it is not clear how this was done, but it seems probable that there was very little difference from modern practice where the mixture of hops and wort is run from the boiling copper into a vessel from which the wort can be run off leaving the spent hops behind), was pumped to large flat vessels called coolers with air propellers suspended overhead. It lay here until it had cooled enough—that is to about summer air temperature—for the yeast to be added. This process took anything from four to nine hours. If the wort had cooled too much some more hot wort was poured in. Cooling in this way was a slow and variable process, and the introduction of wort refrigerators in 1836 must have been a great help in standardizing the brewing time-table. The type of refrigerator employed is not known but was presumably one of the standard types then installed in breweries. Samuel Morewood in his book on brewing refers to wort refrigeration as being in general use in 1838.[1] The cooling water was drawn from a well which produced water of an even temperature in both summer and winter.[2] It seems to have been supplemented from 1864 by the

---

[1] Morewood, *A Philosophical and Statistical History of the Inventions and Customs of Ancient and Modern Nations in the Manufacture and Use of Inebriating Liquors*, p. 627.

[2] Robert Mallet, F.R.S., M.R.I.A., of the Dublin engineering firm of John and Robert Mallet, was consulted by Guinness, and as a result gave the firm 'a supply of water by boring a four-inch hole through the solid rock at the bottom of a well that had given out, and then firing a charge of powder therein by which the rock was shattered, and a supply of water obtained which has never since failed. He also constructed a machine worked by steam for washing casks, and erected a very large sky cooler for the brewery....Steam engines of various sizes were made...from his designs....' (From Obituary of Robert Mallet in *The Engineer*, 11, 18 and 25 November 1881.) In fact the well to which reference is made in the Obituary was abandoned, and another was sunk in 1863-5.

155

James's Gate in the Early Nineteenth Century

use of ice 'collected from the surface of the canal in winter, or obtained by sailing vessels from Norway'.[1]

The hopped wort was next run into fermenting tuns, and yeast from a previous brewing was mixed with it. There were considerable variations in the amount of yeast added, and in the subsequent temperature of the wort. There was an increasing tendency towards a slower fermentation with the use of less yeast and at a lower temperature. The object of this development was apparently to produce a more stable beer. A fermentation that was too fast was known to be bad—'the first Worts this Brewing were set quite too high and altogether were too high which made the fermentation rapid and spoiled the Brewing—it was quite foul and flat 10 days in the vat after starting'. The progress of fermentation seems to have been judged on appearance only. A typical entry from the 1810–12 Fermentation Book is:

1st day	7.00 a.m.	looked strong and fine
	6.35 p.m.	most excellent tuns
	10.05 p.m.	fine tuns
2nd day	6.30 a.m.	looked very well
	tunnage	the tuns were as fine if not the finest that we have had this season but the Heads were not very yeasty—but were coloured—very fleecy and the flavour most excellent.

Tasting at tunnage was a normal procedure—'the flavour was very full but not remarkably vinous'. The present gravity—an indication of the amount of sugar left unfermented—was also determined, but it does not appear that this influenced the time of tunnage. Determinations were made before tunnage only if, judged by the height of the head, the tuns seemed backward.

At tunnage the sugars in the wort had been largely converted into alcohol and the main part of the fermentation process was over. This was followed by the 'cleansing'—the removal of the yeast which had multiplied considerably during fermentation. This operation was automatic. The beer was led from tun into hogsheads placed in troughs. These hogsheads were filled quite full and the yeast worked out from the bung-holes of the hogsheads into the troughs leaving eventually a more or less clear beer, the liquid yeast in the troughs being used as required for store yeast for further fermentations.

[1] George S. Measom, *Official Illustrated Guide to Midland Great Western, Great Southern and Western and Dublin and Drogheda Railway* (London, 1866), p. 163.

The Brewing Process

The periods during which the beer was held in trough varied greatly—anything from forty to ninety hours. Observations were recorded relating to the working of the yeast and to the brightness of the beer when the casks were started; for instance, 'works well but not *very well* rather cloudy when started'. The year 1834 marks an advance towards large-scale production; hogsheads were replaced by 'rounds' or 'pontos' of considerably larger capacity—three to four hogsheads. But the cleansing was still automatic, the yeast being allowed to work itself out as before.

When the greater part of the yeast had removed itself from the hogsheads or rounds, the beer was run to the vat from which it was later sent into trade. In the earlier years it was run straight to the vat, but in 1828 an intermediate vessel, the settling back, was introduced, which allowed a greater control of the clarity of beer sent to the vat.

Little is known about methods of storage and maturation at this time as no Vathouse books have survived. It seems probable, however, that the Town and Country Porters were sent into trade soon after cleansing, and that they were reinforced during the summer months with the higher hop rate Keeping Beer which had been brewed in the cooler months of the year and stored. Extra Superior, on the other hand, was not sent immediately into trade: brewed until about 1840 from November to May only, it was kept in storage vat 'where the whole of the winter's brewing remained until the following summer, when it was sent out from the *original* vat unmixed sometimes as early as April, sometimes as late as October, and so continued unmixed until it was all disposed of and was succeeded by the earliest vats of the next season'. From 1828 more continuity between one season's Extra Superior and the next was obtained by mixing the earlier brewings of each season with the later brewings of the preceding season.

SUBSTITUTES FOR MALT AND HOPS

The slump after the Napoleonic Wars put a financial strain on the brewery, and the response to it ultimately was to improve further the quality of the product and the technique of brewing so as to reduce waste. From 1812 to 1816 hops were 'extravagantly dear' and the quantities used were halved. As a consequence the reputation of Guinness was harmed. There was, in 1814, a bitter campaign against the Dublin brewers arising from allegations that adulterants

157

were used in the beer. The greater part of the attacks were misguided because there was no distinction made between the use of substitutes for malt and hops and the use of adulterants. Substitutes were perfectly legitimate, whether their aim was to reduce the cost of production or to improve the beer, but from time to time certain of them were prohibited to protect the excise. For example, roasted barley was a good substitute for roasted malt, but its use would have evaded the excise on malt. Adulterants, on the other hand, may have been employed by some brewers to deceive the public. There is no evidence at all that Guinness's used adulterants although they used substitutes from time to time. But the reckless charges in the campaign showed as little concern for the distinction between adulterants and substitutes as for the difference between brewers who were reputable and those who were not.

A journalist called Cox led the attack and found an ally in the notorious John Giffard, traditionally supposed to have been brought up by the Dublin brewer Thwaites. He carried his campaign to the Dublin Corporation in October 1814, when in a discussion on baking he declared that while citizens had been the victims of monstrous extortions over a period of years because of the price of corn, the brewers had not suffered.[1] 'The price of corn', he said, 'cannot much affect them for, he verily believed, that they made use of every ingredient in the manufacture of their commodity but—CORN.' '(Hear, hear, hear!)' 'It was a melancholy consideration', he added, 'that everything that is nauseous and nasty, every deleterious drug which either our own country or foreign countries can produce, has a decided preference among the brewers to plain malt and hops.' Another member, Harty, replied that poisonous ingredients had once been used, but not any longer. Giffard scoffed at Harty's reply, and asked when the reformation was effected. 'Will the Hon. Gentleman', said Mr Giffard, 'have the goodness to inform the House how it happens that at this day there are such persons as BREWERS DRUGGISTS? (Hear, hear!)'

Counsellor Richard Guinness 'was astonished to hear [Giffard] speak so about such a respectable and useful class of men, and impose on the community an injury by prejudicing the lower orders against a beverage so conducive to their well-being. He was connected with a brewer, of whom he may be allowed to say that he had

[1] *Freeman's Journal*, 15 October 1814.

Substitutes for Malt and Hops

arrived at the top of his profession and realized an affluent fortune by the practice of every virtue that is estimable in a tradesman or a man.' That brewer would have scorned to 'resort to the expedients which Mr Giffard had attributed to the whole class of brewers'. A Mr McAuley intervened as a well-meaning but inexpert peacemaker. He made matters worse by revealing that in the past 'he had known instances in which druggists were the greatest claimants upon the estates of bankrupt brewers'. No one pointed to the possible connexion between harmful drugs and their users' bankruptcy. Another brewer, Mr Madder, solemnly reminded Giffard of the oath which brewers had been obliged to take to avoid deleterious substances. This provoked Mr Giffard to say that the existence of the oath showed how little the brewers were trusted. Someone else offered to produce a bankrupt brewer's books to demonstrate that his druggist's account appeared much larger than his malt account. The debate was reported in the press and the allegations induced Guinness's brewery to issue statements and affidavits denying that they had adulterated their porter. The *Freeman's Journal* of 7 November 1814 published the following statement in the names of Arthur, Benjamin and Wm. L. Guinness:

James's Gate Porter Brewery

Certain publications have recently appeared in the public newspapers, purporting to be reports of speeches in the Common Council of this city, in which all the persons concerned in the brewing trade are indiscriminately accused of using large quantities of various kinds of poisonous and deleterious ingredients in the composition of their liquors, to the injury of the public health, and entirely in substitution of malt and hops, whereby the revenue is defrauded and the agricultural interest of the country deprived of the natural markets for their barley. We feel ourselves called upon in duty to the public, and to undeceive such persons as may be led to credit these accusations, by giving the most unequivocal proofs in our power of their utter falsehood, so far, at least, as our brewing is concerned which we do in the affidavits hereto annexed.

We shall make no comments upon the motives that have produced these scandalous accusations, because we are at a loss to conceive them; but we cannot forbear reprobating the slander, which if it could be publicly credited, is calculated to do great injury to the community, by bringing into disrepute a manufacture, the prosperity of which is confessedly, intimately connected with the best interests of the country.

An affidavit signed by the three Guinness brothers who were described as 'porter brewers and co-partners in trade' was sworn

159

before the Lord Mayor, Alderman J. C. Beresford, at the Mansion House on 5 November 1814. From 'the commencement of their partnership up to the present hour, a period of many years', read the declaration, 'they had never used, nor permitted to be used, in their brewery, directly or indirectly, any of the deleterious or poisonous articles which a certain member of the Common Council of this city has lately asserted to be generally used in the breweries of Dublin, but they have always brewed their porter of malt and hops, without any mixture of any deleterious or unwholesome ingredients whatever, or any raw or unmalted corn'.

There was a further sworn affidavit along the same lines from John Purser, junior. His association with the firm, he declared, dated from 1799, and he confirmed the statement which the Guinness brothers had sworn about the constituents of their porter over that period. The statement that Guinness had used only malt and hops in the manufacture of porter recalled a remark made thirty years earlier by the first Arthur Guinness, before a parliamentary committee in 1783, when he had said that 'a porter brewer buys none but the best, as none else will answer'.[1]

CONCLUSION

Although there were no really major changes made in brewing technique in the first half of the nineteenth century, there was a great deal of steady progress. The increase in extract during the period was an important feature in the economy of the brewery. The substitution of rounds for hogsheads as cleansing vessels was the first indication of the trend towards larger-scale production. The introduction about 1840 of summer brewings of Double Stout, as the Extra Superior was then called, indicated that the plant available had by then become too small to brew all the Double Stout required between November and May only. But possibly the most significant step was to lay down in 1821 a standard procedure for the brewing of what was to become the firm's chief product—Extra Superior—so that a consistency of quality could be maintained.

The reliability of the product had increased. There had been much saving in malt, fuel and wages. The signs were at hand of the spectacular expansion that was to take place in the following decades.

[1] *Journals of the Irish House of Commons*, 1783, vol. XI, App. f. cv.

[9]

Ireland in the Great Famine and After

...You know my dear Ben that my purse is open to the call. (*The second Arthur Guinness to his son Benjamin Lee Guinness in the Great Famine year of 1849.*)

THE GREAT FAMINE

THE GREAT FAMINE began with the failure of the potato harvest in the autumn of 1845, first in the south-eastern counties, and then spread to rather less than half of Ireland. At first the full magnitude of the disaster was not appreciated and relief measures were small. O'Connell, through the Dublin Corporation, pressed for a ban on the exportation of foodstuffs and for a limitation on brewing and distilling. The original relief measures introduced by Sir Robert Peel were to extend the use of the Poor Law and to begin public works, and by the spring and early summer of 1846 these appear to have been adequate to feed the people. 'The government had done its best within the framework of the existing social structure.'[1] Peel was criticized by Lord John Russell for doing too much, while his high-Tory critics—notably Lord George Bentinck—proposed Prussian schemes of reconstruction involving enormous outlays on railways, arterial drainage and other projects of social development. The famine advanced over Ireland and returned season by season for five years. The country was too stricken to revolt, but the actions of a few desperate men in 1848 were sufficient to alarm people of substance and to make Ireland less attractive than ever as a place for private capital investment.

With the repeal of the Corn Laws Sir Robert Peel's Government fell in the spring of 1846, and was followed by Lord John Russell and a Whig administration which believed that relief must follow from the use of the market mechanism.

In July and August of 1846 there was a second and universal potato blight. 'This had an instantaneous unmistakable effect. For

[1] Kevin Nowlan, 'The Political Background', in R. D. Edwards and T. D. Williams (eds.), *The Great Famine* (Dublin, 1957), p. 143.

Ireland in the Great Famine and After

the first time in Irish history there was a heavy autumn exodus.'[1] In the forefront were the poorest cottiers. By 1847, as the blight continued, about a quarter of the emigrants were of the better-off classes. The potato failure in 1847 was not as complete as that in 1846, when 116,000 people left Ireland, but the fear and terror of famine and disease drove 230,000 people away in 1847. The failure of 1848 was total and complete. 'Panic seized Munster once the full extent of the blight was known. Almost overnight, the ports of the south and east became choked with small farmers clamouring for passages at once.'[2] Between 1849 and 1852 the emigration averaged well over 200,000 people annually, and in 1851 it reached over a quarter of a million. Most of these people came from Connaught and Munster. The crop failed partially in 1849 and slightly in 1850.

The famine was most severe in the west and the south, and much less serious in Ulster and in the eastern coastal belt. Some counties in Munster and Connaught lost over a third of their population by emigration and disease. Above half a million, but less than a million, people died directly from the Great Famine from 1845 to 1851. Probably about a third of the deaths were from typhus, a rather smaller proportion from dysentery and diarrhoea, and the remainder from starvation, dropsy, debility, tuberculosis and scurvy.[3] Over a million people emigrated, mainly to the United States. All told, in five years the population of Ireland as a whole was reduced by a quarter, from 8 million to 6 million, and the population of the non-maritime, rural economy by about a third, from 6 million to 4 million.[4] By 1851 the failure of the potato, and the typhus and dysentery brought about by the Great Famine, had ended.

The appalling tragedy of the Great Famine has often been described. The people lay starving and riddled with disease. Three million of them, nearly half the population, were on public relief. Rural society was totally disrupted. The emigration movement became a torrent that was never stopped despite the horror of the ships on which thousands died from infection brought from typhus-ridden villages, and the cold welcome that awaited many in the New World.

[1] O. MacDonagh, 'Irish Overseas Emigration During the Famine' in Edwards and Williams (eds.), *The Great Famine*, p. 319.

[2] *Ibid.* p. 323.

[3] This paragraph relies upon Sir William MacArthur, 'The Medical History of the Famine', in Edwards and Williams (eds.), *The Great Famine*.

[4] The population of Dublin grew and the population of eastern Ulster hardly fell at all.

The Great Famine

The state spent nearly £9 m. in relief works, and millions flowed in as remittances to pay the emigrants' passages. The flow of incomes was stimulated by public works which employed three-quarters of a million people by March 1847. The total outlay was only just over half of Bentinck's high-Tory scheme for railway development, but it was substantial. Compared, however, with the magnitude of the disaster, the government's efforts were dismally weak.

The social and economic causes of the Great Famine were complex. First and most obviously, the actual failure of the potato was due largely to the overcrowding of the soil with the crop, so that to check the spread of the disease was almost impossible once it had begun. This dependence on a single crop was one important aspect of the subsistence economy. The peasantry relied almost exclusively on the potato, and since their money-incomes were low (gained mainly to pay the rent by the work of one member of the family in the harvest fields of England and Scotland, or in building the railways) they had no alternative food. Because of the lack of money there was no organized retail and wholesale trade in foodstuffs in rural Ireland, and the means of purchase of a substitute for the potato did not exist. The proposals of Peel's Government to relieve distress by public works were clearly right in the long run, as were the suggestions of the Reproductive Works Committee for a wholesale investment by government in railways, land-reclamation, harbours and docks, and other capital projects. They would have spread the method of wage-payment by money, and the retailers would have followed—as they did eventually.

There was a great growth of credit during the year 1846–7.[1] In Skibbereen, forty thousand pawn-tickets were issued in the three winter months in a town of fewer than five thousand inhabitants. Without the 'gombeen man'—the village money-lender—the effects of the Great Famine might have been worse; much distress might have been avoided if earlier there had been more of his retail trading activities. The evils of the gombeen system have been exaggerated and its bad reputation was due mainly to the scarcity of retailing facilities in Ireland, which gave the gombeen man a monopoly and so a power of exploitation.

In the short run, however, the spread of money was neither rapid

[1] T. P. O'Neill, 'The Organization and Administration of Relief', in Edwards and Williams (eds.), *The Great Famine*, p. 229.

163

nor extensive enough to be an effective relief measure. The alternative, suggested by O'Connell, by Mitchell and later historians, that the export of food should have been stopped, was also unlikely to have been successful in its aim. To forbid the export of foodstuffs would have depressed prices in the urban markets of Ireland and reduced the flow of such money as came into the hands of the peasantry, forcing them to rely more than ever on their own subsistence.[1] It would have benefited the townsfolk by keeping down the price of foodstuffs, which in a number of cases had risen—but in the towns there was no great famine. In the circumstances, direct government relief was essential. It came, too little and too late.

The outflow of population from Ireland was probably inevitable in the middle of the nineteenth century though it would not have occurred so suddenly, with such horror, unless the potato crop had failed for five seasons running. The potato failure broke the back of the subsistence economy; it did more, it broke the tradition of the 'extended family' which is so characteristic of a subsistence economy and so great a hindrance to initiative and enterprise. The 'immediate' families of father and mother and children left for America. A year later they sent money for their cousins, or brothers and sisters. The family ties of those who remained were weakened: it became not only permissible for them to leave the plot of land where they had been born, but socially imperative to do so. In the long run this reversal of social values was one of the most profound consequences of the Great Famine. Certainly the old values were among the most potent causes of it, by keeping people at home when they might have left, by causing them to dig a few acres of barren hillside when a new world awaited them.

The landholding system has been condemned often and justly as another potent cause of the disaster. Whether or not it is true that there was a net export of capital from Ireland between 1815 and 1845, it is clear that investment in the land in Ireland was hindered by the landholding system. There was some net investment, of course, because the spread of population shows that land was reclaimed and cottages were built, but it was reclaimed ineffectively and the cottages were bad. There were not many big schemes of improvement.

---

[1] This point was very forcibly made by Campbell Foster, *Letters on the Condition of the People of Ireland*, pp. 612–14. This letter is a most penetrating analysis of the economic problem.

The Great Famine

The landlords were imprisoned in a system of extortion and a land-hungry peasantry; the people saw that their food consumption depended almost directly on the size of their holding; and the soil was exhausted by continuous cropping. Heavy taxation, onerous mortgages and life interests burdened the landlords; family ties and a feudal combination of exploitation and ignorance oppressed the peasantry. The principles of good husbandry were confined to the areas where the market had its influence. Elsewhere the multitudes scratched an exiguous living from a barren soil.

The main cause of the Great Famine was the dependence on one crop, and that dependence is directly ascribable to the lack of a market where other opportunities of advancement would be available. The reasons for the lack of a market in turn reflect the system of land tenure which militated against investment, the ignorance and poverty of the peasantry, and the scarcity of natural resources in Ireland. 'From the outset, the Russell administration worked on the assumption that a well organised retail trade in foodstuffs was established in Ireland, when, in fact, such a trade could hardly be said to exist outside the towns.'[1] As has been suggested earlier, the lack of a market is possibly due to the operations of the monetary system after 1815.

THE MARITIME ECONOMY

The areas unaffected directly by the Great Famine were the maritime economy centred on Dublin, Cork and Belfast. In these towns the mid-nineteenth century saw a considerable industrial growth of small industry, and in Belfast of shipbuilding. These industries relied at least as much upon British as Irish markets. Their growth was characteristic of that in the provincial industrial centres of the British Isles at this time: the steamship took the place of the railway as the means of transport for some of the journey to the markets, but otherwise they relied upon a local banking system whose reserves were kept in London, upon a supply of labour and raw materials not markedly different from that available elsewhere, and upon local business men for initiative and capital. Manual labour in Ireland was usually slightly cheaper than that generally available in Great

[1] Nowlan, 'The Political Background' in Edwards and Williams (eds.), *The Great Famine*, p. 149.

165

Ireland in the Great Famine and After

Britain, but skilled labour was dearer. Indeed, skilled labour was often recruited from England and Scotland. Raw materials such as coal were more expensive than in the north of England because of the sea journey, but no dearer than in London. The maritime fringe of the country was affected by rising food prices, and by unemployment, as a result mainly of the reduction in demand for Irish goods in the British market that accompanied the down-swing of the trade cycle there. 'Rising food prices and unemployment caused much discontent among the artisan class' in Dublin and Cork.[1]

Initially, in 1848, the worst famine year, trade improved temporarily in the maritime economy because of the profits earned from the importation of corn. But soon the country suffered with the rest of the British economy a down-swing of the trade cycle, manifesting itself in falling prices, output and (probably) employment.[2] In Ireland, however, the depression may have been less severe than elsewhere. Only one bank collapsed early in 1848, whereas in England in the previous year there had been financial panic. The mitigation of the effects of the depression in Ireland was due in part to the inflow of capital from England. The fiduciary issue of the Bank of England was exceeded in order to send £200,000 in gold coin to Ireland.[3] The British Government is known to have sent at least £8 m.[4] though the 'total amount of moneys transferred to Ireland for relief purposes' is believed to have been £9 m.

The building of railways in Ireland got under way in the mid-eighteen-forties, but was interrupted, as in England, by the collapse of the speculative boom known as the railway mania. After 1848 it was resumed at a much faster rate,[5] and in due course the country was opened to trade. The railways reduced transport costs, facilitated the movement of people—above all helped in the rapid diffusion of new ideas and the extension of the market economy.

The volume of goods carried by rail was growing; this is in itself an indication of a rapidly expanding market. After 1854 rail traffic in rural Ireland developed to a considerable extent, and the goods carried were cash crops going to Dublin and the markets

[1] Nowlan, 'The Political Background', in Edwards and Williams (eds.), *The Great Famine*, p. 146.
[2] Hall, *History of the Bank of Ireland*, pp. 218–19.
[3] *Ibid.* p. 221.
[4] *Ibid.* p. 216.
[5] *Ibid.* p. 222

The Maritime Economy

in England; goods came in return from Great Britain and the maritime economy of Ireland.

Before 1855, in five or six years, 900 miles of railway had been built in Ireland, at a cost of £17 m. Even in 1854 the receipts for rail traffic were £909,000;[1] 500 more miles were built in the next two years.

Dublin soon recovered from the depression; by late 1848 the boom had resumed. The 'scarcity of provisions' which ended in the autumn of 1847 was not sufficiently long in duration to reduce the sale of porter, and it may be doubted whether the distress among the working class was prolonged or widespread. The Great Famine had taken place as though it were a war in a neighbouring country, while Dublin was a brightly lit, comparatively well fed, slightly anxious neutral territory.

There is extant a letter from the second Arthur Guinness, convalescing at Torquay in his old age, commenting on the Great Famine. It shows the man's piety and liberality, as well as the remoteness of the west of Ireland from Dublin. This confirms the view that the separate economies in Ireland had little connexion:

Undated '1849'—marked 'Torquay'

In *The London Record* of last evening there is a letter from a correspondent who had been visiting Conemara and was just returned to another part of Galway, presenting a picture of the state of destitution in Conemara exceeding in horror and misery anything we have before observed. May the Lord in His infinite mercy direct our Government and all individuals also possessing means to do so to the use of measures to relieve if possible the sufferings of our wretched poor people. I wish to know any mode in which we might be able to aid in the work. You know my dear Ben that my purse is open to the call.

Ever yours,
A. G.

THE CONSEQUENCES OF THE GREAT FAMINE

It is with no sense of callousness that historians have remarked on the tremendous material improvement in the conditions of Irish life after 1850. Much that was bad remained unchanged, but the bandstand on the front at Kingstown,[2] the solid and sensible railway

---

[1] Tooke and Newmarch, *A History of Prices and of the State of Circulation During the Years 1793–1856*, vol. v, p. 377.
[2] Now Dún Laoghaire.

stations throughout Ireland, the acres of small brick houses in the suburbs of Dublin, are monuments to a period of prosperity the like of which had never been seen in Ireland. Later in the century the Royal Commission on Working-Class Housing revealed the details of horrid slums and sordid tenements, and the Guinnesses spent fortunes in giving their work-people decent housing and amenities, but this can too easily lead to a picture of unrelieved squalor. In fact, improvements were taking place with startling rapidity during this period.

The effect of the Great Famine was, after the initial catastrophe, to move the Irish rural economy towards a cash basis. Within four years of the potato failure the market for industrial products had extended to most of Ireland. For those who remained life was materially better than before. The risk of famine was removed because their standard of living now depended on cash crops and remittances. Conditions now resembled those of the maritime hinterland before the Great Famine. For the historian of the maritime economy the Great Famine is almost as remote as suffering on the Niger or the Ganges but its economic consequences were important.

The people died, or fled. Cabins were deserted, villages and towns left desolate and some land was abandoned. On the other hand, those who remained had more land to work. Holdings were consolidated. Most of this change had occurred by 1851. In 1852 Nassau Senior was able to write, 'There seems to be neither poverty nor over-population'.[1] There was a growth of villages in a number of areas as a result of enclosures, although the prevalence of rural tradition still militated against modern agricultural methods, especially rotation of crops, proper manuring, drainage, fences and farm roads, housing for cattle, farmhouses and cottages.[2] This was a failure more of the system of tenure, in which most occupants were annual tenants and many landlords were tenants for life, unable to sell, than a failure of the landlord class.[3]

The elimination of the smallest class of farmer began in 1847 and was substantially complete in 1851. It represented a great increase in the capital/output ratio. This in itself appears to have raised agricultural productivity by giving the survivors more land to work

[1] Nassau Senior, *Journals, Conversations and Essays Relating to Ireland*, vol. II, p. 12.
[2] P.P. 1868–9 [4204], vol. XXVI, *Second Report for the Irish Government on the History of the Landlord and Tenant Question in Ireland*, passim.
[3] P.P. 1868–9 [4204], vol. XXVI, p. 15, *First Report*, pp. 1–2.

and by allowing some landlords to concentrate their demesnes or their tenants' farms. There was a growth of long leases dating from the famine years. In the long run fixity of tenure was a step in the right direction, but the Great Famine was too big a disaster for any cure to succeed quickly.

The recovery from the Great Famine after 1850 was rapid. The flow of emigration continually raised the price of labour relative to land and capital. In Sligo (one of the most afflicted of counties) there was a shortage of labour and wages were rising by 1851. Even in remote Mayo money wages averaged as high as about 6s. a week in 1852 compared with 12s. in County Dublin. There appears to have been a decline in the proportion of paupers and of rural unemployed. The number of large holdings rose dramatically while those under five acres fell from 440,000 in 1841 to 124,000 in 1851. The total cultivated area had been extended largely as a result of the improvement of land by relief works and the inflow of capital. There was also a change in the nature of farming. Crops were produced for the market, and cattle raising and dairying were becoming a staple trade. In 1851 Arthur Guinness's big estates in Wicklow and Wexford were put under new management and two letters from the new agent to Arthur's solicitor, Robert Rundell Guinness, survive.[1] These letters show clearly the rapidity of the improvement that was being undertaken on some Irish estates. Above all, they emphasize the importance of arterial drainage. In his first letter the agent said his intention was to 'negotiate the surrender of farms put them into condition drain and consolidate them with a view of letting them at some future period in large tracts to solvent and improving tenants'.

The increase in monetary transactions dates from before the Great Famine. The importation of corn in 1846 led to good merchanting business and the later slump was followed by a railway boom, so that the Great Famine itself led to no interruption of the process. The opening of branches of the Bank of Ireland at places where Guinness sold beer in large or small quantities took place in the eighteen-thirties.[2]

While the Bank of Ireland's deposits did not rise, because of its mortgage restrictions, those of its joint-stock competitors soared by

[1] The agent was George Waller, a connexion.
[2] Hall, *History of the Bank of Ireland*, p. 185.

Ireland in the Great Famine and After

four times from 1846 to 1864.[1] In the years from 1848 to 1858 the bank opened four new branches (increasing its total from twenty-three to twenty-seven). Other banks opened many more. The contraction in the volume of currency was evidently due to a decline in the circulation of bank-notes and to a rise in the use of cheques,[2] because the total increase of deposits plus coins and notes in circulation rose by nearly three-quarters between 1846 and 1864. At the same time prices were falling. Consequently the total use of money in Ireland probably doubled, and as the population fell by nearly one-third in the period the total use of money *per head* in the twenty years after the Great Famine probably trebled. Only part of this increase is attributable to the growth of Dublin and the other towns, and to improvements in wages. A substantial part of the new wealth found its way into the pockets of the country folk.

Even thirty years after the Great Famine, however, the use of money was not as extensive in Ireland as elsewhere in the United Kingdom. The potato was still the mainstay of the people. Their resources were their indebtedness to the shopkeepers, and to private moneylenders, 'the gombeen men' whose rate of interest sometimes rose as high as 43⅓ per cent. This may seem an extortionate figure, as it did to the clients of the gombeen men, but it must be remembered that the possibility of bad debts was extraordinarily high. The most considerable of Guinness's agents in Ireland died in debt himself.

The poverty of Irish country people after the Great Famine was often attributed to the activities of the 'gombeen man', but it is not clear what these men are alleged to have done with the money they made from their activities. It seems probable, in fact, that in contrast to many of their clients they stayed in their towns and sooner or later spent their money. The general level of prosperity, therefore, was (at the very least) unaffected, though the distribution of income may have been changed in their favour.[3] The 'gombeen man' usually bought a grocery and whiskey shop, so that the two classes of moneylenders coalesced. The factors made advances for cattle and butter.[4] These were still the main source of cash and credit inside Ireland, because the banks lent only at high rates of interest on good security to substantial people. The other sources of cash came from outside Ireland.

---

[1] Hall, *History of the Bank of Ireland*, p. 240. [2] *Ibid.* p. 262.
[3] Campbell Foster, *Letters on the Condition of the People of Ireland*, pp. 305–11.
[4] P.P. 1881 (c. 2778–II), vol. XVI, *Preliminary Report of the Assistant Commissioners for Ireland to the Royal Commission on Agriculture*, pp. 841–8.

The Consequences of the Great Famine

The Connaught and Ulster farmers went to England every year, 'The money brought back from England in this way exceeds the rental'.[1] Between 1848 and 1860 there was a rise in money-incomes in rural Ireland. Some of it came from emigrants' remittances. A class of merchants and shop-keepers emerged; the increase in the number of shop-assistants was a sign of this. There was a growth in the number of agricultural labourers paid in money. There was a remarkable rise in the use of cheap imported consumption goods. Diet habits changed. Food was considerably more varied. The consumption of porter became widespread. There is evidence of an improvement in the standard of living of the country folk in the reports of the various royal commissions which investigated rural Ireland. The economy now rested on a healthier basis. The flight of people from the Great Famine caused profound demographic changes that have never been reversed. Ireland has become a country of the very young and the old, its total population falling decade by decade. In the long run this spelt difficulty for the economy, but in the decades after the Great Famine it spelt nothing but relief from an intolerable pressure. The land-tenure system of the old economy persisted. The almost absolute rights of the landlords, derived both from recent conquest and from the insecurity entailed by a dearth of cash, were often not compatible with the improving farming methods associated with an increasing capital/output ratio. In the popular mind the emigration was a political evil resulting from the landlord system; for these reasons and a variety of others the landlord system came under attack. Because of this the condition of the country folk in the period from the Great Famine to Gladstone's reforms in the eighteen-eighties has been given an unduly black picture. It is true that some landlords were irresponsible tyrants, just as it is true that some were benevolent reformers. The landlord system itself stands condemned as inefficient. It is not true, however, that there was in general ruthless exploitation. All the indices show a rapid rise in the rural Irish standard of living after 1850. The Great Famine had done its work in transforming a society and an economy. In itself it was a horrid disaster. Some of its results were evil. But the standard of living of those who remained after the mass emigration bore witness to some good coming out of evil. It was this reformed society that gave Guinness its great Irish market.

[1] *Ibid.* p. 843.

Ireland in the Great Famine and After

Like the working class in the rest of the United Kingdom, the Irish were benefiting from the flood of cheap goods produced by the fast industrializing economy. Soap, meat, textiles, travel, household equipment—all these things and many others became cheaper and on the whole better. It is against this background that infantile mortality fell more rapidly even than the general death-rate in the decades after the Great Famine.

It seems probable that there was also a continuing influx of British capital. The government spent a great deal, partly financed by loans whose source was in England. The Financial Relations Commission held that until late in the century the balance of taxation was unduly weighted, so that Ireland bore more than its 'fair' share of Imperial expenditure. But the Irish economy benefited from military expenditure and relief works on a larger scale than the other three countries of the Kingdom. The railways were probably largely British-financed. There was an improvement in agriculture which was based on capital investment. After 1860 the Belfast shipbuilding industry grew, harbours and piers were built and steamships crossed the Irish Sea regularly.

It would follow, therefore, that the material condition of the Irish people improved considerably. So did their social condition. This was a great era of church-building. Sir Benjamin Lee Guinness restored St Patrick's Cathedral in the late eighteen-sixties, and innumerable efforts in what was called Hiberno-Romanesque and Hiberno-Byzantine testify to a measure of ecclesiastical affluence. A Pugin spire rises at Ballinasloe as well as at Maynooth. The Irish administration presided over a system of national education that grew only a little more slowly than that of England. Public health measures were introduced and the evolution of local government through the Poor Law and the Resident Magistrates took place at an accelerated rate.

The 1870 Land Act, followed by that of 1881, had little immediate effect. The main result of the first Act was to make eviction more expensive and difficult, and to increase security of tenure. The result of the second Act was to strengthen this tendency, and followed as it was by the Land Purchase Acts a policy was initiated whose consequences were in part to relieve social tension by eliminating, within forty years, the execrated class of landlord. This policy probably had ultimately the effect of diminishing consumption by raising

But Poverty Remained

saving, and possibly of redirecting capital to Britain—but its main effects were later than the period dealt with here.

If the rise in living standards was true of the labouring poor in the towns and in the country, the prosperous middle class was no less benefited by the circumstances of the time. So, too, were the rich and powerful. Ashford Castle and other great houses in the West are monuments to a vanished opulence when private carriages were dropped on request at private stations, and the fashionable were driven to the finest fishing in the country as guests of an aristocracy both old and new.

BUT POVERTY REMAINED

Despite all this, poverty abounded. But there was now a monetary economy and widespread famine could be averted. According to a witness at the House of Lords Select Committee in 1881, R. Wade Thompson, manager of his father's estates near Ballina, County Mayo, the average family income of Mayo peasants, and these were the poorest in the land, was £30 or £40 a year.[1] Out of this they paid £4 or £5 a year rent.[2] They had 'free turf and as much as they can sell for 10s. or £1 a year'.[3]

155,675 mud cabins occupied by 227,379 families, were reported in the 1881 Census.[4] Six million acres of land were surcharged with water and comparatively worthless. On the other hand, rents had not changed for forty or sixty years,[5] and money receipts had risen. Between 1848 and 1864 according to one witness before the 1880 Commission, C. U. Townshend, an 'enormous change had passed over the country'. Agricultural improvement societies had led to better cattle and there was improved machinery on the farms. The railways had been built. Cross-Channel traffic had improved and made markets easier of access.[6]

But the economic improvement was not universal. Another

[1] P.P. 1882 (249), vol. XI, *Second Report from the Select Committee of the House of Lords on Land Law (Ireland)*, Q. 5208.
[2] *Ibid.* Q. 5122.   [3] *Ibid.* Q. 5133.
[4] P.P. 1881 (c. 2778–II), vol. XVI, *Preliminary Report of the Assistant Commissioners for Ireland to the Royal Commission on Agriculture*, Q. 6.
[5] P.P. 1882 (249), vol. XI, *First Report from the Select Committee of the House of Lords on Land Law (Ireland)*, Q. 1511–14. *Second Report from the Select Committee of the House of Lords on Land Law (Ireland)*, Q. 5172.
[6] P.P. 1882 (249), vol. XI, *First Report from the Select Committee of the House of Lords on Land Law (Ireland)*, Q. 1634.

witness before the 1880 Commission, speaking of Mayo, said: 'They have a couple of acres...not of the best land...they grow corn, potatoes, oats and turnips; they have very bad meadows, of course, still they have meadow-land, and they sell butter, and sell it in the Ballina market every week....They have donkeys and horses, and carts; the very small tenants use principally donkeys with baskets. [The labour is done] by their families, as a rule.'[1] In reply to the Duke of Somerset the witness said of their houses, 'They are mud cabins, thatched of course'.

Is the population very numerous in this part of Mayo?
It is very numerous, and great numbers go to America yearly.
Is there much emigration going on now?
A great number go to America every year.
How do they provide for the expense of their emigration?
I cannot tell you; I think they have the money. I cannot tell you where it comes from; we often wonder; they have saved money evidently.[2]

CONCLUSION

Demand was rising fast and supplies of capital and labour were available. But no substantial business class arose to develop the country—Guinness's stood as the greatest mercantile and business family. Why was this? Why was there no rising tide of enterprise and ability that rose higher than shops or small businesses?

A variety of false answers has been given. One is that the majority had been excluded from trade because of their creed and therefore only few commercial talents were available. This is not true, and even if it were there were many members of the Church of Ireland, Presbyterians and Quakers, and the traditional virtue (and a worthy one) of members of reformed confessions is making money. Another answer is that Britain bled the country dry. In fact, however, there was at times an export of capital to Ireland. A third view holds that the falling population discouraged investment. But it is a population's wealth and not its numbers alone that stimulates men of enterprise—though this solution comes nearest to the truth.

The real answer is much simpler. Ireland was a poorly endowed

[1] P.P. 1882 (249), vol. XI, *Second Report from the Select Committee of the House of Lords on Land Law (Ireland)*, Q.5201–6.
[2] *Ibid.* Q.5212–5.

Conclusion

part of a wealthy economic unit. Most men of drive and initiative went to the places where drive and initiative gave the highest returns, which were England, Scotland, America and Australia. Men with small fortunes which they wanted to increase went where they could increase them fastest. Risk capital in emergent economies is often a personal thing. It is the few hundred pounds inherited or saved by an ambitious man and risked by him personally in a business. These men took their money and set up all over the English-speaking world because almost everywhere but Ireland was naturally or socially better endowed. This was not something peculiar to Ireland. It was true of all Scotland except the central Lowlands, all Wales except the two southern counties of Glamorgan and Carmarthen, of the remoter parts of rural England. This was no conspiracy. It was sound sense to let money fructify in the pockets of the people in the nineteenth century. They took those pockets where they could be filled.

The post-Famine economy exhibits all the characteristics of a stable society where dynamic drive was unwonted and unlikely. All the banks were safe, until in 1866 the Overend Gurney crash brought down two by mistake, and then the other banks paid the depositors off. Wealthy people retired to Ireland—they went there to fish. They discovered scenery and built hotels like those at St Moritz. They ate oysters, drank Guinness and bought horses. The army did its exercises in Ireland. It was very different from the mills of Lancashire and the pits and the furnaces of Yorkshire, and it depended for its viability on a steady outflow of its population to Great Britain and America. The social and economic stability rested, therefore, upon a situation which led to political instability, because the politically conscious Irish felt that their country was being drained of its life-blood. As so often, economics and politics pulled in opposite directions—and in the end which was to win?

In such an economy, lacking most of the characteristics of indigenous growth, Guinness's trade was on the eve of its great expansion into parts of Ireland which before the Great Famine had been largely a subsistence economy. The extension of the money economy, the development of rail transport, the increase in income per head, presented opportunities for business enterprise. Some men missed these opportunities through neglect or indifference; others tried but failed to grasp them. Guinness's succeeded. The brewery had rooted

175

itself firmly in the Dublin market and captured trade in England. Now it was offered an extension of its market as a result of the economic changes produced by the Famine. In this new market good management and aggressive selling might convert potential demand into effective demand for a product whose reputation was already established. The old subsistence economy in Ireland was rapidly receding. An integrated economy was coming into existence, in which only local variations distinguished Ireland from widely separated parts of the rest of the United Kingdom.

[10]
Three Guinnesses

You can't expect to make money out of people unless you are prepared to let them make money out of you. (*Attributed to Edward
Cecil Guinness, later the first Earl of Iveagh.*)

BENJAMIN LEE GUINNESS

BENJAMIN LEE GUINNESS was 57 when his father died in 1855.
He had already worked for nearly forty years in the brewery and
for thirty-five of these years as a partner. With his partner John
Purser, junior, he had exercised almost full control for some time
before the death of his father, though the second Arthur never ceased
to take a practical interest in the business, and his son continued
till the end to seek his advice—and usually to take it. Arthur knew
that his son attached great weight to his advice and he was content,
therefore, to leave his son the ultimate decisions. In 1849, for
instance, he wrote from his holiday retreat in Torquay recommending
increases in the firm's stocks of malt and hops while prices of raw
materials remained low, and asking for a 'complete account' of the
firm's financial position. This was followed by another letter in which
he hoped that his advice about the purchase of malt and hops had
not been expressed too strongly. 'I therefore write a line to say that
I feel the utmost confidence in the judgement of my partners in this
matter who possess also local advantages as regards the means of
forming their opinions which I at present do not.'

The pace of the brewery's advance increased after Benjamin Lee
assumed complete control in 1858, when John Purser, junior, died.
In 1865, ten years after the second Arthur's death, the firm's production was exceeded by only four other breweries in the United Kingdom. There were ten other firms making brown stout in Dublin, but
the Guinness output was as great as their combined production.

In 1851 Benjamin Lee was elected Lord Mayor of Dublin. As first
citizen and soon to be head of the city's principal industry he had
a house in the city as well as in the country. Before his father's death
Benjamin Lee lived at St Anne's, Clontarf, a small estate near the

177

sea about four miles from the brewery and two miles from Dublin, and used No. 1 Thomas Street as a town house. In 1856 he bought 80 St Stephen's Green, in one of the fashionable squares of Dublin, and from that time he and his family divided their time between St Anne's and St Stephen's Green. The prosperity of his business and growth of the family fortunes are also attested by the consideration which he gave to 'investing a small sum...(say £20,000 to £30,000) in the purchase of land' in County Mayo in the west of Ireland. He eventually bought an estate at Ashford, County Galway.

After his year of office as Lord Mayor, Benjamin Lee was invited to stand for Parliament, but, while civic duties were useful to a local merchant, party politics was another matter. John Barlow, Governor of the Bank of Ireland in 1851, asked the second Arthur to persuade his son to contest a Dublin seat in the Conservative interest. The second Arthur's reply was characteristic. He expressed pleasure that his son should be so highly esteemed. 'But viewing him as the devoted husband of a wife suffering extreme delicacy of health, and considering the very heavy demands upon his time and mind from the pressure of peculiar family and other relative claims, I feel unable to say that I am prepared to recommend his acquiescence.' The second Arthur advised his son strongly against acceptance of the invitation—'You will recollect', he wrote to Benjamin Lee, 'that on two occasions a similar suggestion was conveyed to me, backed on both occasions by offers on the part of gentlemen who were candidates themselves and who offered to resign in my favour. I then felt, and now feel, that the office of sitting in Parliament for a great city and especially such a city as Dublin where party and sectarian strife so signally abound and more especially if filled by one engaged in our line of business, is fraught with difficulty and danger.' Benjamin Lee took his father's advice. The second Arthur immediately wrote to congratulate him on his decision, expressing 'heartfelt gratification' and blessing 'God for the measure of his Grace which has led you to this happy decision'.

In 1865, however, Benjamin Lee Guinness was elected in the Conservative interest for Dublin City. Many of the considerations which his father advanced against participation in Irish politics had by then lost much of their force. The fortunes of the brewery were firmly established and Benjamin Lee could afford to be less sensitive to the controversies of the day in Dublin. Fourteen years earlier

SIR BENJAMIN LEE GUINNESS, 1798–1868

Artist and date unknown: photograph by Lafayette, Dublin

Benjamin Lee Guinness

prudence might have deterred him from publicly adhering to one political party lest his business should suffer as a result of antagonizing supporters of the other, but by 1865 it seemed in the natural order of things that the head of the house of Guinness should be a Conservative in politics—this was the party of the 'liquor interest'. Naturally, Guinness was a strong Unionist—anything else seemed senseless or worse to the Dublin mercantile class of which Guinness was a recognized leader. There was, it is true, a moderate nationalist movement which respected law and order, but that movement aroused little sympathy or understanding amongst the propertied, business and professional classes in Ireland who identified Irish nationalism with revolutionary terrorism, and the abortive Fenian rising confirmed their worst fears.

Towards the end of 1866 the threat of Fenianism perturbed many people. It was believed that the leaders of the movement had been conspiring in the United States and France to foment a rising in Ireland, and it was feared that a tide of radical republicanism would overwhelm the country. The size and influence of Fenianism were altogether exaggerated. The apprehensions of the time are somewhat apocalyptically revealed in an 'Address to Benjamin Lee Guinness, Esq., M.P., adopted at James's Gate by some persons in his employment' on 13 December 1866. The address was signed by 515 employees including four brewers and forty-nine 'office gentlemen'. James's Gate was as determined as Dublin Castle to defend Ireland against revolution.

...Deriving our subsistence, as we do, from the success which has attended your manufacture, and the enterprise on your part which has raised your concern to such great proportions, we cannot but feel how closely our interests are identified with those of our valued employer, and how entirely they depend on the security and good order which is maintained in the country.

We desire especially at this time to express our abhorrence of those sentiments of sedition and rebellion, and the horror with which we have learned the projects for destruction of life and property, which have been attempted to be introduced into our land by emissaries from a foreign country.

We have seen with deep regret the injury which this dreadful agitation has already done to trade in this country, from the feeling of insecurity which it has caused; and we believe it to be the duty of true Irishmen to use all their influence to put down and expel from among us such mad and pernicious doctrines. . . .

179   12-2

Three Guinnesses

Benjamin Lee Guinness replied in terms which reflected the mood of the address. It is a document of some importance coming as it does from the hand of Ireland's most successful merchant. Most members of the Irish middle class of the time would have subscribed to his sentiments, though not all might have expressed themselves with the same fluency:

It is with no ordinary gratification that I receive the Address in which you have given expression to those sentiments of attachment to the glorious Constitution under which we live, and of your fixed resolve to resist the machinations of those wicked and worthless adventurers who would not only deprive our country of the advantages which, as a part of the British Empire, we enjoy, but who would overturn all the social arrangements of society—would break the ties which bind man to man, and, by a reckless destruction of property and of human life, would deluge our country in bloodshed and reduce the industrial classes to want and misery, and take from others the ability of advancing the onward progress lately so evident in our beloved country.

The address now presented, which has been so unanimously signed, and has emanated solely from yourselves, goes far to show that Irishmen generally abhor the projects of Fenianism; and that the sentiments of sedition and rebellion which its followers inculcate have emanated from a foreign land, and been spread and nurtured in this country by emissaries, who hope by deception and by pillage to grasp from its owners their property, and during the proposed panic to escape with their plunder to whence they came—thus avoiding the just vengeance of society, and to leave to their wretched dupes the sad and direful consequences of the crimes to which they had incited them. . . .

The image of a small band of revolutionaries including in their loot the biggest porter brewery in the world is more than an engaging flourish of the pen. Benjamin Lee's response to the threat of Fenianism may have been unnecessarily exaggerated. But, like other men of property in Ireland of all religious persuasions, he knew that a spectre had been haunting Europe for a generation. He could not have foreseen that when Ireland did become politically independent it would draw its economic principles more from the practices of James's Gate than from the doctrines of the Communist Manifesto.

The Fenian rising took place in 1867, and though it was quickly suppressed the propaganda of the movement and the measures taken by the authorities to deal with it created a profound impression in Britain and in Ireland. From its inception it was openly and avowedly separatist and it never pretended to have any other object.

Benjamin Lee Guinness

Its aim was an Irish republic and its means revolution. It dismissed constitutional agitation as futile and as a result incurred the condemnation of the Churches, as well as the full rigour of the law. At that time Benjamin Lee Guinness spoke for more than his own class and creed when he described Fenianism as 'despicable in its objects, its resources and its courage'.

Like his father and grandfather, Benjamin Lee Guinness devoted himself to public service in benevolent and practical ways, and like them too he had a particular association with St Patrick's Cathedral in Dublin. The cathedral, founded in 1190, is one of Ireland's national monuments. Swift preached there and lived in its gloomy Deanery; within its walls his remains lie at peace. By the middle of the nineteenth century the cathedral bore the marks of the dilapidations of six hundred years; the structure was disintegrating, and the munificence of Benjamin Lee Guinness rescued it from neglect and decay. He acted as his own architect in restoring and repairing it.[1] The task was completed in 1865 at a cost of over £150,000. There was much public appreciation of his benevolence, because the cathedral might have become a ruin if the work had not been done. In extolling Guinness's achievement the Lord Lieutenant of Ireland, Lord Wodehouse, said that 'work which was too great for the Knights of St Patrick, or for the Ecclesiastical Commissioners, or the Bench of Bishops, which the Irish Parliament refused to undertake and which the British Parliament never entertained the thought of executing has been accomplished within four years by a single merchant'. His work was a demonstration of his allegiance to his Church, at that time under strong attack from Gladstone. A Dublin newspaper in 1865 referred to 'Mr Guinness a staunch defender of the Irish Church. The restorer of our National Cathedral is not the man to be found advocating or justifying, with Mr Gladstone, the destruction of the Establishment in this country.'[2] The Church of Ireland was indignant at being threatened with disestablishment, and in the circumstances Benjamin Lee Guinness's generosity was an act of more than local significance. In recognition of this and 'other public service' Guinness was created a Baronet in 1867. He also had plans for reconstructing the area surrounding the cathedral, but this work had to await his successor.

Sir Benjamin Lee Guinness died in London at the age of seventy

[1] The unused plans of a professional architect still survive.
[2] *Daily Express*, 10 June 1865.

181

Three Guinnesses

on 19 May 1868. His last years were varied and eventful. His firm was the leading porter brewery in the industry. He had taken an honoured part in municipal and political affairs. He was the most prominent and successful figure in Irish business life. He was noted for his philanthropy; his unassuming and courteous demeanour recommended itself to all. He was intensely devoted to his family, and his married life was extremely happy although his wife, like many wives of the time, lacked robust health and frequently made special demands on the concern and sympathy of her family. A very close and affectionate relationship existed between his three sons Arthur, Benjamin Lee (known as Lee, who never went into the business) and Edward Cecil and their father. They were all young when he died, for he had married late in life, so he never knew his daughters-in-law or his grandchildren. Whether they were at St Anne's, their quiet house on Dublin Bay, in their handsome town house on St Stephen's Green, or in the wild magnificence of Ashford, County Galway, the atmosphere in which the Guinnesses lived was distinctively pious, serious yet far from solemn. Frivolity was as remote from Sir Benjamin Lee as it had been from his father. Their guiding impulse was high-minded, and their comfortable lives demanded constant recognition of God's grace and thanks for his bounty. Their surroundings were opulent but their lives were sober—in some ways austere—and the day began and ended with family prayers.

SIR ARTHUR EDWARD GUINNESS AND EDWARD CECIL GUINNESS

Sir Benjamin Lee's will was proved at £1,100,000. When provision was made for his daughter Anne, who married Lord Plunket, later archbishop of Dublin, and the second son Lee, who was in the army, the main part of the estate was left equally to Arthur and Edward Cecil. St Anne's and Ashford Castle were left to Arthur. Edward Cecil was bequeathed the town house in St Stephen's Green.[1] The

[1] No. 80 St Stephen's Green was built in 1730 after a design by the famous architect Richard Cassels. It was bought by Benjamin Lee Guinness in 1856, who later acquired the adjoining property No. 81 and converted the two houses into one. This building, later known as Iveagh House, and the gardens behind remained in the possession of the Guinness family until 1939, when the present Earl of Iveagh handed them over to the Irish Government. Iveagh House is now the headquarters of the Irish Department of External Affairs, and the Iveagh Gardens are attached to University College, Dublin. See Craig, *Dublin 1660–1860, A Social and Architectural History*.

182

brewery and all related property was left to Arthur and Edward Cecil as co-partners.

At the time of Sir Benjamin Lee Guinness's death James's Gate was already the largest porter brewery in the world. Business grew rapidly during his proprietorship and the brewery was often enlarged and remodelled. In 1860, though it occupied about four acres on the south side of James's Street and Thomas Street, its capacity was insufficient to keep pace with demand, so portions of adjoining pro-perties were bought to allow for extensions. The rate of growth became even more spectacular in the years ahead, and a huge addi-tion was made to the brewery property when Sir Benjamin Lee's heirs Sir Arthur and Edward Cecil Guinness acquired the ground between James's Street and the Liffey in 1873.

Sir Benjamin Lee Guinness began the heavy investment that made the growth of the James's Gate brewery possible, and he wished this investment to continue after his death. He was typical of many Victorian industrialists, but more far-seeing than most, in his aware-ness of the temptations which great wealth offered the next generation. The terms of his will sought to ensure that the family fortune should remain concentrated in the brewery and that in no circumstances should it be dispersed among his heirs for use outside the business. The sum of £30,000 which a retiring partner might receive under the will was nominal—almost cutting him off with a shilling.

From 1858 to 1868 the brewery was run by Sir Benjamin Lee with the help of his old colleague's son, John Tertius Purser, a man eleven years his junior. There were also the two Guinness boys, Arthur, who was twenty-seven, and Edward Cecil, who was almost twenty-one at the time of their father's death. Since John Purser, junior's, death on 5 April 1858, Sir Benjamin Lee had been the sole owner and no new partnership agreements were made. The two sons inherited the fortune and the business, while John Tertius Purser had a consider-able bequest from his own father, John Purser, junior, a salary and a 'centage' on all the sales of beer. There was great hazard in leaving the brewery in the hands of the two young men alone, but Purser was a guarantee that responsibility and experience would remain at the helm.

Sir Benjamin Lee foresaw, in fact, what eventually took place, that one of his sons might withdraw from the firm, and his will was designed to ensure that if this happened the remaining son should have the capital necessary to continue the process of expansion and

Three Guinnesses

development as his father had done. As Shannon points out, the
dissolution of a partnership was an extraordinarily complex process,
and litigation could go on for years at inordinate expense, sometimes
ruining the company: 'Under a fairly well established rule the Courts
were not likely to interfere in any internal dispute unless at the same
time ordering a dissolution.'[1] Sir Benjamin Lee therefore sought
to limit the power of the parties to undertake litigation by making
dissolution, if it took place by any means, a severe blow to the dissi-
dent party. The following extracts from his will show how he decided
to dispose of the brewery:

...I GIVE DEVISE AND BEQUEATH all my said Brewery concerns...to my
sons Arthur Edward Guinness and Edward Cecil Guinness...AND I
DIRECT that said premises so left and bequeathed to them shall belong to
and be held by them as co-partners in Trade AND I DIRECT and earnestly
hope that my said sons...shall continue to carry on the said Brewery and
the business thereof which has been heretofore carried on at the same place
by their Ancestors for so many years but in case either of them...shall
unfortunately decline to take to and carry on the said business or choose
to retire therefrom and the other of them shall desire to carry on same
I WILL AND DIRECT that the said Brewery concerns shall not be divided
or broken up but shall remain as they now are one concern AND I DIRECT
that my son so declining or retiring from said business shall...make over
his moiety of...the said Brewery Concerns...to his brother so continuing
in said business and to no other person whatsoever so that the entire
interest shall vest in such son so continuing and in case such son so declining or retiring shall neglect or refuse so to do then I REVOKE and make void
all the said devise and bequest to him of said moiety and give devise and
bequeath same to his brother so desirous to continue said business and
I DIRECT that my son so declining or retiring from said business shall on
such transfer...of said moiety to his brother as aforesaid but not otherwise
be entitled to receive out of the said concerns the sum of £30,000 together
with the value of a moiety of the stock then on hands of Porter malt hops
casks cooperage materials and stores drays and horses and of goods debts
bills and cash...AND I DIRECT that the value of said moiety so to be ascertained together with the said sum of £30,000 shall be paid in eight equal
instalments...without interest...but in the event of either of my said
sons becoming Bankrupt...the entire of my said Brewery...shall immediately revert to and become the property of my other son on the same
terms as...if my said son...had retired from said business.

The two brothers were, subject to many trusts, joint owners of
Ireland's biggest business. The elder son, Arthur Edward, inherited

[1] H. A. Shannon, 'The Coming of General Limited Liability' in E. M. Carus-Wilson
(ed.), *Essays in Economic History* (London, 1954), p. 363.

Sir Arthur and Edward Cecil Guinness

his father's baronetcy and his parliamentary seat. In 1868 Edward Cecil was not yet of age, but it seemed likely that he would be the more active partner. While his brother went to Eton and Trinity College, Dublin, he had started work at the brewery at the age of fifteen and then for some years he was a part-time undergraduate at Trinity. He had been nearly six years in the business when his father died and although the entries in the Proprietors Book suggest that Sir Arthur was just as interested in the affairs of the brewery as his brother, he was less expert and soon left the initiative in many matters to Edward Cecil. The brothers were fortunate, of course, in being able to rely on the continued support and guidance of their father's chief lieutenant, John Tertius Purser. After Sir Benjamin Lee's death Sir Arthur and Edward Cecil wrote jointly to Purser asking him to remain in the service of the brewery.

> *27 Norfolk Street,*
> *Park Lane,*
> *London*
> *1 June 1869*

Dear Mr Purser,

We write to thank you for your untiring exertions and the very great assistance you have rendered in closing the many affairs which have now so nearly been completed; and to express our earnest desire and hope that we may long enjoy your friendly and valued co-operation in carrying on the business which now devolves upon us. We have for some time intended asking you to accept as a small acknowledgement of our regard and esteem £2,000 a year in addition to what you at present draw from James's Gate.

We feel that though we have lost the advice and assistance of a father, we may hope to retain that of his friend, whose opinion and candid advice we shall always highly value.

> Ever believe us to be,
> Yours most sincerely,
> ARTHUR E. GUINNESS
> EDWARD C. GUINNESS

Most of the important correspondence was written by Edward Cecil and even the copy of the letter to John Tertius Purser was made by him in the Proprietors Book. Indeed, it would seem that he did the greater part of the work, while his brother usually played a passive role. Sir Arthur had limited experience in business and showed little of his brother's energy, and his periodic intrusions into management meant that the relationship was not an easy one. For Edward

185

Cecil, brewing was at this time his main occupation. He became immersed in the brewery business and addressed himself to mundane practical affairs and questions of general policy with that careful attention which was one of his characteristics. Even when he left to others responsibility for action in comparatively trivial matters he showed his keen administrative sense by insisting on being kept informed of what had been done under his authority. While retaining control he could delegate authority. With him delegation was more than a mechanical or procedural process; it was an attitude of mind. When delegation was exercised the trusted recipient was granted a flexibility of manoeuvre which allowed him considerable freedom in conducting the day-to-day affairs of the business. Nevertheless, Edward Cecil tenaciously retained ultimate control. The aggregate of decisions taken under his delegated authority might influence the policy of the brewery, but he alone determined ultimate policy.

Edward Cecil was an excitable young man, brilliant and gay with an intense vitality, and he found collaboration the most difficult of arts. His sure touch, his quickness and his decision led to irritation and difficulties. Within eight years his brother had left.

Arthur seems to have looked on James's Gate predominantly as a source of income. His father had given him a generous allowance—£420 in July 1864, £630 in November 1865, £1000 in July 1866, £1500 in January 1867. Edward's allowances, though smaller—£170 in 1865, £450 in 1867—were bigger than Sir Arthur's at the same age. After their father's death their incomes leapt forward. In 1868, the first year of their joint partnership, the profits amounted to £102,000. The brothers drew £44,000 for their personal use, of which amount Edward Cecil took only £2000. (He was still under age.) In 1869 profits were £147,000 and each brother drew £10,000. In 1870 they drew between them more than the profit for the year. With the exception of this year their policy was, however, to plough back into the business a large share of the profits.

Sir Arthur was returned unopposed to the parliamentary seat for Dublin which his father held. In the general election of 1868 he was again returned, but next year he was unseated on a petition, it being found that his agents had been guilty of bribery, though bribery was not proved to have been committed by him or to have been committed with his knowledge or consent. In spite of his keen interest in politics he was not returned to Parliament again until

Sir Arthur and Edward Cecil Guinness

1874. In the meantime his brother, Edward Cecil, was invited to stand for Dublin after Sir Arthur's unseating in 1869. He accepted the invitation as 'a generous proof that the goodwill and confidence often before shown to my family by the citizens of Dublin are unaltered', and added, 'My political principles are those held by my father and brother, and I will, if returned to Parliament, support the cause of Conservatism, and the interests of the Church of which I am a member'.

Gladstone and the Liberals were becoming identified with the cause of temperance, and the Conservatives under Disraeli became the brewers' party. The election of 1874, in which Disraeli was returned at the head of a big majority, was allegedly largely won through the influence of the brewers and licensed victuallers.

Edward Cecil withdrew his candidature, however, before the election. He must have had political ambitions to have let his name go forward in the first instance, but it is not possible to say why, on second thoughts, he changed his mind. He was again pressed to stand, not this time by the Dublin business community, but by Isaac Butt, leader of the Home Rule movement which had been launched in May 1870 to seek partial repeal of the union between Great Britain and Ireland. Butt had attracted many conservative nationalists into the movement at the outset. Their motives for joining were mixed, but most of them were opposed to Gladstone's disestablishment of the Church and to his land policy which they regarded as revolutionary. Butt, a moderate nationalist and a constitutionalist, thought that Guinness would be a very useful addition to the nationalist party, and assumed, no doubt, that Guinness's Conservatism would allow him to accept the Home Rule platform. Butt's approach to Guinness shows that Conservatism was not identified at that time with Unionism; indeed, the Guinnesses were probably Conservative because they were brewers and because they were sons of the Church of Ireland. At first the Home Rule party regarded itself as a national party representative of all moderate political interests in Ireland, Conservative and Liberal alike.

Some Conservative and Liberal Members of Parliament declared themselves, in fact, in favour of Home Rule, but the Conservative element declined in importance after 1871 when there was a succession of electoral victories by candidates standing for Home Rule, fixity of tenure and denominational education. But even on the inception of the movement a year earlier, Edward Cecil's Unionism was more rigid than Butt had expected. Edward Cecil was a stricter Unionist than the Conservatives who had joined Butt. Though he worked for the advancement of Dublin and Ireland, he was out of sympathy with the constitutional changes which contemporary nationalists sought, and he would not lend his name to political agitation which aimed at any substantial degree of separation of Ireland from Great Britain. In a letter to Isaac Butt on 25 May 1870 Sir Arthur made a clear statement of his family's political views:

I have showed your letter to my brother & Plunket[1] and I have first to thank you from my Brother and myself for the kind feeling it expresses towards us relative to his candidature for the City. He has resolved not to contest Dublin but I must say, as you have alluded to a rumour that there was a chance of his adopting what are commonly called National views and opinion such was not the case for, while none can feel more strongly a truly National desire for the advancement of Ireland materially and intellectually, we do not and cannot think this is to be achieved by Repeal [of the Act of Union] or by any half measure of Repeal but by the determination of the Irish nation to oblige their representatives to enforce irrespective of party the rights of those they represent which they now almost entirely neglect. . . .

At this time Edward Cecil Guinness was twenty-two years old and these political convictions endured for the rest of his long life.

Although he played so large a part in the organization of the brewery Edward Cecil had many other interests. His father left him his beautiful Dublin house in St Stephen's Green and he had the use of a London flat at 5 Berkeley Square which before Sir Benjamin Lee's death he had shared with his brother. He followed his father's example by taking a leading part in Irish public life and, with Sir Arthur, was amongst those who financed and guaranteed against loss the plans for the great Irish Exhibition of 1872. The Exhibition attracted a good deal of attention, but not enough to be as successful financially as its sponsors had hoped. Nevertheless it enabled Edward Cecil to make a very favourable impression on public opinion and earned for him official recognition for his services in his appointment as Deputy Lieutenant of the City of Dublin.

On 20 May 1873 Edward Cecil married his cousin Adelaide Guinness, daughter of his second cousin Richard Samuel Guinness,

---

[1] Lord Plunket was his brother-in-law, later archbishop of Dublin.

formerly a Member of Parliament for Kinsale and then for Barn-
staple. She was a strikingly handsome woman, highly intelligent,
as energetic as her husband, and, like him, forceful and determined
in character. Their life together until her death nearly forty years
later was one of unusual closeness, identity of outlook and harmony
of temperament. As a bachelor Edward Cecil had already been
known for his social gifts and for his pleasure in using them; his
marriage marked his entry into society on a grand scale; he and his
wife became renowned for the magnificence and sumptuousness of
their entertainment and the brilliance of their entourage. A year
after their marriage their first child, Rupert Edward Cecil Lee, was
born at 5 Berkeley Square.

Edward Cecil and his wife divided their time between Dublin
and London. In Dublin their home at 80 St Stephen's Green became
the most fashionable in the city. Their parties rivalled those of the
Lord Lieutenant himself. It seemed in the order of things that
they should attend the Viceregal court and play their part in the
Dublin season with its racy, but nevertheless imperial, pomp and
ceremony.

In 1874 he bought Farmleigh, a property adjoining the Phoenix
Park at Castleknock, County Dublin, and rebuilt the house. Most
of their Irish entertaining was done in St Stephen's Green, and
Farmleigh was occupied for only a small part of the year. When they
were there, however, Edward Cecil took exercise by walking across
the Phoenix Park to the brewery which he attended every day.
After Punchestown they went to London for the season. Then there
was Cowes, Dublin for the Horse Show, Scotland for the shooting,
and sometimes trips to the Continent were fitted in. They spent the
winter and spring in Ireland. Punchestown Races were then the
leading event in the Irish social calendar. Like the rest of Irish
society the Guinnesses usually had a house-party for the races.
Sometimes they travelled from Dublin on the Viceregal train as far as
Sallins. On other occasions Edward Cecil, who was an accomplished
horseman, would drive his own four-in-hand with relays of horses
all the way from St Stephen's Green to Punchestown.

But however gay his social life, the brewery at James's Gate was
Edward Cecil's abiding interest. Even when he was in London or
travelling in Europe, John Tertius Purser kept him in almost daily
contact with business affairs large and small. He carried with him

wherever he went small notebooks in which he recorded anything
from variations in the price of malt to summaries of household
expenditure. Nothing was too trivial to escape his attention, because
he recognized that in business the smallest matters may be important.
His preoccupation with detail may have been the key to his success
as a brewer. It was certainly consistent with his capacity for delegating the practical management of the brewery to his salaried staff.
He could best communicate his mode of thought and his criteria
of judgement by reference to small concrete matters rather than
generalized abstractions. Success made him neither pompous nor
pretentious; his eyes were never averted from the realities of his
business. In decisions great and small he saw the source from which
the brewery drew prosperity: its ability to sell good stout to great
numbers of customers who were not wealthy but extremely critical.
The order forms of a great diversity of publicans afforded him a
continuous survey of market-research long before modern techniques
were contemplated. The character revealed in his notebooks is that
of a man with a methodical, orderly mind, precise but not pedantic,
exact because it detested carelessness and negligence. He showed
some signs of obsession with detail and he was always worried about
his health. There are indications of an over-anxious and impatient
temperament which may have played its part in making him difficult
to work with.

For nearly eight years after his father's death Edward Cecil seemed
to find no difficulty in combining the active social life which he and
his wife so greatly enjoyed with close personal attention to the
brewery. His partnership with Sir Arthur, under Sir Benjamin Lee's
will, continued, but Sir Arthur showed a declining interest in the
active management of the business. Sir Arthur's wife, Lady Olivia
Charlotte White, the daughter of the third Earl of Bantry, was known
to lack sympathy with her husband's connexion with the brewing
trade. They were childless and Edward's children were heirs to the
brewery. Sir Arthur was in some respects an unsatisfactory partner
for Edward Cecil. A situation in which responsibility and profits were
shared, but most of the work done by one partner could not continue
indefinitely. The heavy penalties imposed under his father's will on
the son who withdrew his share would have involved heavy sacrifices
of prospective dividends in view of the increasing profits of the
brewery. Edward Cecil was, especially after the birth of his son

Sir Arthur and Edward Cecil Guinness

Rupert, anxious to devise a new agreement to replace the will. Sir Arthur, however, showed no desire to alter its terms or indeed even to discuss them though his brother pressed him. When Edward Cecil and his family were in France in the early summer of 1876 he had already made up his mind that changes were imminent in the control of James's Gate, but he had not yet decided on the form which they would take. He wrote to Sir Arthur from Tours on 20 May 1876 urging a revision of the partnership agreement and rejecting his brother's suggestion that the agreement which existed should be renewed as it was. 'I could not', he said, 'renew our deed of Partnership on the present basis, so rather than renew it as it stands I prefer having none.' He wrote to Fred Sutton their Dublin solicitor:[1]

25 May 1876

My dear Fred,

I have been obliged to stay away much longer than I anticipated when I saw you last but the weather has been so severe I found it harder to shake off a stubborn cold but now 'tis quite gone & I hope to be back in Dublin on the 12th June.

Our present deed of partnership expires on the 31st inst. and I feel it w'd not be right for me to renew it as it at present stands. When first it was made the trade was not half what it is at present & therefore the goodwill has now doubled, but the chief reason that influences me is that now I have one child to provide for & probably more coming. I wrote to Arthur asking him to appoint to meet you & me in London early next month to arrange new deed but I have received a note from him saying that he could not consider terms of a new partnership before he returns to Dublin at the end of July & wished me to renew the present one till the 1st Aug. This I am sorry I cannot do as life is very uncertain & if mine lapsed before then I consider I should [sacrifice too much] by signing away too much family property to the survivor besides there would be no chance of arranging terms at end of July as that is the time I hope to go to Scotland & on my return I sh'd probably find Arthur still at Ashford [his house in the west of Ireland]—so I am reluctantly obliged to try & provide by will (until I can get Arthur's time and attention to sign a new deed) as regards my (half) interest in James's Gate....

As Edward Cecil was not yet thirty, too much importance need not be attached to his reflexions on the uncertainties of life. It seems likely that his concern was less with thoughts of death than with the problems of life in partnership with Sir Arthur at James's Gate. The

---

[1] The surviving copy of this letter is a draft and contains alternative phrases.

words in parentheses at the end of his letter to his solicitor suggest a sense of ironical exasperation with his eldest brother which he apparently hesitated to express. His dissatisfaction with the working of the partnership was becoming so acute that he would probably have retired from the firm at that time if he could have done so on favourable terms. Meanwhile the deed of partnership expired at the end of June 1876, and in July Edward Cecil wrote to Sir Arthur of the undesirability of carrying on the business without any deed. He had changed his mind since May when he had written to Sir Arthur to say that he would prefer to have no deed of partnership, rather than renew the deed which had then existed without changing its terms in favour of a retiring partner. 'In case of the removal of either of us the exact position of the survivor as well as representatives of deceased would be placed in uncertainty as regards James's Gate.' He had had, he said, discussions with John Tertius Purser about the valuation of the property, plant, equipment and goodwill at James's Gate.

I have [he added] thought much over the valuation of plant and goodwill and think the following figures would be a very moderate and fair arrangement. I write to ask if you would approve of them, and if so I could get F. Sutton to embody them in a draft of a proposed deed of Partnership say for three years:

Goodwill ... £400,000
Plant ... £400,000

Capital to be called £500,000. Deceased Partner only to be entitled to half of goodwill and plant and half of profits of current year of decease and whatever may be amount of the capital subscribed by him.

So far the purpose of the new deed was to provide for the possible death of a partner; but the terms of the deed would also permit a partner to retire with compensation which at the prevailing profit would have amounted to nearly £480,000. There was no hint, however, from Edward Cecil of retirement and in the event it was Sir Arthur who decided to withdraw.

Edward Cecil in becoming sole proprietor was assuming leadership in industry as well as in society. By default, his brother had conceded his own part in the effective direction of the brewery. Arthur had succumbed to his wife's prejudice against trade. Edward Cecil seemed determined to show that industrial achievement, if sufficiently spectacular, could lead to the highest honours of the realm. He was opening a phase in his career in which social distinction was to become a reflexion of business success rather than an achievement in spite of it. Arthur successfully conformed to the prevailing convention that disinterested philanthropy received more than its own reward. Edward Cecil defied this convention. He became one of the first manufacturers to earn royal recognition for making great wealth which also enhanced the prosperity of the community and raised the standards of an industrial society.

Sir Arthur's decision may have been influenced by the advantageous terms open to a retiring partner under the new deed. It is tempting to think that as he had a diminishing interest in the management of the brewery, the terms of the new deed confirmed him in a course of action to which he had already been predisposed. But this interpretation is hardly consistent with his somewhat uncooperative attitude to Edward Cecil's proposals for drafting a new deed in more lenient terms. It is more likely that Edward Cecil had no intention of retiring himself and that he sought to liberalize the terms of the earlier deed of partnership so as to offer Sir Arthur an inducement for withdrawing from the brewery to more congenial pursuits. Edward Cecil's attachment to the brewery seemed to grow as his brother's active participation waned. His position in the brewery had been strengthened by Arthur's increasing remoteness from it. Edward Cecil's attitude to the direction of the business became more determined and possessive, and this probably intensified his brother's aversion from trade in general. In the control of the brewery Arthur was not yet an outsider in fact, but his behaviour suggested that he was beginning to feel treated as one; and his resentment was not likely to be reduced by the knowledge that he had been the instrument of his own exclusion. The new agreement was signed on 10 August 1876, but it soon ceased to be effective, for just two months later, 12 October 1876, the brothers dissolved their partnership on terms even more favourable to Sir Arthur than those prescribed under the revised agreement of August. He received £600,000 for his share of the business and in addition took his share—£80,000—of the profits of the brewery for 1876. The sum of £680,000 was to be paid over four years in six instalments, the first to fall due on 1 January 1877. The dissolution of the partnership was publicly announced in the *Dublin Gazette* in these terms:

Three Guinnesses

Dissolution of Partnership

THE Partnership between Sir Arthur Edward Guinness Bart., M.P. and Edward Cecil Guinness Esquire, who carried on business as Brewers, at St James's Gate, Dublin, under the style and firm of 'Arthur Guinness, Son & Co.' is this day dissolved by mutual consent. The said Edward Cecil Guinness will continue to carry on the business as heretofore, under the name style and firm of 'Arthur Guinness Son & Co.' Dated this 11th day of December 1876.

ARTHUR E. GUINNESS
EDWARD CECIL GUINNESS

Witness present when signed by Sir A. E. Guinness Bart., and E. C. Guinness Esq.—Fred Sutton, Solicitor, Harcourt Street.

The retiring partner took much more than he would have been able to take eight years earlier under the terms of Sir Benjamin Lee's will—indeed a pound for every shilling. Nevertheless the main object of the will had been achieved. The brewery had been kept intact and under the control of a single proprietor. Edward Cecil, who had served his apprenticeship at James's Gate from the age of fifteen, was sole owner at the age of twenty-nine. It was true that Sir Arthur took over twenty times more out of the brewery than his father had intended that a retiring partner should draw; but sales and profits had grown enormously since 1868, and a good share of these profits had been ploughed back into the brewery to finance the works of extension and expansion which had been going on all the time. Indeed, the sum of £600,000 was a considerable under-estimate of the share of the earning potential of the brewery if the money had been left in it.

The huge profits made by the business are a sign of the dominance of the firm and of its almost invulnerable position in the competitive struggle. During the partnership of Sir Arthur and Edward Cecil, from their father's death in 1868 to the dissolution of their partnership in 1876, the brewery made profits amounting to at least £1,500,000. The Guinness brothers drew over £915,000 between them, £385,000 going to Edward Cecil and £530,000 to Sir Arthur. This was a very great deal of money—during the eight years of the partnership the two brothers drew over 60 per cent of the profits from the brewery, the balance being used to finance development and increase the capital value of the business. In every generation the Guinnesses made a practice of sinking profits in the brewery to

Sir Arthur and Edward Cecil Guinness

expand it, and the policy was to receive most spectacular vindication in 1886 when the firm was sold to the public for £6,000,000 or five times the valuation that had been accepted ten years earlier at the dissolution of the partnership, and even that figure was a serious underestimate, judging from the market value of the shares immediately after their public issue. But there was no thought of selling the brewery to the public when Edward Cecil became sole owner in 1876.

Sir Arthur was bought out on generous terms which, together with what he had received under his father's will and in profits since 1868, left him a rich man. His retirement from James's Gate left him free for his real interests—public life and philanthropy. After 1876 he was able to give money away instead of going on acquiring it and he gave it with the prudence and good sense that the successful Guinnesses always showed. When he advocated or supported a good cause he did so with dignity, integrity and independence of judgement. He gave the impression of giving money away not to please others but to please himself. In his choice of objects for his munificence he showed imagination and an unconventional sense of discrimination.

As a Member of Parliament he spoke occasionally in debates on the brewing trade and the licensing laws, but as a rule his interests were varied and wide. He quickly made friends with the great at Westminster, though the terms of the following letter from Disraeli may indicate more the Prime Minister's oriental extravagance of courtesy than any deep affection for Sir Arthur—in fact, it is just an ordinary three-line whip.

> *2 Whitehall Gardens,*
> *S.W.*
> *5 April 1876*

Private
Sir Arthur Guinness

Dear Sir Arthur

I am always sorry to press my friends but I hope they will admit that, during this severe session, I have never summoned them without a cause and I have always summoned them to victory.

The persevering faction of the Opposition insists on another struggle, virtually on a point which has already been decided and Monday the 10th instant is fixed for the occasion.

Three Guinnesses

I should esteem it a personal favour if you could be present and I will endeavour if possible, by some arrangement to lengthen our holidays so that the House need not re-assemble till the 27th April: Thursday.

Believe me,
dear Sir Arthur,
Sincerely yours,
B. DISRAELI

When nationalist feeling in Ireland was intense and agrarian strife and controversy widespread, Sir Arthur seemed determined to show that a confirmed Unionist in politics could give disinterested and practical service to his country. Even the extreme Irish nationalists respected him for his refusal to seek the popularity which he might have bought so easily by abridging or concealing his principles. He flaunted his Unionism, but much of his benevolence was exercised unobtrusively. Indeed, his Unionist political faith was so firm that it became almost quixotic. He once refused the lieutenancy of the County of Dublin because the offer had been made by a Conservative Lord Lieutenant, Lord Cadogan, at a time when Irish loyalists felt betrayed by Lord Salisbury's administration.

Sir Arthur completed the work which his father began in reconstructing Archbishop Marsh's Library near St Patrick's Cathedral in Dublin. He rebuilt the Coombe Lying-in Hospital, became chairman of the first Dublin organization to concern itself with the housing of artisans, and served for sixteen years as President of the Royal Dublin Society, helping to finance the publication of a history of the Society.

In 1880 he was raised to the peerage as Baron Ardilaun of Ashford, County Galway, where he had inherited a very large estate. He undertook big schemes of afforestation and his efforts brought some prosperity to one of the poorest and most beautiful parts of Connemara. He gave a great deal of work to his tenants and to others and set standards as an enlightened landlord which only a few of his class in Ireland had the means or disposition to emulate. He was among the first to give an imaginative impetus to the tourist industry in Connemara by the simple expedient of maintaining a steamer service on Lough Corrib between Ashford Castle, Cong, and Galway City. He bought the Muckross Estate on the Lakes of Killarney in County Kerry to save it from a 'commercial syndicate', and he presented to the citizens of Dublin the lovely twenty-two acre park, St Stephen's

Green, which was overlooked by his brother's town house where as young children both brothers had lived. The citizens of Dublin put up a statue to him there.

Meanwhile Edward Cecil continued his father's policy of development and expansion. The next ten years were to be the most difficult and arduous of his life. He immersed himself in the affairs of James's Gate and at the same time took an enthusiastic part in public affairs and in society.

The tale of his life will be told in the second book on the history of Guinness's brewery—though to the visitor to St James's Gate it may well be said of Edward Cecil—the first Lord Iveagh as he became— '*Si monumentum requiris circumspice*'.

⌈11⌋

Guinness's Irish Agencies

One must speak for life and growth, amid all this mass of destruction and disintegration. (*D. H. Lawrence to Harriet Monroe in 1915. 'Letters of D. H. Lawrence', ed. by Aldous Huxley (London, 1932), p. 256.*)

INTRODUCTION

MOST IRISH breweries in the maritime economy continued to grow after the Great Famine. Most breweries were, in fact, situated in the maritime economy. Because of the excise enforcement and the spread of the monetary economy, porter was superseding whiskey as a popular drink in parts of the country where it had rarely been drunk before, and it began to compete with illicitly distilled spirits in all but the most remote areas. In 1858 the duty on whiskey was raised to a rate which trebled the tax of a few years earlier. The consumption of porter was further stimulated. The excise men made whiskey distilling difficult, while money was available in rural Ireland for the first time to spend on beer.

The fall in population after the Great Famine produced a contraction in the market for some Irish breweries; usually the fall in population was more than offset by the rising incomes of those who remained, but in some areas where emigration had most seriously disturbed the pattern of production and distribution there was an absolute decline in the market. In general, however, as incomes rose, tastes switched from whiskey, which was still commonly drunk, to beer. The consumption of beer per head of the population was low, and as the sparse population was scattered the costs of distribution were onerous on an industry in which delivery costs were high. Even with the advent of the railways transport of such a bulky commodity as beer was much more expensive over land than sea. Brewery agents had to travel considerable distances and the supply of small quantities of beer to remote areas was unprofitable. The beer was often spoilt by these journeys, and even when the problems of transit could be solved satisfactorily brewers were compelled to tie up an inordinate amount of capital in expensive casks. When the market was

Introduction

concentrated, as in Dublin or Cork, casks could be returned quickly and easily; but the delays occasioned by serving distant rural markets where demand was slight were very costly. This handicap was greater for the small breweries, which were least able to afford it. In Great Britain towards the end of the century for the average wholesale brewer there were only about sixty-five publicans; in Ireland, however, there were on average nearly five hundred public houses (each selling much less beer) for each brewery. Many Irish brewers, therefore, were at the disadvantage of having to supply a great number of distant public houses at which the consumption of beer was comparatively low.

The pattern of production in Ireland was little different from that in the rest of the British Isles. There the big breweries were concentrated in the centres of population, and the cheapness of their products, resulting from the economies of scale, drove out the smaller firms. As the century advanced, Guinness in Dublin and Beamish & Crawford in Cork were increasingly dominating the industry, and their British trade was assuming a growing importance. The advantages of relatively cheap coastal transport relieved them of many of the difficulties which the problems of land transport imposed on rural breweries which served local and inland markets.

In the latter part of the nineteenth century many long-established Dublin breweries were either closing or becoming absorbed by other firms. Soon Guinness and Sweetman would be the only Dublin brewers of note who could claim direct and continuous succession from eighteenth-century founders.

GUINNESS'S SALES

The years just after the Great Famine marked a rise in Guinness's sales in Ireland outside Dublin, and in five years between 1855 and 1860, while the sales of Double Stout in Dublin almost doubled (from 6000 hogsheads to 11,000) and of Single Stout more than doubled (from 8000 hogsheads to 18,000), the sales of Double Stout in the rest of Ireland rose from 10,000 hogsheads to 21,000, and of Single Stout from 7000 hogsheads to 21,000. The sales to England rose from 40,000 hogsheads of Double Stout to 56,000, that is to say by two-fifths. In 1855, therefore, about four-sevenths of Guinness's sales by volume (and more by value) were in England, but by 1860 this proportion had fallen to less than half—56,000 hogsheads as against 67,000—mainly because of a rapid rise in the sales of both kinds of stout in Ireland outside Dublin.

This trend in sales continued between 1860 and 1865. By that year 94,000 hogsheads were sold in England as against 112,000 hogsheads in Ireland (of which 62,000 were Single Stout). Of the Irish sales 63,000 hogsheads were sold in the country (half of it Double Stout) and 49,000 in Dublin. In ten years, the sales of Double Stout in England had risen by nearly two-and-a-half times, in Dublin by nearly three times, and in the rest of Ireland by over three times. The sales of Single Stout had gone up by nearly three times in Dublin, and four times in the rest of Ireland. Clearly, the main factor in the expansion of the brewery was no longer the English market but the Irish market, and the most dynamically growing part of this was the Irish rural market.

By 1870 this was confirmed abundantly. The English sales of Double Stout rose from 94,000 to 120,000 hogsheads, that is by just over one-quarter. The sales of Double Stout in Dublin fell from 17,000 hogsheads to 15,000. In the country they rose by nearly a third, from 33,000 to 41,000 hogsheads. Sales of Single Stout rose in Dublin by less than a fifth, from 32,000 hogsheads to 38,000, and in the country by two-fifths, from 30,000 hogsheads to 42,000. Measured by volume, the English trade was still less than one-half of the total.

In the next quinquennium the English proportion dropped further to just over two-fifths by volume. The sales of Double Stout in England rose between 1870 and 1875 by one-half, from 120,000 hogsheads to 178,000, but the expansion of the Irish sales was even more spectacular. The sales of Double Stout in Dublin rose by three-fifths, from 15,000 hogsheads to 24,000, and the sales in the rest of Ireland doubled, from 41,000 hogsheads to 79,000. The sales of Single Stout doubled as well—from 42,000 hogsheads in the country to 82,000, and from 38,000 in Dublin to 76,000.

A number of general points may be made about this expansion of Irish and English sales. Production rose from 78,000 hogsheads in 1855 to 565,000 in 1879, an expansion of over seven times in twenty-four years. In absolute terms the English market expansion was considerable, but its rate of increase was relatively lower than the increase in sales in Ireland. It is significant that this is not generally

Guinness's Sales

true of other Irish breweries. For other Dublin firms, in fact, the export trade rose faster than their home trade. The exports of Guinness's beers from Dublin rose from 42,000 hogsheads in 1855 to 107,000 in 1868, while the total exports of Dublin beer rose from just under 90,000 hogsheads in 1855 to 255,000 in 1868. Thus at that time all breweries shared in the expansion of the export trade to England, and the other breweries (taken together) expanded their trade as fast as Guinness. Some of them, indeed, progressed faster, notably Jameson, D'Arcy and Findlater, while others, like Sweetman and Manders, were less successful. All in all, however, Guinness did not expand their share of total Irish trade to England.

In Ireland the position was different. The most important development was undoubtedly the growth of Guinness's Irish country trade from 17,000 hogsheads in 1855 (or about 21 per cent of the total sales of Guinness) to 230,000 hogsheads in 1880 (or about 40 per cent of the total trade). While the greater part of this total was porter, 102,000 hogsheads of it was Double Stout, the more expensive of the two beers. By 1864 over half the beer sold in Ireland outside Dublin was Guinness's, and they maintained this superiority throughout the remainder of the century. The crucial time for the conquest of the market appears to be 1860 or a little later.

The reason for this expansion is mainly the upsurge of prosperity in rural Ireland that followed the Great Famine. It is a remarkable feature of Irish economic history. It does not appear that Guinness took trade away from other brewers. There are, indeed, grounds for believing that there was a growth of the sales of other breweries in the country market, although not on anything like the same scale. They suffered a relative and not an absolute decline. A number of small and obsolescent breweries collapsed or were sold out, but the surviving breweries grew in size—though at a lesser rate than Guinness.

Guinness took advantage of the growing market by every means at their disposal. New agencies were opened at a large number of Irish country towns. They were concerned early with canal traffic, and they were pioneers in the development of railways in Ireland. By 1867 the firm owned £86,000 of Irish railway stock. Admittedly these were held largely for purposes of liquidity, but it is significant that the business should have been so deeply involved with Irish railway companies and not with railways in Great Britain, which at

Guinness's Irish Agencies

first sight would seem to have been far more secure and liquid investments. The reasons are clear. The full casks going from Dublin and the returned empty casks played a role in the Irish rural railway economy similar to that of coal in England.

THE EARLY PERIOD

The establishment of Guinness's Irish agencies and the manner in which they grew is a story in itself. There lie in it the reasons for the capture of the Irish market outside Dublin. The detail is insufficient to allow more than a fleeting glimpse of the tactics, but the strategy can be reconstructed from the material available.

Before 1815 sales outside Dublin were small and confined to the neighbourhood of the canals, as at Athy, or in seaports like Belfast and Derry. Sea transport and the canals, especially the latter, were the essential links of the brewery with its markets outside Dublin. The successful agents were to be found at the trading centres which had the biggest trade with Dublin. They were themselves general merchants and sometimes agents for other brewers.

By the early eighteen-thirties the trade outside Dublin was still small. About 800 barrels were sold by Samuel Boyle in Belfast in 1833 and about 250 barrels by eleven customers in Cork in 1835. In 1838 Berry, the canal agents, were operating agencies at Ballinasloe and Shannon Harbour. There is no clear record of the quantities sold, but the canal records show that stout was sent regularly to all the important canal harbours, and that malt came into Dublin from Athy and Mountmellick and was discharged at Canal Harbour. At this time, and well into the following decade, the brewery's trade was almost exclusively in Dublin and Great Britain, but by 1842 there are signs of readjustments in prices and in the terms of the agencies which suggest an increase in the trade, or at least that a greater interest was being taken in it by the firm. The standard adopted in the new agreements was the trade in 1841 and the trade in that year at Ballinasloe appears to have been about 600 barrels. A store was also opened at Galway at the brewery's expense, as part of the Ballinasloe arrangements.[1] The trade at Shannon Harbour was almost the same in 1841 as that at Ballinasloe.

[1] This was a part of the Ballinasloe arrangements, and not a store in the modern sense of the word.

The Early Period

In the later eighteen-forties agencies were opened at Newry and Newbridge. The customers in these towns were by no means given the same treatment as the other agents. It appears that each customer had a special agreement separately negotiated, but the rules of the Dublin brewers affected the terms of agreement in the Dublin 'Vicinity' in which Newbridge fell. The coming of the railway in 1848 made it easier of approach as the following note from the Guinness Brewery Annals makes clear: 'Dublin Brewers have always been in the habit of delivering Porter there. We agree to allow a rebate to Mr George Johnston, a customer, of 9*d*. per barrel on all Porter drawn by rail, as it is more expeditious and convenient. (1 May 1848).'

In 1848 Samuel Boyle's agency at Belfast was discontinued for unknown reasons, and the trade was thrown open to all customers. Possibly 1848 was a year of intense competition because in May 1849 Berry of Ballinasloe were allowed '6*d*. per kilderkin on all Porter sent by them to the town of Tuam, to meet the reduced price at which other Brewers sell in that town'. In 1849 Edward Byrne and Martin Mangan, both of Carlow, were allowed 6*d*. per kilderkin on all porter drawn by them, as a commission.

This is significant for several reasons. First, it represents a much easier extension of credit than the brewery had been in the habit of advancing to its best customers, and secondly it occurs at the beginning of the great growth of trade in Ireland outside Dublin. Taken in conjunction with the preceding note about Newbridge it is possible to conjecture that the brewery was able to offer better terms to its customers where it was not bound by the price agreements that held it in check in Dublin. Certainly in 1850, for example, the brewery was doing things in Shannon Harbour that it could never have done in Dublin: 'We have agreed on a conversation with Mr Hannin, Messrs Berry & Co.'s Clerk, to reduce the Selling price of our Single Stout Porter in Kilds. 3 pence a cask.'

Shannon Harbour lies two locks above the junction of the Grand Canal with the Shannon, near Banagher. A straight reach of water extends under a wide estuary sky as far as the eye can see, then suddenly the road turns over a single-arched stone bridge, dated 1804, beneath a noble and unkempt elm tree to reveal a scene poignant in its dereliction and evocative of past grandeur. Two dry-docks lie idle beside an abandoned warehouse. A wide Georgian building in dark grey stone stands empty and gutted, its stone steps running up to a door within which well-proportioned rooms are open to the sky. This was the hotel. Two smaller four-story houses, lifted from Bath or Merrion Square, stand neglected just behind. Greensward runs to the quiet canal edge where barges formerly unloaded cargoes for Limerick and the surrounding countryside. It was at this spot that much of Guinness's money was made.

Fortunately it is possible to reconstruct the trade at Ballinasloe in 1851 from what is evidently a fairly exact copy of a contemporary memorandum drawn up by Benjamin Lee Guinness and John Tertius Purser. The agent at Ballinasloe was still Thomas Berry, and his clerks—Rourke at Athlone and Hannin at Shannon Harbour—had taken over his sub-agencies. Broadly, a hogshead of Double Stout was usually invoiced at £3. 3s. 10d.; of this, £2. 18s. was the brewery price netted by Guinness's, 2s. was Berry's commission, 4d. was allowed for 'filling' (topping up the casks) and 3s. 6d. for freight. If the proceeds were remitted by the 8th of the month following, there was a 1 per cent discount. The rent of the stores was paid, and allowances were made for the Christmas 'douceurs' to publicans, and for travelling expenses.

Berry's trade was taken over by the Grand Canal Company itself in 1850, because an Act of Parliament in that year allowed the company to act as agent, in order to meet competition from the railways. The beginning of railway competition was worrying the Canal Company, and in consequence they were entering business in a more aggressive way, as the following letter from Guinness's to the Grand Canal Company shows:[1]

James's Gate Brewery
27 December 1850

The Directors of the Grand Canal Co.

Gentlemen,

We would respectfully take leave to ask, as you, we learn, have purchased the interest of our friends and Agents the Messrs Berry on your hire, how our business is in future to be conducted? As the most considerable Shippers by their Boats we should wish to know who are the parties to whom we are in future to be connected with? Who are to be responsible to us for our consignments, as they were not alone our Carriers but our valued Agents?

Allow us to say that the present proprietor of their concern, his father,

---

[1] Grand Canal Company: Court of Directors Minutes, vol. 89.

The Early Period

and other Members of his family, have been closely connected with us in the way of business, between 30 and 40 years, and having been conducted by them with ability and success, we hope that we may still have the connexion carried on, and we trust Your arrangements may be made to correspond with our wish and interest. We are quite satisfied that what is right you will do, but felt it due to Messrs Berry to express our hope that we may still have the advantage of their excellent services.

A. Guinness, Son & Co.

The following reply was sent to Guinness's:

Grand Canal House
1 January 1851

Messrs Arthur Guinness & Co.

Gentlemen,

...I am in reply desired to acquaint you that the Company have been compelled by circumstances to undertake the General Carrying Trade of the Canal, and that they will, in their position as Carriers, be responsible for the safe transmission of all Goods forwarded through the Company's Carrying Establishment.

The Directors are now engaged with the appointment of Agents for conducting the Carrying trade on every part of the Navigation, and at the several Stations on the Shannon from Limerick to Athlone, both inclusive. It is their determination to use every possible care in making these appointments, and they trust that the result will be the completion of their Carrying Establishment on a footing calculated to ensure the utmost regularity and safety, and to prove in all respects satisfactory to the Public....

John McMullen

About the middle of 1851 a conference was held between the Chairmen of the Grand Canal Company, the Great Southern & Western and the Midland Great Western Railways. Its object was to consider the practicability of some arrangement being come to between the Grand Canal Company and railways conjointly with the City of Dublin Steam Packet Company for the establishment of reciprocal rates for the carriage of goods and produce on the canal and on the railways, all parties to be upon an equal footing in respect of the cross-Channel trade. It was agreed that there should be a differential rate in favour of the Grand Canal Company, and it was proposed that a rate of 5 per cent should be allowed. This that Company thought too low. A further meeting was held on 2 August 1851 and an agreement submitted to the bodies concerned. Briefly, this provided that the Grand Canal Company could charge 10 per cent less than the other companies on all rates of freight and passage money which would include the receipt and delivery of goods and merchandise in Dublin, and giving to the Grand Canal Company and the City of Dublin Steam Packet Company a monopoly of certain portions of the Shannon. Both the Grand Canal Company and the railways were to use their influence to procure loading for the cross-Channel steamers of the City of Dublin Steam Packet Company and to 'hand over all goods and merchandise not otherwise consigned'. These arrangements were embodied in a draft Agreement which classified goods and fixed rates. It was duly approved by the Grand Canal Company at their Board Meeting on 3 September 1851.

The terms of the Belfast trade appear in a memorandum written in 1849. From this memorandum it is possible to see that the 1841 trade was still regarded as the datum for calculating the agent's profits: the great expansion had not yet begun. There also appears a growth in the confidence in which the firm held its Irish business contacts, and a much more businesslike approach to the question of pushing sales than had been seen before.

Five per cent was to be allowed for new trade, exclusive of bad debts. Atkinson, responsible for sales in Belfast, was to be paid £20 a year for commercial information, he was to give a bond of £500 as security, he was not to be called 'Agent' but 'Traveller' or 'Correspondent'. His main function, in other words, was to gain business for the brewery, and the brewery would be responsible for arranging to deliver the beer.

This memorandum shows that the deposit of a security was by that time common practice, and that Atkinson's job was to extend trade, not to usurp existing arrangements. Further, the standard terms of 5 per cent were those agreed by the Dublin brewers for the country trade.

These views of the nature of trade in the rest of Ireland were confirmed by a note of Benjamin Lee Guinness in 1853, about the trade practices on empty casks:

The house have repeated complaints from Atkinson of Belfast, and from others also, that other Dublin Brewers paid the freight on empty casks from their customers. After some conversation with several of the trade a document was this day signed, by Mr D'Arcy, Mr Sweetman and ourselves, and sent round to the other houses—that the Brewers are at liberty to charge or not as they think fit, freight on Empty Casks returned from customers in Ireland, or from England.

The Early Period

There was evidently a determined effort to stop price-cutting at the retail level because there exists a copy of a document signed by Guinness's agents in 1858 which expresses in strong terms the brewers' agreements of that time:

Copy of Agreement with Agents in Ireland, not to sell under Brewery price

The undersigned being Agents for the sale of Messrs Arthur Guinness Son & Co's Porter in Ireland are fully aware that they shall not, under any circumstances whatever make sale of Porter at a price under that regulated by the Brewers of Dublin on 27th June 1856, as follows.

Double Stout		Single Stout	
pr. Hhd.	59/–	Hhd.	41/3
Brl.	37/–	Brl.	26/1
Kild.	19/–	Kild.	13/2

And that to the above prices they should add the freight or carriage to place of Sale.

In cases where Discount for prompt cash may be allowed it is not in any instance to exceed *one and a quarter per cent.*

To the above regulation we undertake to continue strictly to adhere.

By 1859 there were Dublin brewers' rules covering the whole of Ireland. As can be seen, the rules were laxly interpreted. They did not apply to agents, and Guinness had been successful in appointing extremely good agents. The following copy of a brewer's agreement of 1859 must be read in conjunction with the document just cited: an interpretation of the two documents may be offered, that Guinness's active agents were attempting to undercut the other brewers, otherwise there would be no point in their giving an undertaking of this sort to the firm. The documents make it clear that there was close regulation of retail prices but not such a close control of agents' commission:

Allowance of Excess in Trade—
to customers in Ireland, *not to apply to Agents.*

A misunderstanding of the rule regulating the allowance of 6*d.* a Hhd. to parties taking 100 Hhds. and upwards in the year having arisen, the undersigned to prevent any misunderstanding for the future, agree that the interpretation of the rule from the 1st January 1859 be

1. That each party taking 100 Hhds. and upwards shall be allowed 6 pence on the quantity taken.
2. If the quantity taken shall amount to 200 Hhds. and upwards, then the allowance of 6*d. only* shall be made on the first 100 Hhds., and an allowance of 1/– on all in excess of the first 100 Hhds.

Guinness's Irish Agencies

Nothing whatever to be allowed to parties unless their business reach 100 Hhds., and this allowance to apply to all customers in Ireland—

Feb. 25, 1859—

Signed: Guinness, Sweetman, Brenan, Rice
D'Arcy, Watkins, & Co.,
Manders, Jameson Pim,

To apply to both
D.S. and S.S.

On the other hand, this rule was soon broken; within three years Benjamin Lee Guinness felt strong enough to make a ruling without first consulting his rivals:

The subject of Discount for Cash having been brought under our notice by several of our Customers, and the question having been duly considered, Mr Guinness has decided that there is no trade rule to prevent the discount of $1\frac{1}{4}\%$ being made to small customers as well as to those whose transactions exceed £100 per annum, and it is quite discretionary to allow it to any customer in the country ledger. In Atkinson's and our other Agents districts we may be particular as we have the Commission to bear, which is not the case in the ordinary accounts.

The attempt to extend the area of the 'Vicinity'—that is of the area around Dublin, ten miles from the General Post Office, in which delivery was free—to the Curragh where there was an extensive military trade, is shown by the following note of 1855:

The price at which Messrs D'Arcy supply their customers residing at this side of Kildare [the Curragh and Newbridge] is:

S.S.	Hhd.	31/2 Brl.	15/7 Kild.
D.S.	„ 68/-	43/6 „	22/6 „

and We agree not to undersell these prices.

This shows that all the time the Guinness pressure was to reduce prices and that their membership of the price-ring was, in some respects, a disadvantage to them.

THE AGENTS—
ROURKE, KENNEDY, BARRETT AND ATKINSON

In the early eighteen-fifties the connexion with Berry's appears to have been formally broken and two of Guinness's most important agents were appointed. These were Patrick Rourke (Berry's former clerk) at Athlone and Ballinasloe, and F. W. Kennedy at Limerick.

Rourke, Kennedy, Barrett and Atkinson

These appointments were crucial and were followed by a great increase in Guinness's country trade.

Ballinasloe is not an exciting town. A church with a Pugin spire dominates it, but in former years the quietude was broken annually by the noise of the biggest horse-fair in Ireland. There stout was sold in great quantities, and the canal terminus, where the faded words 'Grand Canal Company' may be seen outside Guinness's Store, was a scene of great activity. In the days of Patrick Rourke this was a most important site of Guinness trade.

Rourke and Kennedy were allowed 5 per cent on all sales, and the rent of their stores and their travelling expenses were allowed. Kennedy gave a £500 bond to the brewery as security. These rates of payment were reasonably generous; the relationship was turning into a more exclusive one between the signatories in the agreements on the part of the brewery to pay the rent and to pay cartage.

These two men, Rourke, on the whole an unsuccessful business man though a good salesman (he died over £5000 in debt to the brewery), and Kennedy, who was both a good business man and a good salesman (he died worth over £6000), were instrumental in extending the sales of Guinness in the west of Ireland. Together with Atkinson in Belfast and Barrett in Cork they were the four great Irish salesmen, on a par with Samuel Waring and Sparkes Moline in England.

The Cork agency was developed mainly after 1859. The first agent, Wigin, held the appointment from November 1858 to March 1859 but then resigned because Bass, his other proprietors, objected to the Guinness connexion. James Barrett was then appointed on fairly standard terms. By this time, in contrast to ten years earlier, the agent took over existing customers and the security was very much greater. His agreement was the same as Rourke's and Kennedy's, with a quantity discount as well, a cash discount of 1¼ per cent, and a £3000 bond of security.

The size of the deposit is an indication that the Cork trade of the brewery was already substantial, and a possible sign of the weakness of some of the formerly strong Cork porter brewers is given by the strength of Wigin's connexion with Bass, which must have been stronger than his prospects of profit from Guinness. There is other evidence for this decline of the Cork brewers in the laments in the press of the time.

The end of the eighteen-fifties and the early eighteen-sixties was, therefore, a critical time for the conquest of the Irish market. There were new agencies at Parsonstown, where 1500 barrels were sold in 1859, and at Carrick-on-Shannon and Roscommon: in Waterford and in Longford the agencies were reorganized. The Dublin brewers' maximum-price agreements about selling beer outside Dublin evidently came to an end. Cork, centre of a number of strong brewers, was an important market. Evidently the Irish provincial brewers were negligible competitors and the agreements with those in Dublin were rejected. Advantageous trade terms played their part in extending Guinness's trade and certainly aggressive salesmanship by the agents was a vital factor. How far the product was better than its rivals is uncertain. What is clear, however, is that the coming of the railways and the rise of rural incomes led to the growth of the market which Guinness conquered.

Before his death in 1861 Patrick Rourke had played a conspicuous role as a salesman. After his death his sub-agents took over in Athlone, Ballinasloe, Carrick-on-Shannon and Roscommon, showing what a wide area he had developed, how rapidly the trade had grown (for his sub-agents all became full agents), and how wisely he chose his men. Like Samuel Waring he was foolish in his personal finances and his debt to the brewery was never paid off; on the other hand, the profits made by the brewery from his work were enormous.

By 1864 the conquest of some parts of the Irish market appears to have been so secure that the agency system could be changed. After Rourke's death, and the loss of £5797 by the brewery because of it, his sub-agencies became agencies, with his son left at Ballinasloe to run the agency in County Galway, centred on Ballinasloe and Galway. John P. Rourke, the son, died in March 1864 with only about £140 of the debt paid off, and his uncle, Thomas Hogan, his assistant at Ballinasloe, was made manager of the store, then taken over in its entirety by Guinness's, and Thomas Hogan's son John became manager of the Galway Store. From this it may be deduced that initially the concept of brewery stores, as depots run by the brewery, as opposed to agencies, was not necessarily due to any advantages of a brewery store over an agency as such, but to Patrick Rourke's having died in debt to the brewery, and to John Rourke's having died before the debt could be paid off. This accidental change, however, became established practice.[1]

---

[1] See below, p. 212.

Rourke, Kennedy, Barrett and Atkinson

By 1863 the English trade was £213,000, of which £61,000 was with direct customers, £64,000 with London, £49,000 with Bristol, £22,000 with Liverpool and £18,000 with Manchester. In Dublin the brewery sold £100,000 worth of beer, with £39,000 worth in the 'Vicinity' (the bulk of this trade was in south Dublin), while in the Irish 'country' £202,000 of trade was done. Thus, by 1863 nearly two-thirds of the brewery's trade was in Ireland, and well over one-third was outside the Dublin area.

Of the country trade in Ireland, which was more than one-third of the brewery's total trade in money terms (and more by volume), £81,000 was done by the agents in 1863 and £120,000 by ordinary customers. Thus, already by that date the agents had fulfilled their primary function of creating a market, and their trade was increasingly taken over by other local people, while the agents became the local storehouses for Guinness's stout and porter.

Some idea is given of the relative importance of the various agencies in the year 1868 by the following figures: London and its 'outports' had a trade of over £80,000, Bristol had a trade of almost £60,000 a year, followed by Liverpool and Manchester with £31,000 and £26,000 respectively. In Ireland, Limerick, Cork, Belfast and Ballinasloe had a trade of about £20,000 a year each, followed by six agencies with trades of £4000 or less. It will be seen that not one of the Irish places is as important as the smallest English agency.[1] It will also be clear that the railway centres of Ireland were becoming important. In 1867 Sir Benjamin Lee made an agreement with the Midland Great Western Railway to transport porter to Galway, and this appears to have been but one of several such agreements. Certainly by 1867 towns in the 'Vicinity' were being supplied regularly by rail.

By 1872 the brewery's total trade reached £1 m. Of this £0·45 m. was in England, £0·25 m. was in Dublin and the remainder in the rest of Ireland. Over two-thirds of this was through the agents. Partly the remarkable increase over 1863 was due to the replacement of some customers by agencies, but it is indicative of the powerful drive that still remained behind them.

The conquest of the rural Irish market coincided with a change in

[1] The actual figures were: Limerick, £22,223; Cork, £20,319; Belfast, £20,297; Ballinasloe, £18,578; Shannon Harbour, £4427; Galway, £4291; Carrick-on-Shannon, £3228; Athlone, £3060; Roscommon, £1987; Portumna, £1817; Bristol, £59,933; London, £59,682; The 'Outports', £22,649; Liverpool, £31,589; Manchester, £26,447.

the nature of Guinness's wholesaling arrangements. Instead of appointing new agents when their old agents died, they were often replaced by stores administered directly by the brewery. This is surprising when it is recalled how amazingly successful the agents like Rourke had been in promoting the brewery's trade. Indeed, the change cannot have been made primarily because the agents were failing in their job, or because Guinness wanted a forceful selling policy from its own store managers. As has been seen, initially the change was due to John Rourke's early death,[1] but within a few years so great were the sales of Guinness's beer in the Irish hinterland that almost every wholesaler and retailer had become a Guinness salesman. Consequently, the relationship became a more mechanical one, less dependent on the personal efforts of the salesmen to push Guinness's beers. In 1863 the agents sold only two-fifths of the Irish trade outside Dublin, and the remaining three-fifths were sold to wholesalers and publicans directly from the brewery. There was, therefore, a need for stores away from the brewery to deal with this huge provincial traffic. The agents became, in fact, holders of stocks. By 1872, when trade was 50 per cent greater than nine years before, the agents and stores had two-thirds of the stout delivered to them.

The refounding of the Shannon Harbour agency on 1 January 1875 allows a glimpse of the standard treatment of the agents now that the conditions of trade had settled down. They reveal a careful relationship based on sales on commission analogous to those paid for malting barley, and they no longer had an extra commission paid for increasing sales. The documents also show the extent of Shannon Harbour's decline. The store rent was very low, the security given in deposit was only £1000, and in 1876 it was reduced to £500, and the towns to be supplied were only 'Shannon Harbour, Banagher, Ferbane, Cloughran, & Frankfort, with liberty to sell in Portumna and Eyrecourt'. Mr Hannin's fine house is no longer occupied and the birds nest where the stout was discharged.

At the same time for the year 1874 there is a list of the Irish agencies in terms of their annual turnover. From this it is clear that Limerick had long since overtaken Ballinasloe and Shannon Harbour as a centre for distribution. The growth of Limerick city after the Great Famine has often been noted; its connexion with America and the Continent was not unimportant.

[1] See above, p. 210.

Rourke, Kennedy, Barrett and Atkinson

Belfast and Cork ranked after Limerick as important agencies, followed by Ballinasloe, Galway and Shannon Harbour. Thereafter all the agencies were small.[1]

DUBLIN

The expansion of trade in Dublin is partly a reflexion of the growing incomes of an expanding city, and also of a remarkable capture of trade from other firms. The Double Stout business in Dublin multiplied by four-and-a-half times in the twenty-five years from 1855 to 1880, but the porter trade increased by sixteen times. This was, in particular, a feature of the eighteen-seventies, and by the success of Guinness in capturing the Dublin porter trade the other breweries had their 'bread and butter' taken from them. It is the success of the Dublin porter in this decade, coupled with the solid achievement in rural Ireland, which provide the background to Guinness's eventual domination of the Irish brewing industry.

Prices throughout this period were agreed by the Dublin brewers. They regulated the prices for Dublin beer sent to England in 1851. In 1854 they agreed to raise prices because of the war-time malt tax, and they brought them down in 1856 because of its withdrawal. In 1859 the brewers regulated the excess in trade allowance—an indication that price rebates and trade conditions were regulated at a comparatively late date in the nineteenth century. It is not clear when the decisions of the Dublin brewers became merely formal acknowledgements of Guinness's own price policy; clearly, the probability is that it was when Guinness became the dominant Dublin brewer. This happened in the mid-eighteen-sixties. In 1868 Manders, their rivals, left the Dublin brewers' agreement. The presumption is, therefore, that by that time Guinness were in fact dictating the price policy in Dublin. It was from this decade that Guinness hardly altered its basic price. By the end of it, too, they were seeking to reduce to uniformity the various agreements and trade discounts by which their trade was conducted. The size of the brewery's sales before these indications suggests that the uniformity and steadiness of price was a consequence and not a cause of their dominant position in the Dublin trade.

[1] The actual figures were: Irish Agents' trade 1874; Limerick, £55,200; Belfast, £38,000; Cork, £35,383; Ballinasloe, £24,570; Galway, £14,550; Shannon Harbour, £13,200; Carrick-on-Shannon, £4800; Athlone, £4730; Tuam, £4634; Carlow, £4200; Mullingar, £3960; Roscommon, £3800; Oranmore, £3460; Longford, £3000.

Guinness's Irish Agencies

The strategy of the conquest of the Dublin market is not clear. The growth of Guinness's English trade was not greater before 1870 than that of three of the other Dublin brewers, although they started with the advantage of having nearly half the trade in 1855, and probably more before then. The conquest of the Irish market outside Dublin gave the firm a basis for further expansion. Inside the city it was a big brewery with an unconquered market on its doorstep. The conquest of the city market was not due to the ownership of tied houses. In the eighteen-thirties Guinness owned only eleven, and by the eighteen-seventies the number was down to seven.

Other possible explanations may be advanced. The price competition in Dublin may have been keen, in the sense that Guinness clipped profit margins because of its own low costs, and that this drove other brewers into difficulties. The withdrawal of Manders from the trade agreement is suggestive of this. There is also the later bankruptcy of Manders and of several other brewers. A further possible explanation of the Guinness success may have been the quality of the porter. There is clear evidence after 1869 that the quantity of returned porter was very low. (Returned porter is beer returned to a brewery from trade as unsatisfactory, and is usually an index of bad brewing or bottling.) There creeps in after this date a self-congratulatory air about the stout—all sorts of explanations are later noted in Guinness internal memoranda of how its peculiar flavour first attracted public notice. It is also the case that sugar was not used, while other Dublin brewers are known to have used large quantities of it.

There is no evidence of any less-respectable means by which the firm may possibly have sought to capture the Dublin trade. Exclusive dealing arrangements with bottlers appear to date from before 1862, when the 'Harp' trade-mark labels were first used.[1] Photographs of Dublin a little later also show public houses which 'sold no other stout' than Guinness. On the other hand, the brewery was adamant in refusing special terms to individual customers.

There is some guide to the solution in an analysis of the sales of beer in various parts of Dublin. Between 1863 and 1872 the value of sales in Dublin rose from £139,482 to £246,700. The expansion of £106,000 was attributable to a £50,000 growth in 'south town',

---

[1] The Harp was registered as the Guinness trade mark on 5 April 1862, and the first labels were issued on 18 August of that year.

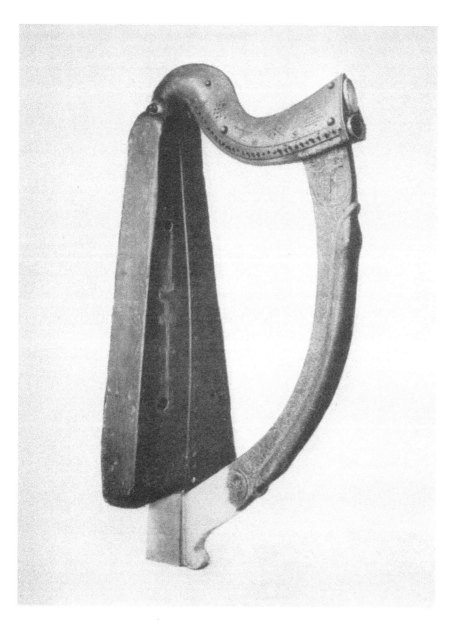

THE O'NEILL HARP

Popularly known as Brian Boru's harp and preserved in the Library of Trinity College, Dublin. The design of the trade mark used by Guinness's Brewery since 1862 has been based on this harp.

Dublin

and £40,000 in the 'Vicinities', or the newly growing suburbs. The 'south town' area was territory in which Manders had formerly sold, while the 'Vicinities' were areas into which the population was moving because of the growth of suburban rail traffic and the opening of horse-tram routes in 1872. Guinness went to great trouble to favour their customers in the 'Vicinities', making careful arrangements for free delivery and negotiating the most meticulous contracts with the railway company for Howth, Dundrum, and other suburbs where the consumption was at first very low.

In 1864 Guinness did 53 per cent of Dublin brewing.[1] Of this, they sold 61·5 per cent of the total Irish trade in the country and in Dublin, and 45·5 per cent of the exports to Great Britain and elsewhere. It is likely that their share of the Dublin trade itself was not more than 45 per cent, though the exact figures cannot be established. They were now doing over three-quarters of the Irish trade outside Dublin, because the Dublin trade was at least half of the total Irish trade. In 1864, therefore, the position was that Guinness had conquered less than half the British and the Dublin trade (of all Dublin brewers), but had taken about three-quarters of the Irish market outside Dublin.

After 1872 the leap in Dublin sales was comparable to the leap elsewhere. Indeed, it came to overtake the growth of English and other Irish sales. Objectively what had happened was that Guinness's great trade gave it advantages inside Dublin against which its rivals could hold out for some time but not for ever. Beneath this simple generalization, however, lies the confused story of the actual conquest of the Dublin market.

By 1869 the competition in Dublin appears to have become severe. Manders denounced the brewers' agreement and left it. Within a few years they were bankrupt. Other grave signs are not apparent in the Guinness records—save perhaps the following note of 1872:

Phoenix Brewery Prices:
The president of the Canteen 14 Hussars informed Mr Beare that the Phoenix Brewery deliver Porter into the canteen at Newbridge for 42/3 a Hhd. S.S. and also supply pint Measures, Sawdust and Spittoons, free of charge, the value of which for 4 months came to £15.

There was a fall in the number of Dublin brewers at this time. Possibly, also, the amount of returned porter was evidence of other

[1] Year ended 30 September 1864.

215

difficulties suffered by the Dublin brewer. In England the average payment for returns per £100 of sales of Guinness beer was about 12*s*. in 1872, and 5*s*. in the Irish country. In Dublin and the 'Vicinity' it was 42*s*. The beer was sold in Dublin, however, in the best condition and under fairly close supervision, so that the high rate of returns is surprising. Almost certainly, therefore, other brewers' beer was being sent into the brewery by retailers as returned porter, and it would therefore appear that the returned porter figures were a sign that the other Dublin brewers were going through a bad period at this time. The other brewers certainly relied very heavily upon their tied houses for their trade, as the following note by George Beare in 1874 shows. It refers to the sale by a publican in North Earl Street of Foreign Extra Stout, which Guinness's brewed for their foreign trade:

Mr J. Kenny, North Earl Street, has been latterly putting an advertisement in the Dublin papers and Railway Guides, calling attention, among other articles, to our 'XXX' Porter as supplied to him. His transactions are of a most trivial kind and are confined to 6 or 8 Barrels of Foreign Extra in the year. Mr Beare had a conversation with him and told him that he did not like such advertisements, as it placed us in an unpleasant position with our other customers, as we had not a stock of Foreign Export, beyond what is required for that particular branch of our trade, and that it is not adapted for home consumption. He also reminded Mr Kenny that he got neither D.S. nor S.S. from us, and Mr Kenny said his house belonged to Sweetman, with whom [he] is under an engagement to deal. Kenny promised to withdraw the Advertisement. Sweetman allow him to sell Foreign as they cannot supply this article. 9 September 1874.

From 1860 to 1880 the profit margins on Guinness's beers fell substantially, probably from 30 per cent to 20 per cent and most of this fall took place in the eighteen-seventies.[1] This suggests that the terms offered to the firm's main customers may substantially have improved during the period of the conquest of the Dublin market. Certainly after 1860 or so there is a change in the reaction of the firm's activities during years of generally bad trade. In great contrast to the years before the Great Famine the rate of growth of output was not reduced —sometimes it was accelerated—at these times, but the profit margin fell substantially. It is possible, therefore, that at times of bad trade Guinness cut its margins in order to keep up output and in so doing put pressure on its rivals whose profits were not sufficiently high to

[1] See below, p. 224.

stand a cut. A change of this kind in the nature of the market is the most likely explanation of the conquest of the Dublin trade.

The other brewers were not competing in the free market and Guinness's attitude to its own tied houses, of which eight still remained in 1873, was in striking contrast. On the basis of a transaction in that year the following laconic note was made:

House in Capel St.
    Unexpired lease 53 years—

head rent	£55.	7.	8.
let to Mrs Fitzpatrick for	100.	0.	0. a year
Profit	44.	12.	4.

    She offers to purchase for £1,500.

Guinness's victory was so complete that Mrs Fitzpatrick could be as free as she wished.

[12]

The Physical and Commercial Expansion of the Brewery

Interest republicae ut quilibet re sua bene utatur.

INTRODUCTION

THIS CHAPTER presents the anatomy of Guinness's business in the period of its great expansion. It begins with a study of the brewery's methods and passes to an analysis of its costs in relation to its sales. Then follows an examination of its management, and lastly a brief survey of its physical growth.

One main lesson may be drawn from the narrative: no sudden or dramatic changes in direction took place; conscious policy was reflected mainly in the aggregate of many day-to-day decisions. The firm concentrated on brewing and kept out of retailing and to some extent out of wholesaling, largely because of short-term financial advantages. In what follows are some examples of this main theme.

THE BEERS

As already stated, the five beers brewed in 1840 were Town Porter, Country Porter, Keeping Beer, Double Stout and Triple Stout. In the next few years three significant changes were made. First, the firm ceased to brew Country Porter. This was probably an indication of improved conditions of transport and quicker turnover of the country trade. It was no longer necessary to brew porter with a higher hop rate for the country trade. The lower hop-rate Town Porter was quite adequate. Secondly, in 1846 Double Stout was brewed to go into trade without maturation. It was no longer sent out unmixed; it was blended with a higher hop-rate Keeping Beer brewed, like the old Double Stout, in the cooler months of the year. Henceforth, until almost the end of the century, there were to be two Double Stouts for consumption in Ireland and Great Britain,

218

The Beers

Current Double Stout and Store Double Stout. Finally, Keeping Beer, which had been used for reinforcing porter in the summer months, was no longer brewed. Not only was Town Porter stable enough for the country trade but it was also stable enough to endure the summer months. It would henceforth be sent out unmixed, and its new-found reliability was marked by its name being changed to Single Stout.

A third Double Stout, for foreign export, made its appearance as a regular feature of the trade sometime after 1824. This beer, Foreign Double Stout as it was called, was the lineal descendant of West Indies Porter and Triple Stout, which before had been brewed at irregular intervals only.

There was little change during this period in the strength of these beers except for some diminution in the case of the Double Stouts. The hop rates varied within wide limits but remained relatively the same for the four qualities, with Single Stout the lowest, Current Double Stout about twice the rate of Single Stout, and Store and Foreign Double Stout higher again. The colour of the beer seems also to have varied widely, rising between 1840 and 1852, and then falling to the 1840 level.

THE PROCESS

The mashing and sparging procedure remained unchanged for the most part during these years, but there was a very significant development in the introduction of two new mashing devices. One of these, first used in 1863—the Steele's Mashing Engine—is important because it was the prototype of the mashing engine to be installed when the new brewhouse was erected in 1875 (and which is still in use in the brewery today). The ground malt and mashing liquor were mixed in a horizontal cylinder commanding the kieve, and containing inside the cylinder a set of revolving spikes, the mash being projected into the kieve by means of a chute leading from the cylinder. But it was installed over only one kieve and the old procedure continued throughout the period.

Mechanization of the copper furnaces was introduced in 1863, the coal being burned on a revolving hearth so as to give more even and economical results. About this time, too, the amount of wort boiled off was considerably reduced. These two changes must have

Expansion of the Brewery

led to a great saving in fuel. Sometime after 1867 an artificial-cooling plant was installed, making the importation of ice into the brewery unnecessary.

The course of the fermentation seems to have continued to be judged by the appearance of the head, although present gravity seems to have been determined more often than previously. There was, however, a major advance in the technique of cleansing. Sometime not long before 1866 the rounds were replaced by long flat open vessels called skimmers, from which the yeast was removed as it rose to the top by a metal bar made to travel over the surface of the beer by a system of racks and pinions. This mechanical contrivance seems, however, to have proved unsatisfactory as it was subsequently replaced by hand skimming with wooden boards.

The yeast separated during cleansing is a mixture of yeast and beer which was originally disposed of as a by-product. From about 1867 the yeast was separated mechanically from the barm beer, the yeast being sold as a by-product as heretofore, but the barm beer was collected and mixed off in the beer for trade. This appears to have given a considerable saving in material.

The practice of adding unfermented wort in order to hasten the subsidiary fermentation producing the foam when the beer was draughted from cask or poured from bottle seems to have been common practice by 1838.[1] It is not known when this was first done by Guinness, but it was not done for the Double Stout until 1853 and apparently only then because of 'the present desire on the part of the customer that the beer should get very quickly up in bottle'.

It is clear that this period in James's Gate was very largely one of mechanization. The copper furnaces, the ice production, the yeast cleansing and the yeast separation were done mechanically for the first time. The machinery for mashing and for cooling the worts was improved. No doubt more attention was paid to the details of the process. The beginnings of a need for laboratory analysis of materials and product are discernible. The extract obtained from the malt did not increase much but it was a good deal less variable, pointing to an increased control of the process. The main efforts seem to have been directed toward changes which would increase the capacity of the brewery—the amount of beer that could be produced in a

[1] Morewood, *A Philosophical and Statistical History of the Inventions and Customs of Ancient and Modern Nations in the Manufacture and Use of Inebriating Liquors*, p. 626.

The Process

given space or with a given plant. From the late eighteen-thirties the plant was being driven harder than was really desirable. The change from brewing Double Stout mainly in the winter months to brewing it in the summer months is a clear indication that this was so. In a memorandum of 1869 John Tertius Purser wrote: 'The large quantity of beer that we have now to make in the summer months is evidently brewed at a disadvantage. And even in autumn, spring and winter the present plant is overworked. Increased power is requisite to conduct the manufacture with comfort and efficiency.' The need, now acute, had probably been felt increasingly for many years.

MALT AND HOPS

The malting of barley was a fundamental part of the brewery's activities because so much depended on the quality of the malt. The firm's initiation into the business of malting and its main sources of barley in Ireland and England have been described in an earlier chapter. By the eighteen-fifties malt was being made in Dublin by Guinness's themselves, and also on their behalf on commission in a number of other Irish towns—notably Mountmellick, Charleston and Enniscorthy by the early eighteen-fifties, and Castlebridge and Wexford later. The barley came partly from Ireland and partly from England and Scotland. In years of bad harvests during the Napoleonic period the barley had come almost exclusively from England, while during years of abundance the proportion of Irish barley appears to have been high.

From the eighteen-fifties the market for barley in both countries was dominated by the growing output of beer, and in Ireland this meant increasingly that it was dominated by the firm of Arthur Guinness. By 1880 over half the Irish barley crop was being bought by the brewery, which got over half its barley from Ireland. Much of this barley was bought directly by the brewery and malted in its own maltings or on commission by maltsters to whom it gave credit. There were other independent maltsters as well, of whose output Guinness bought the major part.

In 1878 the brewery bought 43,000 barrels of malt from Sheare at Mountmellick, 15,000 from White, 33,000 from Carter's, at prices varying between 2s. 6d. and 3s. for the malting operation. 50,000 barrels were made in Cooke's Lane at the brewery's own maltings. There were maltings at New Ross, Wexford, Bagenalstown, Charleston and Enniscorthy. Some barley came from Sweden and Chile as well. In all, the brewery bought 203,000 barrels of malt at a total cost of £349,000. Of the average price per barrel of 34*s.* 4*d.*, 21*s.* 4¾*d.* was for barley, 10*s.* 7*d.* for excise duty, and about 2*s.* 4¼*d.* for the cost of malting. The price paid for malt was negotiated individually with each maltster, and there were slight variations. During the period from 1860 to 1876 the usual price appears to have varied from 32*s.* to 35*s.* a barrel.

The brewery used English hops predominantly, so far as the records indicate, until well into the eighteen-forties. In 1842, for instance, all the hops came from Kent. In 1853 small quantities of Bavarian hops were bought, and by 1858 American hops were being used as well. This use of foreign hops coincides with the beginning of the brewery's expansion. By 1869 the memorandum book had a formula 'one-third British, one-third Bavarian and one-third American', and this became a regular buying policy except in years when British prices rose because of scarcity.

SUBSTITUTE MATERIALS

According to a House of Commons Return in 1878, the breweries using malt entirely without sugar or other substitutes were Guinness, Combe, Truman, Whitbread and Meux. Other brewers used quantities of sugar or other substitutes running into the order of 10 per cent of their total raw materials. These breweries were catering for a mass-market cheap beer, and much of their production was considerably weaker than that of the brewers who sold beers made exclusively from malt and hops.

Guinness's, despite their position as the biggest brewer employing malt only, stood midway between the high-class brewers and the manufacturers of cheap beers. The average strength of its combined products was considerably less than that of Combe, Truman and the others. This was because its English market was one for a strong expensive stout, whereas in Ireland it sold a great deal of a much weaker porter. The average of the two pulled Guinness down to a position between an expensive and a cheap brewer. In England Guinness's stout was the working man's champagne, in Ireland its porter was his staple drink.

Why did Guinness's insist on using 'pure' materials exclusively,

Substitute Materials

when the nature of their Irish market might have suggested a different approach? It is interesting to speculate upon the reasons for the
'purity' of Guinness's porter when in fact the firm was catering in
Ireland for a market at least as cheap as the one that in England was
leading to the use of more sugar. For many years the brewery had
protested its innocence of adulteration. Its reputation, therefore,
was based partly on complete absence of substitute materials. This
was the foundation of its reputation in England; and in Ireland
the memories of the allegations about adulterants may have been
still vivid. Next, the brewery produced both Double and Single Stout
on the basis of a common process, so that the complications of adding
to one beer without interfering with another might have been considerable. Above all, the brewery prided itself on its beer, on its
reputation for quality and on its employment of raw materials that
were publicly recognized to be above suspicion. That this was sound
policy is shown both by the figures of sales and profits, and by a
consideration of the pace of the expansion. By being single-minded
about the product the problems of increasing the size of the brewery
were simplified. It is easier to concentrate on improving an existing
product and specify new capacity for it than to invent new products.
The public was more than satisfied with the product it knew. This
is the context within which Guinness's grew in the last half of the
nineteenth century.

COSTS AND SALES

It is possible to reconstruct the cost structure of the brewery for a
period of six years from 1871 to 1876. In a table in the Proprietors
Memorandum Book for 1877 the firm's main items of receipts
were followed by the main items of expenditure. In the six years
£7·0 m. were received, of which £6·8 m. was for the sale of beer
(divided as to about three to one between stout and porter). Out
of this a surplus of £0·9 m. was left. The remaining £6·1 m. was
made up of £4·5 m. for materials, £0·5 m. duty, £0·3 m. salaries
and wages, £0·1 m. maintenance, £0·1 m. cooperage, £0·1 m. carriage, and a variety of other charges.[1]

The main element of cost was raw materials. This charge was
divided into £3·6 m. for malt and £0·9 m. for hops. Following this

---

[1] The cost structure was based on a sale of 2·5 million hogsheads of beer during the
six years, rising from 0·3 million in 1871 to over 0·5 million in 1876.

Expansion of the Brewery

came the duty. The other items were extraordinarily small. The major labour cost, for example, was for salaries and not for wages, and no less than one-fifth of the brewery wage bill was the estimated value of the porter given to the men. This is a fascinating sidelight on the importance of drink in working-class budgets of the day, and of the money that could be made out of selling beer to the ordinary people.

The profit figure rose year by year and was the sole source of liquid capital for the expansion of the firm. According to one memorandum the amount invested annually rose from £10,449 in 1869 to £74,031 in 1873. In one year in the later eighteen-seventies it exceeded £100,000 and in three years it was over £90,000. The average expenditure from 1868 to 1879 was £68,000 a year, most of it in net investment, not merely replacing worn-out plant. At the same time the Guinness family disposed of enormous sums outside the firm. The variations in the profit rate are of great interest. There are available figures of output, of gross profits and gross investment for the years 1860–79. From them it is possible to deduce that the profit margin fell over the period, from 14s. or 15s. a hogshead to less than 10s. The variation in the rate of profit was associated with the trade cycle—it fell in 1873–4, years of depression, it fell again in 1878–9. It rose in 1865 and 1876.[1] This is true to some extent, too, of changes in the rate of investment. In the years 1871–6 taken together, the firm's income after tax was disposed of as follows—rather more than £600,000 to the partners, rather less than £400,000 to investment and about £300,000 in wages and salaries. This is equivalent to a high rate of investment and the heavy bias towards profit to be expected in an industry with (to use technical language) a high capital/output ratio. In consequence the average of incomes resulting from the brewery's activities gave rise naturally to a relatively low demand for consumption goods and to high savings. The workers had a high propensity to consume, and the partners a low propensity to consume. Since the partners' share of the total income was so high, the average propensity to consume was low. This may be compared with an industry like cotton manufacture, where wages formed a high proportion of the product. The income of the average brewery worker was high; but in brewing relatively little labour was employed per unit of capital, in contrast to such contemporary Irish industries as agriculture, linen and furniture making.

[1] Rostow, *British Economy of the Nineteenth Century*, p. 179.

Costs and Sales

All these vast sales of stout, costing millions of pounds to make, and yielding six-figure profits, were based on a wholesale price of 1s. 2d. for stout and 9¼d. for porter, *per gallon*. The retailer bought the one for a little under twopence, and the other for a little over a penny *a pint*. The retail selling prices were usually about 5½d. and 3d. *a quart*. The first was above the price for ordinary beer, and the latter considerably below it. Therefore in stout Guinness's had a quality or prestige market; porter sold because it was cheap.

It was in the eighteen-seventies that Guinness's marketing policy settled into its classical pattern. The firm remained very decidedly manufacturers. They abandoned their retailing—by 1875 they were making only £40 a year profit on the rents of public houses, and the total rents were only about £370. Most of them were legacies of expansion when they had been incorporated in the brewery territory, or of bad debts. In this respect Guinness's were almost alone as brewers. Most breweries owned a large number of tied houses, or had close or exclusive relations with them. Next, Guinness's abdicated any of their remaining role as transporters of their own beer. They based all their prices after 1879, as far as they possibly could, on the basis of f.o.b. Dublin, except that they maintained a free delivery area within ten miles of the centre of the city—the 'Vicinity' as it was defined by the Dublin brewers.[1] Guinness never advertised as brewers, although retailers advertised their stout. Finally, the firm sought to extricate itself from a system of exclusive dealing with agents in the major British ports.

The usual explanation of this movement towards an almost complete concentration on brewing to the exclusion of marketing and retailing is that the firm found it more economic to do so. Unless this is a pure tautology, the argument must lie upon a basis of economic reasoning something like this: a firm that specializes makes more profits than one that does not, and Guinness's specialized as manufacturers and not as retailers of beer. Therefore, by specializing, they became the lowest-cost manufacturers, and other firms had to use the tied-house system as a device to limit Guinness's expansion.

Guinness's were good brewers—although there may be doubt about their being the least-cost brewers in the sense that their products were remarkably cheap or remarkably good compared with those of some

[1] See above, p. 208.

Expansion of the Brewery

firms in England. Guinness's expansion owed more to their response to the sudden and unexpected growth of demand in rural Ireland after the Great Famine than to any great technological advance or to any magic formula for stout which made their product extremely cheap. The economies of scale may explain the cheapness of the porter compared with other beer, and these arose from an expansion of the brewery in response to demand and not in anticipation of it. The market in Ireland expanded, Guinness's was able to equip itself to meet the demand (and therein, of course, lies the secret of its success). In the process the brewery became very big. As a result of its size and the competence of its management the beer was very cheap to brew. Specialization was not necessarily the product of any single decision in broad policy-making. Circumstances created a situation to whose needs the Guinnesses had the business sense and the resources to make an adequate response. The response was well timed and earned prodigious rewards.

The absence of tied houses outside Dublin has first to be explained. In order to do this two matters have to be discussed. The first is the economic basis of the tied house, and the next is the organization of retailing in rural Ireland.[1]

In another work the economic basis of the tied house has been analysed, and it is unnecessary to repeat the arguments in detail.[2] The tied house is an arrangement for exclusive dealing by a retailer in a brewer's beers based either on full ownership or heavy finance of the licensed premises by the brewer. It seems that three elements are necessary for a growth of the tied-house system. First, the capital assets of the brewer must be much bigger than those of the publicans so that he can afford to act as a supplier of credit. This means that beyond the stage of the ordinary publican-brewer the brewery has to reach a certain size before it becomes possible for it to act as a source of finance. This size, in fact, is associated with a degree of mechanization that was not characteristic of many brewers outside Dublin, Cork and Waterford at any time. For a brewer to act as a source of capital, too, there has to be an element of restriction in the retail market, otherwise he will be giving capital almost indiscriminately to a large number of retailers; in a restricted market the number of applicants is limited and a publican, once tied, cannot be

---

[1] See above, chs. 2 and 7.
[2] John Vaizey in P. Lesley Cook (ed.), *Effects of Mergers* (London, 1958).

226

Costs and Sales

challenged by a new publican setting up nearby.[1] There has to be
a limit to the number of public houses imposed either by town-
planning or by licensing or some other device. If there is not, then
the brewer has less incentive to cut out his rivals by exclusive dealing
arrangements (because they can always open up in opposition to him)
and he is also faced with a prospect of financing an almost unlimited
number of small retailers.

This was precisely the position in Ireland. The licensing laws had
never been stringent and there was a plethora of public houses.
Further, the rural parts of Ireland had a primitive economy in which
specialist retailing was unknown. Many people were retailers, or
their equivalent, and they sold many things. This is still the case.
Few bars in the country parts of Ireland are exclusively bars. It
follows that any attempt to finance the retailing of beer in the develop-
ing economy of Ireland after the Great Famine would have meant
taking control of the major part of the retail trade in Ireland, and
hence of becoming the complete arbiter of the whole economy,
because it was through retailing that the maritime economy made
its rapid strides after 1850.

Along these lines, therefore, almost certainly lies the explanation
of Guinness's lack of involvement in retailing outside Dublin. But
there is a danger of having proved too much. There were exclusive
dealing arrangements for Guinness's beers and there are photographs
of public houses that show that the right of exclusive dealing was a
well-advertised privilege. These arrangements appear to have been
based upon a discount system (which became codified after about
1879). These discounts appear gradually to have become concentrated
on wholesalers. It is possible that the easy credit terms given to
customers in Ireland may have helped the growth of Guinness sales
after 1850, but this is entirely a matter of conjecture.

The position in Great Britain was different. There, Guinness was
not a local beer, and its sales were usually a minor part of the
turnover of any one publican. The problems of management whether
of property or debts would have been serious had the firm decided
to buy public houses.

It seems, therefore, that the relative absence of involvement in
retailing is explicable by the circumstances in which Guinness found
themselves. In both parts of their market the acquisition of tied

[1] *Ibid.* p. 397.

houses was too big an operation for a firm of their situation to undertake. Their gradual withdrawal from the delivery of their beer outside Dublin is also explicable more in terms of the contingent than in terms of any subtle consideration of the advantages of specialization.

One item of cost in which the firm took a great interest was coopering. The costs of making and repairing casks rose faster than the sales of beer because the greater sales of beer in more distant parts added to the time that the average cask was away, increased the possibility of damage in handling and also very considerably added to the chance of loss. Consequently the item of cooperage charges tended constantly to rise while every other charge was falling. By 1880 there were 151,000 casks in the possession of the brewery which meant that each cask was used about four times a year on average. Various devices were suggested for getting the casks back. In 1877 Purser wondered 'whether it would be as well to take off an additional new system slip of returned casks and stamp it for the day on which such casks might reasonably be expected to be returned, and place in a pigeon-hole—dated for such day—and on that day revise the cards with a view of seeing what casks were overdue and then asking for same'. In June of 1877 three of the ten important matters under review concerned casks.

The effective life of a cask appears to have been about ten years or more, so that the real problem of cost was obviously the problem of returning the casks to the brewery. This question came to dominate the discussions of transport, and was the major element in the decisions that were taken about it. The brewery was spending about £26,000 a year to make about 34,000 casks, break up 9000, and keep 100,000 in repair. Each cask, therefore, appears to have cost about £1 over its life at that time: but by two years later it was estimated to cost about £2. By increasing the usage of each cask in trade this item of costs could be cut very substantially. It appears, too, that the issue was not merely one of cost but of management. Judging from the number of entries in the memorandum books of the time the problems of managing the cooperage were disproportionately great, and therefore there was a constant pursuit of simplification of the methods of control and increase of cask usage.

The brewery enforced payment for lost casks. In 1875 these prices were raised by 20–25 per cent to nearly the economic price, and also a system of compensation for damage was insisted upon. This appears

Costs and Sales

to have been fairly successful, but the main difficulty was getting the casks back to Dublin from England. The brewery decided in the same year to pay the return freight on empty casks from England, which was a new decision.

The system of sale free on board to England (other than to the English stores) had been adopted in the early eighteen-seventies, but the payment for the return of the casks made this arrangement unsymmetrical. The brewery absorbed all transport costs in Dublin where they were much higher than by railway, canal and steamboat to the rest of Ireland and to England. There was no trade discount in Dublin, only one of 1¼ per cent elsewhere in Ireland, and 2½ per cent in England. The brewery also paid all carriage costs to the rest of Ireland, not merely the cost of returning empty casks as in the English trade. The difference in treatment of England and Ireland in this matter is explicable mainly by the problem of getting casks back.[1] Where Guinness's delivered in Dublin they had considerable control of the return of casks.[2] By making arrangements for the return of casks by rail from the main centres in Ireland (which they did centrally with each railway) they also exercised control over the Irish trade. But in England the position was obviously more difficult. The sales of Guinness in any one area were not sufficient to justify special arrangements with the railways, except in the immediate vicinity of the main English stores. Consequently the brewery was able to contract with the shipping companies to return casks from the English stores, but there was no efficient method whereby Guinness could arrange for the transport of its full casks from its stores to the retailers, and of its empty casks from the retailers to its stores without setting up an extraordinarily expensive and elaborate system to do so. It therefore seemed easiest to reduce their absorption of transport costs in England since, if they had agreed to bear all transport costs they would have entered into an extremely complex and expensive system which would not necessarily have increased the rate of return of casks.

The withdrawal from the agencies was part of the same procedure, and could be interpreted as a policy of increasing as much as possible

[1] It may also be that in Ireland there were advantages to be gained by contracting for big lots of casks to be transported, but that there were few opportunities to do so in England because the sales in any one place were small.

[2] In 1869 the average Dublin cask was only out for one month, which was but one-third of the time for the whole trade.

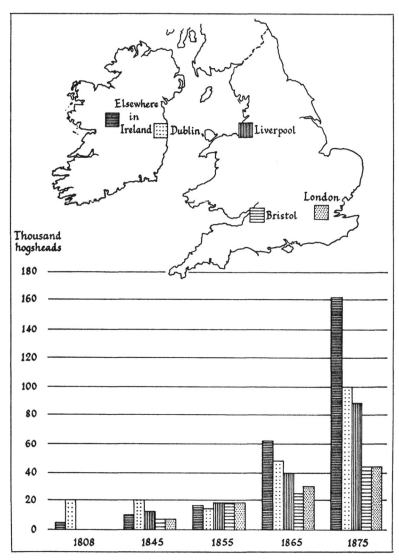

Distribution of Guinness sales: 1808–75. (*See* Appendix.)

Costs and Sales

the number of sellers of Guinness.[1] It may perhaps be at this point—
about 1875—that the withdrawal from extra-brewing activities became a conscious one. The increase of sales in England had outstripped
the original agencies there. From 1810 to 1850 sales in England
were fairly steady. Then they rose slightly. Between 1860 and 1880
they rose at a fantastic rate. New times required new arrangements.

It has been explained that in England Guinness's stout was a
quality beer, selling in small quantities compared with the beer sold
on draught by most English brewers. Moreover it was usually sold
in bottle. The customers for Guinness appear to an increasing extent
to have been wholesale bottlers as well as wholesale beer dealers.
The original fifteen exclusive agencies were at Liverpool, Barrow-in-
Furness, Blackburn, Preston, Bolton, Maryport, Newcastle upon Tyne,
Sunderland, Huddersfield, Derby, Shrewsbury, Nottingham, Leicester, Douglas and Jersey. There were also the stores at Liverpool,
London and Bristol. By 1884 the whole of Scotland was open and
a concerted move was afoot to terminate the agencies for exclusive
dealing.

The management of the Liverpool Store involved the brewery
in costs of about 10s. a hogshead, of which the greater part was
possibly local delivery costs. In Liverpool about one-quarter of the
stout was sold at 60s. net, and about three-quarters at 61s. 6d. net
(there was no discount because transport costs were absorbed). The
average net receipt per hogshead was 51s. 2d. (f.o.b. Dublin) for
Liverpool. For London the stout was sold at 58s. 6d. less 2½ per
cent discount, or 57s. a hogshead (f.o.b. Dublin). This gave the firm
5s. 10d. advantage in its London trade despite the fact that the
price competition in London was probably strong. Therefore the drive
to reduce exclusive agencies arose as much from the advantageous
terms given to the local agents in terms of free delivery as from any
wish just to be quit of the bother of fetching and carrying.

The effect of this kind of calculation was to make Guinness's sales
policy one of giving value for money. It had the effect of enabling
the brewery to concentrate on keeping down the costs of brewing
and keeping up the quality of stout, while the wholesalers had every
incentive to reduce wholesaling costs.

[1] See above, p. 225.

231

Expansion of the Brewery

ADMINISTRATION

The family were helped in the administration of the brewery for eighty-seven years by the Pursers. According to the second Arthur Guinness the families first met in 1786 or 1787.[1] The eldest Purser, John Purser of Tewkesbury, came from London in 1776 to brew porter for James Farrell of Dublin, and died in 1783, after making a name for himself as a porter brewer for some of the leading Dublin firms. His son, John Purser, senior, came to the brewery in 1799 as chief clerk, and by 1802 was earning £150 a year with occasional bonuses of £25. It is said that after an argument with the first Arthur Guinness he left to work for Cairnes in Drogheda and was brought back by the second Arthur, thus increasing his power in the brewery. In 1820 he became a partner of the Guinness brothers and sons, together with his own son, John Purser, junior, who had become an apprentice brewer in 1799. In 1821 John Purser, senior, had all the secretarial and cash side of the brewery firmly in his hands: the cashier reported to him, and the cask accounts were kept by him. He died in 1830.

Benjamin Guinness, brother of the second Arthur Guinness, appears to have been an important figure in the brewery; he shared the management until 1820 with his brothers Arthur and William Lunell Guinness, and after 1820 with the Pursers. He died in 1826, leaving the brewery to the management of his brothers the second Arthur and William Lunell and to John Purser, junior; in this they were actively helped by Arthur's sons Arthur Lee and Benjamin Lee. Another brewer, St Leger Palmer, was employed after 1800, and in 1828 he was a Warden of the Brewers' Guild, but he seems to have had little influence on policy. It is probable that the day-to-day management of the brewery between 1820 and 1830 was in the hands of John Purser, junior, because most extant memoranda are addressed to him. The second Arthur, however, exercised a continuous watchful care and in several important instances changed a policy recommended by John Purser, junior. From 1810 to 1830 he exercised most meticulous control of the brewing. After 1835, almost certainly, John Purser, junior, Arthur Lee and Benjamin Lee ran the brewery, until Arthur Lee's retirement in 1839. Thereafter John Purser, junior, and Benjamin Lee were in effective control

[1] See above, p. 116.

232

JOHN TERTIUS PURSER, 1809-93

Photograph by Elliott and Fry, London: Professor J. Purser's Collection

Administration

until the former's death in 1858. His position, but not his share in the partnership, was taken over by his son John Tertius Purser, then Head Brewer. When John Purser, junior, died in 1858 at his home, Rathmines Castle, he left less than £40,000. This is possibly indicative of a subordinate position in the partnership because the second Arthur Guinness (who died in 1855) left £150,000, but this included the residue of profits earned from flour-milling and banking as well as from brewing.

The close relations of the Guinnesses and the Pursers are shown by the fact that not only did members of both families live in the brewery in adjoining houses, but the sons of the second Arthur Guinness and of John Purser, junior, were taught together by private tutors.

It is not possible, in view of what has been said about the growing amount of brewing talent in the firm, to assign the improvements and changes in the mid-nineteenth century to any one person. All that can be said is that there was no division in the firm between brewing knowledge and business acumen. The second Arthur Guinness possessed both, and so did his son Benjamin Lee. There is no ground whatever on which it could be alleged that John Purser, junior, had a monopoly of brewing ability, although he appears to have specialized in the brewing operations and to have been less concerned with the buying of raw materials and selling the beer.

In the earlier days of the firm, when output was small, the Guinness family and the Pursers appear to have run the brewery—to have engaged and paid the staff, supervised the brewings, bought the raw materials, interviewed the customers and negotiated with the politicians. The emergence of a distinct managerial class known as brewers is associated with the growth of output after 1845 and with the gap which developed after the second Arthur's virtual withdrawal from the brewery in the mid-eighteen-forties. This gap existed between the direction of policy by Benjamin Lee and John Purser, junior, on the one hand, and on the other the hour-to-hour supervision of the brewing which would in future be carried out by the brewers. By the eighteen-fifties the 'night clerk' system had begun, by which a level of management was recognized which ran the brewery at all hours under the supervision of the brewers, and the apprentice brewers had begun to fulfil the role of doing the actual brewing under the ultimate supervision of the brewers.

Expansion of the Brewery

Before the advent of this new managerial class the partners had employed a group of clerks who were paid (when grown men) from £70 to £200 a year. The senior of them was the cashier, and there was a fairly rapid turnover, but whether this was due to dishonesty, to illness or other cause, never emerges from the records. Occasionally the cashier became confidential clerk to the senior member of the Guinness family (when his salary fell partly on the brewery and partly on the family); and the man's position in the brewery hierarchy is hard to determine. Associated with the clerks were a number of younger men and youths known as apprentice clerks and then as apprentice brewers. In this list were included at various times John Tertius Purser and his brother Benjamin, sons of John Purser, junior, and Captain R. B. Ussher who became head book-keeper and then confidential secretary to Arthur Guinness. About 1820 or so, some clerks were called brewers—the first so to be called was St Leger Palmer, but there were soon others, and these eventually came to be regarded as superior in authority to the ordinary clerks.

One of the most interesting of the clerks was Dionysius Lardner Boursiquot (named after the popular educator), the alleged son of a Huguenot draper in Dublin and of an ambitious mother who kept a boarding-house in Haddington Road. A personal friend of some of the Guinnesses, he left the brewery when he was about eighteen, in 1840, became an actor under the name of Lee Morton, and wrote a play called *London Assurance* which was put on at Covent Garden in 1841 with immediate success. Dion Boucicault, as he was by then known, was a successful actor specializing in character parts. Most of his plays were of the Irish genre, but two—one of them was *The Corsican Brothers*—were in the French historical manner.[1] Later in life he settled in America, where, as the *Dictionary of National Biography* has it, his 'brilliant literary and histrionic qualities were not supported by any very rigorous moral code'.[1]

A number of apprentices were always in the brewery, in the hope that some of them might become partners and brewers. Most of them appear to have been connexions of the second Arthur Guinness. A high proportion of them were brothers or nephews—John Grattan Guinness who left to join the Liverpool Agency in 1825, Edward Guinness who became bankrupt and went to the Isle of Man to

---

[1] *The Colleen Bawn*, his best known 'Irish' play, based on Gerald Griffin's *The Collegians*, was first produced in New York in 1860 and soon became a great popular success.

234

Administration

escape his creditors, Richard Lyons Darley who left Dublin in disgrace and Arthur Burke who is included in a much later list of those who 'turned out badly'. Then there was John Grattan Guinness, junior, who left the brewery in 1838, was set up in a brewery in Bristol, went bankrupt and unsuccessfully sued Benjamin Lee Guinness in 1858. He had been dismissed in 1838 because according to 'Mr Purser our brewer' he was 'given to mixing with degraded society', and he was required to leave Dublin. Through Wetherman's kindness a Bristol brewery was bought for him, but this collapsed in 1845.[1] By 1858 he was living in abject poverty and sued Guinness's for his allegedly wrongful dismissal twenty years earlier. Benjamin Lee gave evidence and the suit was immediately dismissed.[2] Many of the apprentices were unsatisfactory. The nephews of the second Arthur, John Burke (son of Mary Anne) and John Guinness (son of Hosea), took to drink, and Richard Guinness (son of Edward and brother-in-law of Benjamin Lee) went mad. These occurrences show how extraordinarily difficult it was to ensure a succession of adequate managers. In 1839 Arthur Lee Guinness decided to leave the firm.

In 1843 the second Arthur Guinness protested to his niece Eliza O'Grady[3] that 'the claims upon us from many, very many Relations, not a few of them Brethren with very large Families, is very great... I can only repeat what I said before on the subject of employment that there is no vacancy here for a Clerk'. The family was prolific, but the problem of choosing managers correctly was a serious one. The business needed probity and skill and the combination of the two was rare indeed. Good men were scarce and the Pursers were highly valued, as their positions and incomes show.

By the eighteen-fifties Benjamin Lee and Arthur Lee were partners with John Tertius Purser, though Arthur Lee, whose interest in the brewery was never great, had retired and soon died. Below this level of management was the head book-keeper, or cashier, and a number of brewers, one of whom was known as the head brewer. Simeon Ussher, son of R. B. Ussher, appears to have been the first person so called. There were below this a series of night-clerks, who supervised the brewing by day and at night, and a number of out-

---

[1] Wetherman was the Bristol agent. See above, p. 134 (footnote).
[2] *Saunders' News-Letter*, 26 June 1858, p. 2.
[3] She lived at Stillorgan with Arthur Lee Guinness.

clerks who travelled for trade in Dublin and elsewhere. There were also the clerks, and below them were the labourers and draymen.

The death of the second Arthur Guinness in 1855 left the brewery in the hands of his son Benjamin Lee Guinness, with John Purser, junior, as a partner. Arthur's other sons enjoyed annuities. John Purser, junior, died in 1858 after thirty-eight years as a partner. John Tertius Purser, who joined the brewery in 1824, became head brewer. His knowledge of the brewery in which he had grown up was as intimate as that of the Guinnesses of that generation, and of Benjamin Lee Guinness's sons.

With the death of Sir Benjamin Lee in 1868, Sir Arthur and Edward Cecil, both young men in their twenties (and Edward Cecil still an undergraduate at Trinity College, Dublin) became the proprietors. John Tertius Purser assumed a position of authority because of his age and experience. Within eight years Sir Arthur withdrew: probably his period of influence lasted only for three or four years because references to him in the memoranda became fewer and fewer in the early eighteen-seventies. At the same time, as already explained, Edward Cecil's power grew very quickly.[1] He was a dynamic, restless man, remarkably like his father, with a capacity for quick decision, a flair for business, and an intuitive understanding of men's characters. In 1876, after the protracted negotiations already described, he became the sole proprietor.

By the eighteen-sixties the brewers had finally emerged as a separate category, distinct from and more highly paid than the clerks. But they were still largely recruited from the Guinness and Purser families. In 1870 the leading brewers were Edward Cecil's cousins George (who was head brewer) and Edmund Waller, and John Tertius Purser's two nephews Thomas Grace Geoghegan and William Purser Geoghegan (who became head brewer on George Waller's retiring in 1880). These were followed by Edward Purser and Samuel Geoghegan, who were also nephews of John Tertius Purser (Samuel Geoghegan was W. P. Geoghegan's brother and later became chief engineer to the firm).

Purser's power through his family connexion and with his experience and influence was therefore considerable. G. H. Beare the Secretary (as the head clerk was called) was well under his thumb. He also knew the agents intimately and interviewed them whenever

[1] See above, ch. 10.

236

trouble arose. Gradually, however, the notes of these meetings imply that Edward Cecil was usually present, and as the Irish agencies lost their independence and were transformed (usually on the death of the agent) into stores, the personal connexion became less important. Gradually the Purser influence waned. None of John Tertius Purser's nephews ever acquired his influence or power. Only three brewers outside the Guinness and Purser families were taken in between 1870 and 1880, but it was on one of these, Christopher Digges La Touche, that the mantle of John Tertius eventually fell. That is another story outside the period of the present work.

An expansion of trade of the scale experienced by the brewery required a continually changing administrative structure. A new administrative system had been evolving since 1862. It was an interesting example of the complex office organization which had replaced the earlier simple system of clerks who worked under the partners. There was an Audit Office to check all payments and receipts, and a large office called the Registry, which was the department responsible for checking and signing the accounts of each department. It also contained the work records of the brewery employees as well as keeping the records of the various pension payments. In general, the Registry appears to have been an embryonic Labour Department. In the Secretary's Department all the correspondence and invoicing, which was growing each year to monumental proportions as the surviving contents of the safes indicate, was looked after. The Secretary was George Beare, and it was his function to keep a general eye on the solvency of the customers and to bring to the attention of the firm any possibility of loss by insolvency. There was also a book-keeping department and a Cash Office, which was a sort of bank for the whole brewery, where all the wages were paid, and where the town customers paid their accounts. In 1879 the administration of the brewery was further overhauled. It was divided into eight departments: Engineering, Works, Delivery, Cooperage, Accountant's, Secretary's, Registry and Brewery Office.

The brewery had at this time enjoyed for many years a reputation of being a good employer, and the provision for tradesmen and labourers—as the skilled and unskilled workers were called—was extremely generous. Their wages were generally above those prevailing

237

in Dublin, and their security of employment was substantially greater. This was an important point at a time when unemployment often averaged ten or twelve weeks a year for the ordinary worker. The firm provided medical attendance and medicine free for its workers, and also paid for them to go to a convalescent home and to hospitals. The sick were given full wages or two-thirds of their wages if they were in hospital. There was also a death benefit which was of considerable importance because a great deal of working-class poverty at that time was attributable to lavish expenditure on funerals and the unscrupulous exploitation of death by insurance companies who solicited weekly payments which many families could ill afford to make. The brewery also provided pensions for its labourers' widows, ranging from 2*s.* to 6*s.* a week. The tradesmen had two Friendly Societies of their own to which the firm made contributions. There was one for the coopers, who were the most considerable body of tradesmen employed, and another for tradesmen such as carpenters. At this time annual holidays were unknown for the working class, and the most that they could expect was an excursion on a day off: the brewery paid £600 a year at a date somewhat later than this towards the excursion undertaken by their employees.

A flexible organization for sales was a prerequisite of the expansion. By the late eighteen-seventies the Dublin district was defined and carriage allowances abrogated. Dublin had no longer to be treated as a special market to be watched and protected. The local agencies were closely defined, presumably because their areas had been overlapping. The giving of discounts was systematized and reduced, and the agency allowances were cut. The exclusive rights of the agencies were abrogated, and porter was made available at the brewery to any customer who ordered it. Guinness's no longer absorbed transport costs, except to the stores, because the price of beer was becoming normally f.o.b. Dublin. Nevertheless, the brewery paid the carriage from any port or any railway station of all casks returned to it. This was evidently because it was cheaper to do so than continually to replace casks. The aim by this time was to open the trade and gradually to discontinue the agencies. Soon the whole of Scotland was 'open'. In England a number of places were still 'closed'—that is to say the brewery had in those areas agents through whom alone it sold. Thus, just as the tied-house arrangements made by Guinness had become redundant by about 1850, so less than thirty years later the trade was so considerable and Guinness's stout had become so familiar a product that local exclusive agents were no longer required. The stout could be sold to anybody because everybody bought it.

THE REBUILDING

The expansion of trade pressed increasingly on the brewery plant and buildings, and between 1870 and 1876 the brewhouse was almost completely reconstructed. A new building was erected containing the bins, elevators, mills and hoppers necessary for storing the malt and preparing it for brewing. The four kieves in existence in 1865 were increased to eight. The other plant necessary for brewing and fermentation was correspondingly increased, including the provision of new tuns and skimmers and five new vathouses, these last increasing the number of vats available for storage and racking from 62 to 134.

Much of this building was done on existing premises but the space available was already too small. By 1872 new ground had been acquired to the south and new stables and another vathouse erected there. A large tract of land between James's Street and the Liffey was bought in 1873, almost doubling the space available, and by 1874 a large maltings, a new cooperage, and new cask cleansing and racking sheds were being erected there. It also provided a frontage on the River Liffey from which barges could be sent to the docks where the sea-going ships were tied up. The new arrangements set the pattern for the modern brewery whereby the beer was brewed and fermented around the original premises to the south of James's Street and racked and dispatched from the new premises to the north.

These buildings were all connected by a steam narrow-gauge railway (designed by John Tertius Purser's nephew Samuel Geoghegan), a spiral tunnel being constructed to bring it down to the level necessary to run under James's Street and emerge on the lower ground to the north.

By 1869 the available water supply had become insufficient. In that year a big main was built bringing water from the River Dodder through the canal into the brewery. For about £400 a year the brewery had a complete supply of 150,000 gallons of Dodder water a day. In 1870 the brewers found that the Dodder water was

Expansion of the Brewery

unsuitable, so for a cost of £9000 to the Corporation and the Canal Company a new basin and filter-bed for the supply of canal water was built. In fact in 1870 the brewery used over 300,000 gallons a day at a cost of £800 a year. Supplies were still insufficient and in April of that year the brewery began to obtain Vartry water, which inquiry of Mountjoy Brewery had shown to be entirely suitable for brewing purposes. By 1876 the consumption was about 750,000 gallons a day at a cost of £2300 a year.

There was still a shortage of residential and office accommodation. The family had moved out of No. 1 Thomas Street by 1855 and the space was given up to offices and the accommodation of 'a resident gentleman having as far as possible the charge of the services of the various personal attendance of the Brewery Staff' with 'a number of rooms suitably furnished for the residence of such Gentlemen as may require rooms in consequence of early or late duty requiring their presence'. No. 101 James's Street was opened as a house for resident unmarried employees. By 1872 an additional block of offices had been erected in the brewery yard. Finally, by 1874 a large new office block had been put up fronting on James's Street.

All this had resulted in a considerable increase in the value of the firm's premises. In 1869 John Tertius Purser assumed that the value of the brewery was £80,000. Over the next eight years £400,000 was spent on investment in fixed plant and buildings, and of this only £110,000 was for depreciation. Thus at the most conservative estimate Guinness's spent only just less than £300,000 on new capital in the brewery in eight years, which was nearly four times its value before rebuilding.

By 1876 the brewery was again too small. In eight years sales had more than doubled. New hop stores and grain stores, and refuse, manure and offal stores were built. The boundary wall was renewed and to this end a number of pieces of property contiguous to the brewery were acquired. Further additions were made to the brewhouse and fermentation plant; but most important of all, a new brewhouse was erected (at the westerly limit of the James's Street premises) with the four kieves and ancillary plant as the nucleus of what would later become the largest brewhouse in the world.

These additions again increased the value of the brewery estate. By 1879 the land was valued at £100,000, the buildings at £200,000,

240

The Rebuilding

and the plant at a further £200,000. The total of £500,000 compared with a value in 1803 of £20,000 for the flour-mills as well as the brewery. Probably the value of the estate had risen by twenty-five times or so in eighty years during a period in which prices had on the whole fallen.

In forty years the size of the brewery had increased by over ten times; in eighty years the value of the concern's physical assets had multiplied twenty-five times. The value of the business as a going concern had increased probably by at least a hundred times. This was the result of the activities of the men whose business lives this study has sought to depict. The increasing incomes of the population had offered the Irish brewing industry prospects of a growing market. Guinness converted these prospects into realities by grasping their opportunities more rapidly and effectively than their rivals. They adjusted their methods and adapted their techniques to move with the rising tide of changing and improved economic conditions. In the wise choice of agents and managers, and in alert attention to making and selling they outpaced competitors who were less responsive to the opportunities of the time or less capable of availing themselves of these opportunities. The Guinness tradition of preoccupation with detail established an attitude towards cost control which intensified the rewards of enterprise as operations in the brewery became more complex and output increased. Internal organization was rationalized as growth rendered obsolete old and simple methods of administration. And always the ability to perceive was accompanied by the capacity to adapt.

[13]

Conclusion

Be not the first by whom the new are tried,
Nor yet the last to lay the old aside.
(*Alexander Pope, 'Essay on Criticism'.*)

A HISTORY of money-making has its own fascination. Getting and spending, the long years of accumulation, interrupted by occasional disasters and the dissipations of spendthrifts, are Balzacian themes. The first Arthur Guinness seems in his last portrait to be a keen and shrewd old Irishman, but a picture of him as the father and originator of all the success that was to come needs infinite detail—which is lacking. We know that he was intelligent, energetic and tenacious in the conduct of his business, that he was active in public affairs with a high sense of public duty—a virtue often lacking in eighteenth-century Ireland—and that he was loved by his family. We see a man riding out in his old age to his new mills at Kilmainham; we see him abhorring the 1798 rising; we see a man in a small business who moved into his country estate and surrounded himself with fine portraits and good furniture—all this is suggestive but not revealing.

The second Arthur Guinness is a man we can realize more fully. Deeply pious and affectionate, full of versatility, accomplishment and style, proud and dignified, respected by his fellow citizens and by his workpeople, he inherited a good business and left a thriving one. His decisions, informed by shrewdness and intuition, implied business techniques quite rare in his day. His son Benjamin Lee inherited a modest competence and died rich. His wealth brought him honours—Lord Mayor, Baronet, restorer of the cathedral, and the renown of a liberal benefactor. His ability, mature, self-confident, and calm, presided over a steady growth of business that became a dazzling rocket-like climb into millions of capital—the Balzacian apotheosis. A story unfolded in infinite detail, a family chronicle rich in character, measuring that character all the time against money ('I pray you to be careful in keeping your personal accounts'), showing the generosity, the jealousy, the connexions, the wit, the

242

Conclusion

charm and the courtesy that great wealth often attracts and breeds, might end on a wistful note as we look back at a picture of Lord Iveagh and King Edward VII, with their ladies, in a shooting party at Elveden, perched on a motor-car, jaunty, gay, confident—an age so soon to pass.

This is the history we might have written. We have chosen to write otherwise. Our story has been for the most part dry and technical, because an objective account of a great business's evolution in an economy whose main outlines are often misunderstood had for us a greater value. The rise from a small, poky brewhouse on the outskirts of the city of Dublin to a six-million pound joint-stock Company was more within our competence than the rise from the misty riverside at Leixlip to the ostrich feathers, the satins and the jewels of a Viceregal reception.

Looking back over our narrative we can select certain themes as dominant, and certain problems as recurrent. Looking forward, beyond our closing date, we can see them mingling with new problems barely or not at all thought of at that time. In this last chapter we take stock.

Possibly the most important point is the most elusive. It is the character of the proprietors. The Guinnesses who owned the brewery were very dissimilar, but they had some characteristics in common. 'In the management of this commercial enterprise to the minutest details of which he personally attended', wrote the contributor to the *Dictionary of National Biography* about Benjamin Lee, 'he manifested a remarkable power of organization, the effects of which were visible in the steady growth of his fortune, and in the comfortable condition and fidelity of his workmen'. This was true of all the Guinnesses who ran the brewery. It is evidenced by their constant appearance in the firm's books, noting this, ordering that, and by their clear mastery of the details of brewing and of business.

This was no narrow devotion, no obsessional love of vats and casks. Their interests were wide. The Church, of which they were all devoted sons, Dublin, the brewers' societies, charities, the Bank of Ireland for the second Arthur, Parliament for his son and grandson, all claimed their time. In these activities they showed diligence and enthusiasm. They were all devoted family men, loving not only their own children, but caring for their cousins and uncles and aunts who were often tiresome and usually hard-up. Their love and care took practical

Conclusion

forms—they managed investments, they gave legal advice, they got jobs for their relations. In every way these four Guinnesses appear to have been mature and wise men, of the type who make good fathers, and successful headmasters, bishops and judges. In their day they were the best of men—dignified, intelligent, good and intensely religious.

The brewery was usually their main concern, except perhaps for the second Arthur, but they did not lavish their fortunes on it, rejoicing in gleaming machinery while their children went barefoot. Self-indulgence—well within the limits of their incomes—appears to have been a Guinness characteristic. They bought good houses, good lands, good furniture and good pictures. They dressed well, and their women were elegant. They ate well and had many servants. In the days of affluence Lord Iveagh became famous for his high style of life, for his superb collection, for his magnificent hospitality and his shoots at Elveden—according to King George V the best in the country. His brother, Lord Ardilaun, owned great estates and great houses as well.

If their aim was to make money in order to spend it, they were cool and rational in their calculations. The brewery—especially after 1830—was the place they put their money in when its trade was good. But they always held stocks and shares in other concerns like the Bank of Ireland, and the railways, and between 1814 and 1830 a main source of income was from consols. They bought land extensively and they managed it well. The successful members of the family, too, had to look after the black sheep. One fled to the Isle of Man to escape his creditors; others emigrated. Many widows and unmarried daughters had claims on what seem to have been innumerable trusts, and when Arthur Lee Guinness withdrew to Stillorgan his father and his brother became solely responsible for them all.

The growth of the brewery, then, is due to the Guinnesses' diligence and intelligence, but not to their single-minded devotion. They always looked above and beyond James's Gate. They show no sign of genius, or of great learning, though they had a shrewd common sense and were always convinced by a clear demonstration of a case. In one respect, however, they were remarkable. They chose men wisely. There are two indispensable conditions of outstanding success in business: the leadership that provides a confident sense of direction, and the capacity to select men with the qualities of mind

EDWARD CECIL GUINNESS, 1847–1927
Later first Earl of Iveagh. At age of 35

Conclusion

and character for executing policy. Like many other masters with the faculty of choosing servants of great ability the Guinnesses themselves remained none the less masters. But they treated their staff generously and sympathetically, and never reproached them for their limitations. Their first Bristol agent, Samuel Waring, built their trade for them in Bristol. They trusted him, consulted him, relied on him and learnt a great lesson when he almost went bankrupt. Thereafter they were much more cautious in their agency business, but they never reproached Samuel Waring. Their greatest choice was the Purser family. The eldest looked after the books. The second became a partner who knew how to brew as well as they did, and possibly better, and who acted with them in their commercial arrangements. The third carried the tradition to its height, and retired wealthy and respected. There were other connexions like this. Simeon Ussher became head brewer after his father, Captain R. B. Ussher, had been chief clerk, and Simeon's son and grandson were also in the brewery for many years. Connexions of the Pursers, the Geoghegan family, at the end of our period, were others who worked hard for the Guinnesses, and there were many of more lowly rank.

This capacity for choice is seen as the remarkable thing it was in the context of the nineteenth century. Men were then often violent and unreasonable; they took to drink, they went mad, they stole and abused positions of trust far more easily than in this century of mental health and efficient accounting. Business life was more chancy; it was prone to greater swings; and while it may have been easier to climb the ladder of financial success, there was no net to catch those who fell off.

Those whom the Guinnesses had chosen were treated well. From the earliest times they appear to have paid good wages, and by the eighteen-sixties they were in the vanguard of good employers, taking an enlightened interest in their workmen's health, housing and old-age, in the welfare of their families, in the regularity of their employment and in their hours of work. For nearly a century James's Gate has given some of the best jobs in Ireland to workers of all levels of skill. All the Guinnesses seem to have subscribed to the maxim attributed to Edward Cecil: 'You can't expect to make money out of people unless you are prepared to let them make money out of you.'

Conclusion

If one man were to be singled out of so many as the main architect of the firm it would be the second Arthur. But his son, Benjamin Lee, also played a leading part. He was born in his father's house in the brewery in 1798, he went into partnership in 1820, he ran the brewery during his father's frequent absences, he presided over its meteoric rise from 1840 on, and he died a millionaire in 1868, leaving his son a baronetcy and sufficient wealth to turn it into a barony a few years later. Lord Mayor and Member of Parliament, rebuilder of St Patrick's Cathedral, philanthropist and good employer—in all his public life he was the archetypal Guinness. In his family life, too, he was successful. He was a man remarkable in his wise benevolence and in his understanding—as his errant brother, Arthur Lee Guinness, had good reason to know. He married late, at the age of 39, and left when he died two young men, his sons Arthur Edward and Edward Cecil, lavishly endowed with money and moral precept. Edward Cecil, above all, inherited his father's character and ability, and his career shows how great the similarity was.

A remarkable family, then, lay behind the growth of this business. Their circumstances, perhaps, were propitious. Beer was one of the earliest industrialized products and the Guinnesses were early industrialists. Initially they were local brewers and they rose to prominence probably about forty years after they were founded. Like the other Irish brewers the firm benefited from the relief of beer from taxation in 1796, and from the devaluation of the Irish pound from 1797 to 1815. Then, for the next fifteen years, they suffered from the deflation and from the revaluation of the Irish currency that in the interests of financial stability Arthur Guinness, as a banker, so enthusiastically supported. In 1824, however, they picked a good agent in Bristol. On the basis of this experience, and the sharp lesson of his near failure in 1837, they chose agents wisely all over Britain. They were well placed for the growth in lower-middle-class incomes in the eighteen-forties and in all incomes that marked the eighteen-fifties and eighteen-sixties. In the same way they benefited from their business associates in canal and railway companies in Ireland, and from their Irish agents, during the great period of expansion of Irish incomes after the Great Famine. In the eighteen-fifties Guinness came to dominate the Irish market. On the basis of these two successes—Ireland and England—they came, by the eighteen-seventies, to dominate Dublin.

246

Conclusion

In all this their wisdom appears to have consisted in making good beer, and then choosing capable agents to sell it. They were hardly at all concerned with retailing, and they retreated quickly from any direct involvement in wholesaling as such, although their agents worked on a commission basis and were fairly closely controlled by the firm. The relative failure of the Liverpool connexion, based in part on a blood-relationship, at the same time as the Bristol agency succeeded so brilliantly, seems to have been a lesson well learned. The 1837 crisis taught them, too, never to extend credit to any great extent. This left them with their circulating capital to spend on the brewery.

The technical superiority of the brewery appears to date from Benjamin Lee's time, or possibly from the time that Edward Cecil took over at James's Gate. It seems, almost certainly, to have followed rather than to have preceded the great increase in sales. The continual increase in output seems to have left them always a little breathless; the brewery was always too small, and its haphazard rebuilding while they continually did a bigger trade seems to suggest that the legend of great technical skill and foresight is based more on *post hoc* reasoning than on evidence.

If high ability is to be discerned, then, it is less in the internal organization of the brewery than in the arrangement of its commercial activities, in the way that the firm responded to market trends and opportunities and learnt rapidly from experience. At first it was a local brewery in the maritime sector of the Irish economy. Then it took advantage of the sea-routes to Bristol and Liverpool and the rise in artisans' incomes in England and Scotland that accompanied the building of the railways. After the Great Famine the use of money spread like a tide through a depopulated Ireland whose remaining inhabitants had higher incomes than ever before. Guinness's was the first business to conquer this market. Within twenty years after the Great Famine there was hardly a shop without a stock of porter. Then Dublin itself succumbed. It is this conquest of the opportunities given by the rising incomes of the people first in England then in Ireland that is the great achievement of the commercial policies of the firm.

In a different, more subtle way, too, good management is to be discerned. There is a notable absence of religious, political or industrial trouble in the history of the firm. The O'Connell boycott and the

247

Conclusion

rivalries with other breweries on the Grand Canal are almost the only disturbing incidents in a history full, otherwise, of laudatory comments. In a troubled country, and a troubled century the Guinnesses never hid their strong allegiance to the Union and to the Church of Ireland, and they never suffered from this allegiance. They never suffered because they were scrupulously fair and extremely generous to those who would otherwise have been their opponents. They were supporters of Catholic emancipation, and in a sense they regarded their wealth as a trust from God; they developed agriculture, they improved their city and they advanced the welfare of their workers and helped their poorer neighbours.

They were outstandingly generous in paying their clerks and brewers, and their senior employees, by the end of the century, were educated gentlemen living like senior officials of the Indian Civil Service; high salaries gave them lavish quarters, membership of the Kildare Street Club, yachting at Kingstown, hunting and coursing, and good marriages. The workmen, too, were the aristocracy of the Dublin working class. Secure in their employment, they were given good wages, double that of country labourers and several shillings higher than that generally paid in Dublin; after the expansion of the brewery under Benjamin Lee Guinness they got medical treatment and benefits, pensions and family care, while some of them were given better housing. Guinness achieved in Ireland a reputation equal to that of the great Quaker proprietors in England, and this reputation, disinterested and benevolent in origin, paid dividends in social and political peace and public favour.

Their philanthropy as a family was remarkable. St Stephen's Green, the Guinness Trust, donations to hundreds of charities and good works greatly overshadowed their activities as politicians who were rowing against the nationalist and popular tide. Edward Cecil Guinness's defeat in the Dublin election of 1885 went almost unnoticed in the general applause at his later elevation to the peerage. They were not alone among British industrialists in the good use they made of their wealth, for many others did as much as they did, nor was their generosity at the cost of their own high standards of living, but they were rare in Ireland both because of their riches and of their benevolence.

The formation of the public company ten years after Sir Arthur's withdrawal from the partnership coincided with another change in

Conclusion

the administration of the business. The brewers were not Guinnesses, nor were they Pursers. The Board had its share of Guinnesses, and Sir Edward Cecil and Claude Guinness dominated the firm, but Purser was gone and other men came in. By the turn of the century the intimate day-to-day control of the brewery was passing into other hands—hands trained in the brewery, but not born into it. This change in administration we have seen in embryonic form in the emergence of a complex managerial structure to control a big concern. Its fruits, however, were reaped many years later when the brewery became more of a constitutional monarchy and less the domain of its lord.

The age into which the Company moved was more radical, more socialist, more political. Its wealthy shareholders spent more time at Westminster; the new age gave the brewery new problems. Trades Unions grew up. State social services were already imitating the brewery's social services. Above all, the new age was more technical and complicated. Brewing was put on a scientific basis, so the firm had to recruit graduate scientists. A big business required a complex administrative structure. This in itself posed a whole series of new problems.

The conditions of the market were also changing. Within twenty years the working-class consumption of beer in Britain was at its height and thereafter the expansion of one firm's sales often meant the contraction of another's. The Guinness flotation touched off a 'brewing mania', dozens and then hundreds of brewing companies were founded on the amalgamations of old firms, vigorous pushing of sales took place, and above all the competitive buying of public houses for the exclusive retailing of the brewer's own beers. In all this Guinness's had a very complicated route to follow. They owned no licensed houses, and they sold their product in those of the other brewers. Perhaps their greatest success in the period after the founding of the public company was in surviving this threat.

Their stronghold was Ireland where they had sold by far the greater part of the beer since their conquest of the countryside in the eighteen-sixties and of Dublin in the eighteen-seventies. There, at least, they were secure so long as they repulsed the invaders from England. In the long run, however, they were threatened by less tangible but greater dangers. The population of Ireland dwindled every year and they had to sell more beer to fewer people. The Great Famine's

Conclusion

dark shadow fell forward into the twentieth century. Not only that, but the year 1886 was almost the last year that Parnell's solution of the Irish political problem might have been successful. Thereafter, for thirty-five years of intense struggle, breaking out at times into violence, and ending in a tragic civil war, Ireland had to find its own path to nationhood. Few situations are more dangerous than to come to be regarded as a wealthy alien in a land inflamed by nationalist passion, and yet at the end of thirty-five years the firm remained where it had been for a century and a half, and the Unionist family were as respected as ever.

In this book we have shown the foundations, or as much of them as we have been able to uncover. In our last chapter we have described the beginning of the years of success. There remains to be told the story of the years of triumph. Essentially, however, business history consists in the surmounting of obstacles, for those who succumb rarely leave trace.

GLOSSARY OF SCIENTIFIC AND
TECHNICAL TERMS

ALE AND BEER Fermented drinks made from malted barley. The original distinction between ale and beer was that ale was brewed without hops, and beer with hops. This distinction has, however, long been lost and by the eighteenth century 'beer' and 'ale' were being popularly used to denote such drinks with little or no colour, as opposed to 'stout' and 'porter' which were black due to additions of roasted malt or caramel. 'Beer' as used by the brewer, however, denoted the whole class of fermented drinks made from malted barley, including 'stout' and 'porter'.

BARM Yeast multiplies itself many times during the fermentation. The surplus removed during the cleansing process is called barm and consists of a suspension of the yeast in beer. A part of the barm may be used as store yeast, for pitching a subsequent brewing. The rest is separated, by some filtration process, into its constituent parts of yeast and barm beer, the yeast then being disposed of as a by-product and the barm beer being added to the current racking.

BARREL In Guinness's brewery a cask of 32 imperial gallons was used until 1881 (elsewhere 36 gallons). There was also an Irish barrel of 42 Irish gallons which equalled 32·96 imperial gallons. The barrel is a unit of measurement of weight of barley and malt (224 lb. for barley and 168 lb. for malt) as well.

BREWING The ground malt is mixed with hot water and this mixture allowed to stand for about an hour. During this time the reactive system inside the malt corn converts most of its starch into malt sugar. Further additions of hot water complete the extraction and the resulting 'wort' is separated from the mash and boiled with hops. The 'hopped wort' is then cooled to atmospheric temperature and yeast added. Yeast is a living organism (a rudimentary plant) which secretes a reactive system capable of converting malt sugar into alcohol and carbon dioxide. When the fermentation has proceeded to the desired extent the yeast is allowed to separate itself from the beer (or by a more modern technique skimmed off the surface of the beer). Further clarification is effected by addition of preparations of isinglass, and finally the beer is prepared for trade by maturation in vats, during which time the small amount of yeast left in the beer will continue to ferment, producing the characteristic foam when the beer is draughted from the cask, or more quickly by adding a small proportion of wort which has just begun to ferment.

BUSHEL A unit of measurement for barley and malt (56 lb. for barley and 42 lb. for malt).

251

Glossary

CAPITAL/OUTPUT RATIO   The relationship between the total capital employed and the value of a given output. An industry with a high capital/output ratio uses far more fixed capital and pays much less in total wage payments than an industry with a low capital/output ratio.

CLEANSING   The removal of yeast from the beer when the main fermentation is over.

COOLER   The vessel to which the hot wort is run after the hops have been separated. As its name implies, it was originally a shallow vessel in which the wort was allowed to cool before the yeast was added; but this function has long since been made unnecessary by the use of refrigeration machinery, and the cooler is now merely a storage vessel for hot wort between hopback and the wort refrigerators.

COPPER   The vessel in which the wort is boiled with hops.

DASH   The addition of hot liquor to the kieve after the stronger wort produced by the mashes has been run off. The invention of the sparge arm early in the nineteenth century made it possible to replace the discrete quantities of hot liquor added in the dashes, by a continuous 'sparging' which spread the hot liquor evenly over the top of the goods in the kieve.

EXTRACT   The total amount of dissolved matter produced from a given quantity of malt, this being measured by the excess weight of a given volume of wort over the weight of an equal volume of water.

FERMENTATION   The conversion of the wort sugars into alcohol and carbon dioxide caused by a complex series of chemical reactions set up by various substances secreted by yeast.

FININGS   Jelly-like material added to the beer before racking which, falling to the bottom of the vat, drags down floating particles so that the beer racked is clear and bright. Traditionally a mixture of isinglass (prepared from the dried swimming bladder of certain large tropical fish) and old beer.

FIRKIN   In Guinness's brewery a cask of 8 gallons (elsewhere 9 gallons).

GOODS   The ground mixture of malt and roast malt in the kieve.

HOGSHEAD   In Guinness's brewery a cask of 52 gallons (elsewhere 54 gallons).

HOPBACK   The vessel in which the wort is separated from the hops after boiling. It contains a false bottom of slotted plates through which the wort passes leaving the spent hops behind.

INVESTMENT   The creation of fixed capital goods and the building up of stocks.

KIEVE   The vessel in which the goods are mashed and sparged. It contains a false bottom of slotted plates through which the wort passes, leaving the goods behind for further mashing and sparging. It contains also the 'carriage', a set of rakes which move round the kieve as they revolve on a horizontal axis, mixing the goods and the liquor during the mash; and the 'sparge arm', a pipe containing small holes which

252

Glossary

rotates about the centre of the kieve sprinkling the hot liquor over the surface of the goods during sparging.

KILDERKIN   In Guinness's brewery a cask of 16 gallons (elsewhere 18 gallons).

LIQUOR   Water used in the brewing process.

MALTING   The use of barley for brewing depends upon the ability of the maltster to treat it so that the hard woody structure of the barley corn is dissolved away making the starch, of which the corn mainly consists, readily available to the action of the hot water which will be poured over the ground malt in the first stage of the brewing process. This occurs in nature when the barley corn germinates in the field, together with the production within the corn of a reactive system which can transform the starch into sugar so as to provide food for the infant plant. The art of the maltster is to effect these changes under controlled conditions in his malthouse; and to this end the ripe barley is harvested and kept dry during storage until the maltster is ready to convert it into malt. This he does by first immersing it in water and then spreading it out on the malt floor, regulating its temperature by thinning or thickening the layer until the barley has germinated to the right extent to effect the changes set out above. Finally, the 'green malt' is heated on a kiln over a coal fire so as to stop any further germination and make the malt safe against deterioration during storage.

MASH TUN   This term is the same as 'kieve' which was peculiar to Irish breweries. It is still used in Guinness's brewery.

MASHING   The mixing of ground malt with hot liquor at a suitable temperature, either in the kieve by adding hot liquor to the dry ground malt on the floor of the kieve, or (a more modern method introduced into Guinness's brewery in 1863) by making the mixture outside the kieve in a Steele's masher, in which an upward flow of hot liquor meets the ground malt as it falls from the hopper, and from which the mixture is run into the kieve (the 'carriage' being used in both cases). A second mash is subsequently made in the kieve by adding a further quantity of mashing liquor to the goods after the sweet wort from the first mash has been run off.

NET INVESTMENT   Investment after allowing for the replacement of worn-out capital and used-up stocks.

ORIGINAL GRAVITY   The strength of the wort before fermentation measured by the excess weight of a given volume of wort over the weight of an equal volume of water.

PITCHING   The addition of yeast from a previous brewing to the cooled hopped wort.

PORTER   The eighteenth-century term for a beer made from malt and roast malt, so used because it had become popular with London porters.

PROPENSITY TO CONSUME   The proportion of income spent by the receiver on consumption goods.

PROPENSITY TO IMPORT   The proportion of national income spent by a country on imports.

253

Glossary

QUARTER   A unit of measurement for barley and malt containing eight bushels.

RACKING   Filling the beer into cask for trade.

SKIMMER   The vessel in which the yeast is removed from beer after the main fermentation. (Also called 'round' or 'ponto'.)

SPARGING   The addition of hot liquor to the goods subsequent to the mashes (see 'dash' and 'kieve'). Also the liquor used for this purpose.

STOUT   A stronger porter. First used in Guinness's brewery at the beginning of the nineteenth century in the sense of 'a stouter Porter'.

TUN   More fully, 'fermenting tun', the vessel in which the main fermentation takes place after yeast has been added to the cooled wort.

TUNNAGE   The removal of the beer from tun to skimmer towards the end of fermentation.

VAT   A vessel in which the beer is stored (and where necessary matured) before going out into trade.

VINOSITY   An obsolete term presumably referring to the wine-like flavours which develop in beer after long storage.

WORT   The liquid run from the kieve after the solution of various constituents of malt (mainly sugars) in the mashing and sparging liquors. It is called 'sweet wort' before boiling with hops and 'hopped wort' thereafter.

YEAST   A microscopic unicellular plant which secretes various substances which are able to turn the wort sugars into alcohol and carbon dioxide. Brewers' yeast has the particular properties which make it easy to handle in the brewing process.

LIST OF REFERENCES

ORIGINAL SOURCES

In the breweries

The ST JAMES GATE records divide themselves into three groups: material in the strong room off the Chairman's room; material in the basement underneath the Cash Office and the Post Office; material elsewhere in the brewery.

The strong room contains a large number of manuscript books, mostly personal account-books of members of the Guinness family from the second Arthur to the first Earl of Iveagh. They vary greatly in the degree of their concern with brewery or purely personal finance. Some of them concern both. There is also a long run of brewery ledgers, beginning in 1791–2.

The strong room contains about a thousand letters. They deal with a wide variety of subjects and though they cover the whole nineteenth century they are most numerous between 1840 and 1870. Many of them are mainly of family interest, but throw light upon the conditions of life in the firm at the time.

There is a series of volumes called 'Brewery Memoranda' entered up nearly at the times to which they refer, and giving much information about equipment, buildings, etc. There is a volume for 1869, one for 1875, and a series complete till 1885, except 1883 which is missing.

There are a few letter-books, which are extremely badly preserved.

There are some 'worked-over' or secondary records, such as the 'Brewery Annals', a manuscript book which purports to begin in 1800 and continue to the present day, but was in fact retrospectively entered up for more than half of the period. The late Henry Seymour Guinness's two typescript books of notes for the *Brewery Guidebook* are also of secondary authority, but these secondary sources do occasionally contain information not available in primary records, which had to be taken on trust.

The basement contains a prodigious accumulation of books and papers, the latter in boxes and chests. The books include letter-books which amplify those in the strong room, but are similarly disappointing in scope; Specie Books and Charges Ledgers, which are epitomized in the Yearly Ledgers in the strong room; Brewers' Calculation Books from 1814 to 1873; personal account books similar to those in the strong room; and a miscellaneous collection of books bearing on the day-to-day running of the brewery.

There are enormous numbers of papers including: papers relating to the English Agencies; papers relating to the Irish Stores and Agencies; receipts, vouchers and dockets and bills of lading, returned cheques and stubs, mainly of the first Lord Iveagh; inter-departmental memoranda,

255

References

and memoranda which are the raw material of the Brewery Memorandum Books in the strong room; books and papers relating to the 1869 Dublin elections (Sir Arthur Edward Guinness); over 4000 letters; appeals to Sir Benjamin Lee Guinness for charities; Acts of Parliament, Bills, insurance policies and legal documents of the early nineteenth century—bonds, indentures, leases touching real estate and business relations; advertising folders mainly about brewing machinery of the period 1855–70; bank correspondence contemporaneous with the retirement of Sir Arthur Guinness from the business; miscellaneous small books.

The material at PARK ROYAL includes the Guild records which relate to the Dublin Guilds of Smiths and Chandlers and the Dublin Guild of Brewers. It seems that the Smiths' records were acquired because early members of the Guinness family engaged in goldbeating and ironmongery. The reason for the inclusion of the Chandlers' does not appear.

The Brewers' Guild records are less informative than might be wished. They are very incomplete, and it is evident that the official regulation that all active brewers must be members of the Guild was widely ignored.

There is also to be found the manuscript of *The Family of Guinness* by H. S. Guinness, which is mainly of genealogical interest but contains also some correspondence beginning in 1798. These letters appear to have been kept for the light they throw on interesting events or periods—the 1798 rising, the award of a peerage to Edward Cecil Guinness, and the like. Part of these typescript volumes is the basis of the printed *Family of Guinness* by the same author. *The Guinness Family* in two volumes by H. S. Guinness and Brian Guinness is also indispensable as a guide to the convoluted family pedigree.

The notes on various members of the family are mainly excerpts from original documents. The most important files are those of Richard Guinness of Celbridge; Richard Guinness of Leixlip, brewer; the first Arthur Guinness; the second Arthur Guinness; Benjamin Guinness; William Lunell Guinness; Hosea Guinness and his family; William Smythe Lee Grattan Guinness; Benjamin Lee Guinness; and those of various families intermarried with them, notably the Darley and Smyth families. There are also the calendar of Lord Iveagh's collection of family papers and records, and the calendar of the Plunket papers.

Outside the breweries

Anglesey papers in the Northern Ireland Public Record Office, Belfast.
British Museum Manuscripts.
British Parliamentary papers.
Calendar of the Ancient Records of Dublin, (ed.) Gilbert (Dublin).
Calendar of State Papers (Ireland).
Corporation of Dublin: Reports and minutes of correspondence.
Customs Ledgers of Imports and Exports (Ireland) 1698–1829, in the Public Record Office, London.

References

Dictionary of National Biography.
Directories for Dublin, London, Belfast, Manchester, Bristol, Liverpool and Glasgow.
Dublin Custom House Records of Exports and Imports for Ireland 1764–1823 (Abstracts).
Foster papers in the Northern Ireland Public Record Office, Belfast.
Grand Canal Company papers at Canal House, Dublin.
Historical Manuscripts Commission, Dublin: Reports.
Journals of the House of Commons.
Journals of the Irish House of Commons.
Massereene papers in the Northern Ireland Public Record Office, Belfast.
Peel papers in the British Museum.
Registry of Deeds, Dublin: papers.

OTHER PRINTED SOURCES

A BREWER OF EXTENSIVE PRACTICE. *The Complete Brewer* (Dublin, 1766).
AGRICOLA. *Letters to the Rt Hon. the Chancellor of the Exchequer* (Dublin, 1791).
ASHTON, T. S. *The Industrial Revolution 1780–1830* (London, 1948).
BERESFORD, W. *The Correspondence of the Rt Hon. John Beresford, Illustrating the last thirty years of the Irish Parliament, selected from his original papers, and edited, with notes, by his grandson, the Rt Hon. W. Beresford*, 2 vols. (London, 1854).
CARUS-WILSON, E. M. (ed.). *Essays in Economic History* (London, 1954).
CLAPHAM, J. H. *The Economic History of Modern Britain*, 2nd ed. (Cambridge 1930).
COMBRUNE, MICHAEL. *The Theory and Practice of Brewing* (London, 1762).
CONNELL, K. H. *The Population of Ireland 1750–1845* (Oxford, 1950).
COOK, P. LESLEY (ed.). *Effects of Mergers* (London, 1958).
COYNE, W. P. (ed.). *Ireland, Industrial and Agricultural* (Dublin, 1902).
CRAIG, M. J. *Dublin 1660–1860, A Social and Architectural History* (London, 1952).
DYOTT, WM. *Diary 1781–1845* (London, 1907).
EDEN, Sir F. M. *State of the Poor* (London, 1797; reprinted, abridged, London, 1928).
EDWARDS, R. D. and T. D. WILLIAMS (eds.). *The Great Famine* (Dublin, 1959).
FETTER, F. W. *The Irish Pound* (London, 1955).
FITZPATRICK, W. J. (ed.). *Correspondence of Daniel O'Connell, the Liberator* (London, 1888).
FOSTER, T. CAMPBELL. *Letters on the Condition of the People of Ireland* (London, 1846).
GRAY, MALCOLM. *The Highland Economy, 1750–1850* (Edinburgh, 1957).
HALL, F. G. *History of the Bank of Ireland* (Dublin, 1949).
HOBSBAWM, E. J. 'The British Standard of Living 1790–1850', *Economic History Review*, 2nd series, vol. x, no. 1.

References

KERR, BARBARA M. 'Irish Seasonal Migration to Great Britain, 1800–1838', *Irish Historical Studies*, vol. III (1942–3).

KINGTON, JOHN BARNETT. *Trade of Bristol by a Burgess* (Bristol, 1834).

LATIMER, JOHN. *The Annals of Bristol* (Bristol, 1887).

MACARTHUR, Sir WILLIAM. 'The Medical History of the Famine' in Edwards and Williams (eds.). *The Great Famine*.

MACDONAGH, O. 'Irish Overseas Emigration During the Famine' in Edwards and Williams (eds.). *The Great Famine*.

MCDOWELL, R. B. *Public Opinion and Government Policy in Ireland 1801–1846* (London, 1952).

MATHIAS, P. *The Brewing Industry in England 1700–1830* (Cambridge, 1959).

MEASOM, GEORGE S. *Official Illustrated Guide to Midland Great Western, Great Southern and Western and Dublin and Drogheda Railway* (London, 1866).

MOORE, THOMAS. *Memoirs, Journal and Correspondence*, ed. by Lord John Russell (London, 1853–6).

MOREWOOD, SAMUEL. *A Philosophical and Statistical History of the Inventions and Customs of Ancient and Modern Nations in the Manufacture and Use of Inebriating Liquors* (Dublin, 1838).

NASSAU SENIOR. *Journals, Conversations and Essays Relating to Ireland* (London, 1868).

NOWLAN, KEVIN. 'The Political Background' in Edwards and Williams (eds.). *The Great Famine*.

O'BRIEN, GEORGE. *The Economic History of Ireland in the Seventeenth Century* (London and Dublin, 1919).

—— *The Economic History of Ireland in the Eighteenth Century* (London and Dublin, 1918).

—— *The Economic History of Ireland, From the Union to the Famine* (London, 1921).

O'NEILL, T. P. 'The Organisation and Administration of Relief' in Edwards and Williams (eds.). *The Great Famine*.

PEEL, Sir ROBERT, Bart. *Memoirs, published by Lord Mahon and the Rt Hon. Edwd. Cardwell, M.P. 1828–1846* (London, 1856).

POSTAN, M. M. 'The Rise of a Money Economy' in Carus-Wilson (ed.). *Essays in Economic History*.

ROSTOW, W. W. *British Economy of the Nineteenth Century* (Oxford, 1948).

SHANNON, H. A. 'The Coming of General Limited Liability' in Carus-Wilson (ed.). *Essays in Economic History*.

SILBERLING, N. J. 'British Prices and Business Cycles, 1779–1850', *Review of Economic Statistics* (October, 1923), Prelim. vol. V, suppl. 2.

SMITH, ADAM. *Wealth of Nations*.

STANIHURST, RICHARD. 'Description of Dublin', *History of Ireland* (London, 1577).

TIZARD, W. L. *The Theory and Practice of Brewing*, illustrated 2nd ed. (London, 1846).

TOOKE, T., NEWMARCH, J. J. and W. *A History of Prices and of the State of the Circulation During the Years 1793–1856* (London, 1838–57).

References

VAIZEY, JOHN. 'The Brewing Industry' in Cook (ed.). *Effects of Mergers.*
—— *The Brewing Industry 1886–1951* (London, 1960).
Victoria History of the County of Gloucester (London, 1907).
WAKEFIELD, EDWARD. *An Account of Ireland, Statistical and Political* (London, 1812).
YOUNG, ARTHUR. *Tour in Ireland*, vol. II.
Historical Manuscripts Commission, Fourteenth Report, App. Part V, vol. II (London, 1894).
Home Office Papers, Col. 1766–69. Sec. V, 436.
Second Report of the Association for the Suppression of Mendicity in Dublin (Dublin, 1820).

PARLIAMENTARY PAPERS

1810–11 (222), vol. V, *Petition of Dublin, Cork and Waterford Brewers.*
1816 (436), vol. IX, *Report from the Select Committee on Illicit Distillation in Ireland.*
1818 (399), vol. III, *Report from the Select Committee on Public Breweries.*
1819 (409), vol. VIII, *Second Report from the House of Commons Select Committee on the State of Disease, and Condition of the Labouring Poor, in Ireland.*
1823 (561), vol. VI, *Report from the Select Committee on the Employment of the Poor in Ireland.*
1826–7 (245), vol. VI, *Report from the Select Committee of the House of Lords to Inquire into the State of the Circulation of Promissory Notes under the Value of £5 in Scotland and Ireland.*
1828 (440), vol. XVIII, *Exports of Beer 1809–1828.*
1831 (60), vol. XVII.
1835 (17), vol. XXXI, *15th Report of the Commission of Excise Inquiry.*
1842 (338), vol. XIV, *Report from the Select Committee on the Spirit Trade (Ireland).*
1868–9 [4204], vol. XXVI, *First Report for the Irish Government on the History of the Landlord and Tenant Question in Ireland.*
1868–9 [4204], vol. XXVI, *Second Report.*
1881 (c. 2778–II), vol. XVI, *Preliminary Report of the Assistant Commissioners for Ireland to the Royal Commission on Agriculture.*
1882 (249), vol. XI, *First Report from the Select Committee of the House of Lords on Land Law (Ireland).*
1882 (249), vol. XI, *Second Report.*

NEWSPAPERS AND JOURNALS

Bristol Mercury.
Cox's Irish Magazine.
Daily Express.
Dublin Evening Post.
Dublin Gazette.
The Engineer.
Faulkner's Dublin Journal.

Felix Farley's Bristol Journal.
Freeman's Journal.
Gore's General Advertiser.
Milesian Magazine.
The Pilot.
Saunders' News-Letter.
The Times.

APPENDIX

SALES OF GUINNESS, 1800–76
(Bulk barrels of 36 gallons)

Year	Barrels	Year	Barrels	Year	Barrels
1800	10,026	1826	34,270	1852	105,082
1801	14,533	1827	33,864	1853	109,719
1802	23,126	1828	42,384	1854	110,080
1803	22,479	1829	43,066	1855	116,424
1804	25,144	1830	40,158	1856	131,088
1805	27,660	1831	53,965	1857	156,658
1806	28,886	1832	56,977	1858	162,747
1807	29,520	1833	68,357	1859	184,179
1808	39,790	1834	80,984	1860	198,478
1809	61,872	1835	76,578	1861	234,769
1810	56,988	1836	74,010	1862	241,195
1811	48,160	1837	71,519	1863	263,149
1812	54,232	1838	73,192	1864	296,957
1813	65,009	1839	87,322	1865	331,176
1814	66,017	1840	79,924	1866	322,477
1815	66,672	1841	73,369	1867	310,198
1816	56,164	1842	68,178	1868	350,411
1817	50,535	1843	68,664	1869	393,598
1818	36,374	1844	74,249	1870	423,080
1819	32,569	1845	81,441	1871	475,961
1820	27,374	1846	100,895	1872	540,535
1821	30,519	1847	95,750	1873	559,595
1822	30,922	1848	89,563	1874	631,665
1823	27,185	1849	94,278	1875	725,791
1824	27,987	1850	100,111	1876	778,597
1825	31,309	1851	106,369		

INDEX

Index

Banker, family, second Arthur Guinness as, 105, 107, 125
Banking system in Ireland, 24
Banks, Irish: after Great Famine, 175; connexion with London, 18; increase in branches 1848–58, 170; system of, 24
Barclay, Liverpool brewer, 138
Barclay, Perkins' Extra Stout, 131
Barclay, Robert, report to House of Lords, 56–7
Barley, 127, 129, 221–2; roast, 150
Barlow, John, Governor of Bank of Ireland, 178
Barm, 251; barm beer, 220; sale of, 130
Barrel, 251
Barrett, James, Guinness agent at Cork, 7, 208–13
Barrow-in-Furness, one of original Guinness agencies in England, 231
Bass, Burton-on-Trent, 82: objection to Guinness connexion of their agent in Cork, 209
Bath Pale Beer and Porter Brewery, 131
Beamish and Crawford, Cork brewers: agent complains that country rivals evade tax, 83; Cork Porter Brewers, 89–90; open agency in Liverpool, 139; sell barley to Guinness, 129; trade twice Guinness trade 1826, 132
Beare, G. H., 215–16, 236–7
Beaumont, Co. Dublin, 5, 71, 74, 104, 113
Beaver, Sir Hugh
Beckett, Professor James E., viii
Beer, 251; bounty on, 151 n.; characteristics of Guinness's, 150–3; determinants of its characteristics, 149; English, superiority and cheapness, 43; exports of Irish after 1795, 80–1; imports to Ireland in eighteenth century, 52–3; nature of Irish market, 47; quality of Dublin, 40; quality of Guinness's, 6; quality of Irish, 46; revenue from Irish, 54; strength of Guinness's, 219; taste for turns from whiskey, 198; types of, 38–40 *See also* Keeping Beer
Beer duties: abolition of excise in 1795, 67; significance of abolition, 68
Beer, small, restriction on brewing, 55
Beerhouse Act 1830, 102
Belfast, 202–3; decline in number of breweries after 1850, 98
Belfast, Guinness agency: being supplied 1821, 124; terms of Guinness's trade with 1849, 206; trade in 1868, 211 n.; trade in 1874, 213 n.
Belfast Porter and Strong Ale, 138

Bentinck, Lord George, and Great Famine, 161, 163
Beresford, Alderman J. C., Lord Mayor of Dublin: Brewers' Guild support in election, 66; Guinness swear affidavit before, 1814, 160
Beresford, John, 65–6; as Chancellor of the Exchequer, 58; as Commissioner of the Revenue, 59
Berkeley Square, London, no. 5, 188
Berry, Francis, Director of Grand Canal Company, 79
Berry, Thomas—also Berry & Co., Guinness agencies Ballinasloe and Shannon Harbour, 202–5
Bethesda Chapel, Dublin, 5, 103
Bewley and Nevill, Guinness agents at Liverpool 1826, 119, 138–9
Bibby's Dublin Porter, 138
Blackburn, one of original Guinness agencies in Britain, 231
Blackburne, Thomas, Guinness agent in Liverpool, 147
Blight in 1845–6 and 1848, *see* Potato
'Blue Last', The, Shoreditch, London, 39
Bodleian Library, Oxford, viii
Bolton, one of original Guinness agencies in Britain, 231
Book-keeping department, James's Gate, 237
Bottle, sales in, England, 231
Boulton and Watt, engine-makers, suppliers of first steam-engine to James's Gate 1809, 154 n.
Bounties on corn sold in Dublin, 41
Bounty: on beer, 151 n., on British beer exports, 50
Boursiquot, Dionysius Lardner (also Boucicault, Dion), 234. *See also*, Morton, Lee
Boycott, O'Connell, 247
Boyle, Guinness agency, 123
Boyle, Samuel, Guinness agent in Belfast, 202–3
Bradford Strong Beer and Porter, 131
Brenan, Charles, and Phoenix Brewery, 91
Brenan, John: and O'Connell's Brewery, 91; his reflexions on, 92; partner in brewery in Kilkenny, 94
Brenan, Rice & Co., sign Dublin Brewers' Agreement 1859, 208
Brennan, Dr, 143
Brewers, Cork, decline of, 209
Brewers, Dublin: Agreement 1859, 207; fall in number after 1869, 215; Guinness dominant, 213; Guinness leading by 1810, 80; mergers in late nineteenth

Index

Brewers (cont.)
century, 199; Price Agreement ended, 210; regulate prices and allowances, 213; Resolution 1831, 98; separate category of management at James's Gate, 233–6; social status, 37–8
Brewers, Irish: competitive position, 2; growth in Maritime Economy after Great Famine, 198; rivals to Guinness, 89
Brewers, London, 3; compete in Dublin, 55
Brewers' Associations and competition, 98–101
Brewers' Corporation or Guild, 38; its activities, 45; Dublin, as political force, 57; first Arthur Guinness, Master 1767, 71; first Arthur Guinness receives silver salver, 104; Grattan and, 58; petitions to Parliament, 46; succeeded by associations of brewers, 98; and tied houses, 48
Breweries, commercial: fall in numbers after 1838, 80; fall in numbers after Great Famine, 201; fall in numbers after 1850, 78; numbers large relative to total output, 79
Brewers' Druggists, 158
Brewery Office, James's Gate, 237
Brewhouse, James's Gate, reconstructed 1870–6, 239
Brewing, 251; art of, 149; change in structure of industry in nineteenth century, 78; commercial advantages, 40; connexions with agriculture, 41; in Dublin in eighteenth century, 37–8; industry, location, 40–2; Guinness's reasons for concentration on, 225–7, 231; legislation affecting, 38; organization, 45; private (domestic), 78, 131; process at James's Gate, 154–7, 219–21; technique, 42–4. See also Output and Specialization
Brewing, capital/output ratio of, 17
'Brewing Industry', 226 n.
Bristol: agent's crisis in 1837, 133; Guinness agency there in 1824, 119; Guinness's trade with 1868, 211 n.; original venue of Guinness's expansion, 130–4
Bristol Central Library, viii
Bristol Journal, 145
Bristol Mercury, 132
Bristol Port records, 80, 123
Bristol Trade Directory, 1825, 132
British Economy of the Nineteenth Century, 33 n., 224 n.
British Museum, viii
'British Prices and Business Cycles, 1779–1850', 29 n.

'British Standard of Living 1790–1850', 33 n.
Brittan, S., viii
Brophy, distiller, 48
'Browning Malt', improved method 1815, 153
Burke, Arthur, 235
Burke, The Reverend John, 104
Burke, John, 235
Burton Ale, 132, 138, 140
Bush and Ware, London hop merchants, 130
Bushel, 251
Business ability lacking in Ireland in nineteenth century, 174
Butt, Isaac, presses Edward Cecil Guinness to stand for Parliament, 187
By-products: barm beer, 220; yeast, 220
Byrne, Edward, Guinness agent at Carlow, 203
Byrne, John: purchases Anchor Brewery, Dublin, 92; supports Guinness, 143
Byrne and McNulty, Dublin brewers, 100

Cairnes, brewer, Drogheda, 232
Cairnes, William, founded Drogheda Brewery, 97
Cambridge University Library, viii
Campbell, Andrew, 39
Canals, 5: basis of Guinness's second great expansion, 141; Circular Road, 23; Grand, 22–3, 79, 94; Royal, 22–3; traffic on, 79, 94, 201–2
Capital/output ratio, 17, 168, 224, 252
Capital: export of, 15, 164; Guinness possibly short of after 1815, 124, 126; imports into Ireland, 28; movement, 27; supply of, 13
Caramelization of malt, 153
Carbon-dioxide, 251, 254
Cardwell, Rt Hon. Edward, M.P., 9
Carlow: Guinness agency there in 1812, 124; trade in 1874, 213 n.
Carnarvon, first Arthur Guinness considers setting up brewery there, 55
'Carriage', 252–3
Carrick, D., viii
Carrick-on-Shannon, Guinness agency, 210; trade in 1868, 211 n.; trade in 1874, 213 n.
Carus-Wilson, E. M., 28 n., 184 n.
Casey's Brewery, Drogheda, 97
Cash Economy, 9–10, 12
Cash Office, James's Gate, 237
Casks: carriage paid by Guinness from any port or railway station, 238; costs of, 228;

263

Index

Index

Cox attacks the Guinnesses on alleged use of adulterants, 158
Cox's Irish Magazine, 143
Coyne, W. P., 92 n.
Craig, Dr M. J., vii, 71 n., 182 n.
Credit: extension of by Guinness, 203; growth of in Ireland during Great Famine, 163
Creywell Brewery, New Ross: established, 94; history, 96
Crop, failure of potato during Great Famine, 162
Crosbie, Mathew, Dublin publican, tied house agreement with Guinness, 141
Culture, Gaelic, 10
Curragh, Co. Kildare, 208
Currency: effect of revaluation, 36; effect of sound currency on economic growth, 31–2; relationship between Irish and English, 29
Current Double Stout, Guinness's, 219
Customers, Guinness's allowances to, 207–8; Guinness's terms to, 127
Cyriax, G., viii

Daily Express, 181
D'Arcy, Dublin brewer: expands export trade 1855–68, 201; signs brewers' agreement 1853 in respect of freight on empty casks, 206; signs brewers' agreement 1859 in respect of allowances, 208
D'Arcy, John, Dublin brewer, buys Anchor Brewery 1818, 92
Darley, Frederick, 103, 111
Darley, Richard Lyons, 235
Darley family, 71 n.
Dash, 252
'Dash-box' and 'Dashes' at James's Gate, 154
Davis, Strangman & Co., Waterford brewers, 94
Day, The Reverend Dr Samuel, 133 n.
Deasy Brewery, Clonakilty, 94
Death benefits, Guinness employees, 238
Deflation in Ireland after 1815, 33–4
Delafield, Joseph, report to House of Lords, 56–7
Delegation of authority—Edward Cecil Guinness's attitude, 186
Delivery Department, James's Gate, 237
Demand, growth of in Ireland, 226
Dennison, Professor S. R., vii
Depression 1815–21, 6, 32–6
Derby, one of original Guinness agencies in England, 231
Derry, Guinness agency, 119, 123

'Description of Dublin, 1577', 74 n.
Differential rates in transport, 205
Discounts, Guinness, 207–8, 227, 229, 238
Disease during Great Famine, 162
Disraeli, B., letter to Sir Arthur Guinness, 195–6
Distillation, illicit: becoming dangerous and expensive, 78; decline in, 6; detrimental to brewing industry, 49–50, 88
Distilling, suspension 1808–11; Correspondence Spencer Perceval and John Foster, 84–6; second Arthur Guinness writes to John Foster, 86–7; revival causes temporary recession in brewing, 99
Dodder, river, 239
Double Stout, Guinness's, 123, 152, 160, 199–201, 213, 223: brewed for blending 1846, 218. *See also* Current Double Stout, Foreign Double Stout, Store Double Stout, Extra Superior Porter
Douceurs, 48
Douglas, Isle of Man: one of original Guinness agencies in Britain, 123, 231; temporary home of Edward Guinness, 111
Doyle, The Reverend Dr, Bishop of Kildare and Leighlin (J. K. L.) urges government to encourage brewing, 88
Dresser, W., viii
Drogheda Brewery, founded by William Cairnes 1825, 97
Druggists, Brewers', 158
Dublin: brewers' petition, 79; brewers' rules in 1859, 207; eighteenth-century, 10, 18; expansion of Guinness trade, 213–17; Georgian, 23–4, 30; Georgian, brewers in, 38; size of market, 37
Dublin Ballast Board, second Arthur Guinness and, 105
Dublin Brewers' Society controls prices, 98, 213
Dublin Brown Stout, 138
Dublin Chamber of Commerce, second Arthur Guinness president, 105
Dublin, Common Council of City: 45, first Arthur Guinness brewers' representative on, 72
Dublin Corporation: and complaints against brewers, 158; dispute with first Arthur Guinness over water rights, 75–7
Dublin Evening Post, 142 n.
Dublin Gazette, terms of dissolution of Guinness partnership, 193–4
Dublin 1660–1860, A Social and Architectural History, 71 n., 182 n.

Index

Dublin Society, later Royal, 21, 37: encourages advances in brewing, 43–4; industrial role in eighteenth century, 73; offers prizes for cultivation of hops, 41; second Arthur Guinness and, 105; Sir Arthur Guinness and, 196
Dún Laoghaire (Kingstown), 167, 248
Dundalk Brewery at Cambrickville, 97
Duties: attitude of British Government in 1791, 59–61; evasion of, 81; on beer, abolished, 67; on beer, demand for repeal of, 54; on Irish beer reduced in 1775, 55; on Irish trade with British Colonies, 19; on malt, 56–7, 67; on spirits, 89, 198; on strong beer, 62
Dyott, William, *Diary* quoted, 89 n.

Economic History of Ireland in the Eighteenth Century, vii
Economic History of Ireland in the Seventeenth Century, vii
Economic History of Ireland from the Union to the Famine, vii, 11 n., 27 n., 34 n.
Economic History of Modern Britain, 15 n., 131 n.
Economic History Review, 33 n.
Economic integration, emergence after Great Famine, 176
Economies of large scale, 3, 42, 199, 226
Economy, Cash, 9, 10, 12. *See also* Maritime Economy, Irish
Economy, Irish Maritime, *see* Maritime Economy, Irish
Economy, Irish Subsistence, *see* Subsistence Economy, Irish
Eden, Sir F. M., 130 n.
Edinburgh Ale, 140
Edward VII, King, at Elveden Hall, 243
Edwards, Professor R. Dudley, viii, 161 n., 162 n., 163 n., 165 n., 166 n.
Effects of Mergers, 226
Elveden Hall, Norfolk, 243
Emancipation, religious, 20
Emancipation, Catholic: second Arthur Guinness an advocate of, 105–6; view of first Arthur Guinness, 73; views of second Arthur, Benjamin and William Lunell Guinness, 142
Emigrants' remittances, 171
Emigration during Great Famine, 162
Engineer, The, 155 n.
Engineering Department, James's Gate, 237
English trade, Guinness's, reason for growth, 140

Enniscorthy maltings, 221
Enterprise lacking in Ireland in nineteenth century, 174
'Entire' or 'entire butt', 39
Espinasse, Paul, 70
Essay on Criticism, 242
Essays in Economic History, 28 n., 184 n.
Eton College, 185
Excise, protection from untaxed malt, 158
Exclusive dealing, 214, 225
Excursions for Guinness employees, 238
Exhibition, Irish of 1872, 188
Exodus from Ireland in 1846, 162
Expenditure, state during Great Famine, 163
'Extended family', Great Famine breaks tradition, 164
Extra Superior Porter, Guinness's, 157: its effect on firm's trade, 151; standard procedure for brewing, 160. *See also* Double Stout
Extract, brewing, at James's Gate: changes in, 154; increase during first half nineteenth century, 160; less variable, 220; definition, 252

Famine, Great, see Great Famine
Famine, Great, 78, 161–76, 216: causes of, 163, 165; deaths in, 162; disease during, 162; effects of, 167–76; effects on brewing, 7; emigration, 162; export of food during, 164; and 'extended family', 164; fiduciary issue and money transfers during, 166; Foster, Campbell, on, 11; 'Gombeen man' in, 163, 170; growth of credit during, 163; and Guinness's Irish market, 171; and Guinness, second Arthur, 167; Guinness sales rise during, 141; and landholding system, 164; and Maritime Economy, 165; pawning during, 163; public works during, 163; railway development during, 163; recovery from, 169; social values and, 164; and Subsistence Economy, 163
Farming Society of Ireland, and second Arthur Guinness, 105
Farmleigh, Castleknock, bought 1874, 189
Farrell, James, Dublin brewer, 232
Father Mathew, *see* Mathew, Father
Faulkner's Dublin Journal, 69 n.
Felix Farley's Bristol Journal, 145 n.
Fenianism, 179–81
Fermentation, 149, 220, 252
Fermentation Book, James's Gate, extract from, 156

266

Index

Fetter, F. W., 26 n., 34 n., 35 n.
Fiduciary Issue, Bank of England, exceeded during Great Famine, 166
Financial relations, between Ireland and England, 26–8: capital imports to Ireland, 30; capital transfers, 27
Findlater, Dublin brewer, 201
Finings, 252
Firkin, 252
Fiscal disadvantages of Ireland in the eighteenth century, 18
Fiscal policy, 2
FitzGerald, Garret, viii, 90 n.
Fitzgibbon, Lord, letter to John Beresford, 1795, 59
Fitzpatrick, P. V., letters from Daniel O'Connell 1832 and 1839, 144–5
Fitzpatrick, W. J., 144 n., 145 n.
Flour Mills, Guinness's, see Hibernian Mills
Foreign Double Stout, Guinness's, 219
Foreign Extra Stout, Guinness's, 216
Foster, Campbell, 11–12, 164 n., 170 n.
Foster, Rt Hon. John, Chancellor of Irish Exchequer, later Lord Oriel: letter to Sir R. Heron, 41, 41 n.; correspondence with Spencer Perceval about effects on Irish agriculture of suspension of distilling, 84–6; letters from second Arthur Guinness, 86–7
Foster Papers, 29 n., 84 n., 85 n., 86 n., 87 n.
Foster's Corn Law, 41 n., 121 n.
Foxford, thirteen brewers there in 1830 (!), 97
Freeman's Journal, 109, 158 n., 159; advertisement 1814, 100; comments on Grattan, 57; denies report of death of first Arthur Guinness, 71
Freedom Box presented to Henry Grattan by Dublin Brewers' Guild, 58 n.
Freight costs at James's Gate, 145–8; on barley, 129; on empty casks from England 1875, 229; to Bristol 1826, 131; to London, Liverpool and Bristol 1838, 140
French, R. A., viii
Friendly Brothers of St Patrick and first Arthur Guinness, 71
Friendly Societies and Guinness tradesmen, 238
Fuel saving at J. G., 220

Galway: Guinness agency, 9; Guinness open store, 202; trade in 1868, 211 n.; trade in 1874, 213 n.
Geoghegan, Samuel, 236, 239

Geoghegan, Thomas Grace, 236
Geoghegan, William Purser, 236
George IV, King, state visit to Ireland 1821, 105
George V, King, 244
Georgian buildings at Shannon Harbour, 204
Georgian Dublin, see Dublin
Giffard, John, Dublin journalist, 142, 158–9
Gin, 44, 64
Gladstone, W. E.: his reforms, 171; identified with cause of temperance, 187
Gloucester, Victoria County History, 130 n.
Gold: circulating medium in Ulster, 26; circulation in Ireland in 1797, 27; coin sent to Ireland by Bank of England, 166; scarcity, 30; suspension of payments by Bank of England and Bank of Ireland 1797, 28
'Gombeen man' and Great Famine, 163, 170
Goods, 252
Goodwyn's London Porter, 138
Gore's General Advertiser, 138
Connott, Lieut.-Col., 31 n.
Grain, little known in Ireland, 12
Grains sold to distillers and farmers, 130
Granard, Guinness agency there in 1812, 124
Grand Canal, Guinness's trade on, 79, 94, 96, 123
Grand Canal Company, 94, 206, 209: correspondence with Guinness, 205; and railway competition, 204; receives letter from Guinness on rivalry between brewers, 79
Grattan, Henry, 5; connexion between his family and Guinnesses, 71 n.; his concern for brewers, 20, 54, 57; his sentiments towards Brewers' Corporation, 58; his speech 1791, 58; his views on decline of Irish brewing industry, 62–3, 66; receives freedom of Dublin Brewers' Guild, 58
Gravity: of beer, 156, 220; original, 253; specific, determination of, 43
Gray, Malcolm, 10 n.
Great Famine: 'Irish Overseas Emigration During the Famine', 162 n.; 'Medical History of the Famine', 162 n.; 'Organization and Administration of Relief', 163 n.; 'Political Background', 161 n., 165 n., 166 n.
Great Famine, see Famine, Great
Great Northern Brewery, Dundalk, 97

Index

Great Northern Railway, 97
Great Southern and Western Railway, 205
Greer and Murphy's Irish Porter, 131
Grenville, Lord, 57 n., correspondence on Irish beer duties, 60
Grey, D. E., viii
Growth: economic, 2; requirements of, 14; of towns, 30
Guilds in Dublin, Cork, Belfast, 21
Guinness, Adelaide (1844–1916), marries Edward Cecil Guinness, 188
Guinness, first Arthur (1725–1803), 5, 69–74, 242: brewer to Dublin Castle 1779, 71; contemplates brewery in Holyhead, 55; died 1803, 74; dispute with Dublin Corporation, 75–7; founder member Hibernian Insurance Company, 121; gives evidence to House of Commons 1799, 63–4; marries 1761, 71; Master, Corporation of Brewers 1767, 71; supports religious emancipation, 73; will, 104
Guinness, second Arthur (1768–1855), 5, 103–18, 232, 242, 246: architect of firm's fortunes, 7; assists father, 72; association with Bank of Ireland, 105, 126; banker, his views as, 7, 35–6; character, 104; claims on, 104, 112, 125, 235; and currency school, 126; denies use of adulterants 1814, 159; died 1855, 177; estates, 169; in family crisis 1839, 113; joins Yeomanry 1798, 74; main interest banking after 1815, 120; marries 1793 and 1821, 104; on Great Famine 1847 and 1849, 107, 167; probate of will 1855, 147; on religion 1847, 107–8; succeeds father in brewery 1803, 6; supports brewers' petition due to increase in spirit drinking 1811, 79; supports Catholic Emancipation 1813, 142; travels on bank business, 126; withdraws from active management 1839, 114
Guinness, Arthur Edward, later Sir Arthur, subsequently Lord Ardilaun (1840–1915), 8, 182–97, 236, 244: and afforestation, 196; and Ashford Estate, Co. Galway, 196; and Coombe Hospital, 196; created a baron 1880, 196; decides to retire from James's Gate, 193; declining interest in the brewery, 190; and Disraeli, 195; inherits father's baronetcy 1868, 185; interest in philanthropy, 195; marries, 190; and Marsh's Library, 196; and Muckross Estate, Co. Kerry, 196; retires 1876, 193–5; and Royal Dublin Society, 196; and St Stephen's Green,

196; and Salisbury, Lord, 196; states family's political views, 188; unseated from Parliament 1869, 186
Guinness, Arthur Lee (1797–1863), 6, 113–16, 232, 235, 244: died 1863, 115; exertions during Great Famine, 116; in family crisis, 113; at Stillorgan, 115
Guinness, Benjamin (c. 1730–c. 1778), 70
Guinness, Benjamin (1777–1826), 5, 6, 73, 79, 87, 103–4, 112, 140, 142, 232: denies use of adulterants 1841, 159; died 1826, 103 n.
Guinness, Benjamin Lee (Lee) (1842–1900), 182
Guinness, Benjamin Lee (later Sir Benjamin Lee) (1798–1868), 6–7, 177–82, 232–6, 242–8: assumes complete control of brewery 1858, 177; created baronet 1867, 181; died 1868, 182; elected M.P. 1865, 178; in family crisis 1839, 112–14; invited to stand for Parliament 1851, 178; letters from second Arthur Guinness 1847 and 1849, 107, 167; Lord Mayor of Dublin 1851, 177; receives Address of loyalty at James's Gate 1866, 179–80; reconstructs St Patrick's Cathedral, 172, 181; signs Dublin Brewers' Agreement 1859, 208; visits Bristol agent 1837; 133; wealth, and will, 182–4
Guinness, Claude (1852–95), 249
Guinness, Edward (1772–1833): business failures 1811, 108–10; family difficulties 1814, 111–12; firm pays final settlement for his bankruptcy 1815, 124 n.; joins Yeomanry 1798, 74; newspaper tribute 1812, 108–9; solicitor and iron-master, 103–4; works in brewery and receives annuity, 112, 115
Guinness, Edward Cecil (later Lord Iveagh) (1847–1927), 182–97, 236, 243–8: character, 186, 190; continues policy of expansion and development at James's Gate, 197; control of business, 193; his Unionism, 188; marries 1873, 188; preoccupation with administrative detail, 190; sole proprietor 1876, 8, 192–4; withdraws candidature for parliamentary election, 187
Guinness, The Reverend Dr Hosea (1765–1841), 5, 74, 103–4, 107, 112, 125, 235
Guinness, John Grattan (1783–1850), 103–4: fails in business with his brother Edward 1811, 108–9; letter on output from second Arthur Guinness 1825, 80; Liverpool agency, becomes partner 1825, withdraws 1826, 138–9, 234

268

Index

Guinness, John (1817–?), 235

Guinness, John Grattan, junior (?–1870), 235

Guinness, Richard (c. 1690–?), 69

Guinness, Richard (?–1806), 69, 104

Guinness, Richard (Counsellor) (1755–1829), 109, 143, 158

Guinness, Richard (?–?), 235

Guinness, Robert Rundell (1789–1857), 169

Guinness, Rupert Edward Cecil Lee (later Lord Iveagh) (1874–), see Iveagh, Earl of

Guinness, Samuel (c. 1761–1826), 109

Guinness, William Lunell (1779–1842), 5, 6, 79, 103–4, 126, 232: denies use of adulterants 1814, 159; joins Yeomanry 1798, 74; on Managing Committee of Association for the Prevention of Mendicity in Dublin 1819, 33; supports Catholic Emancipation 1813, 142

Guinness, The Reverend William Smythe Lee Grattan (1795–1864), 113, 125 n., 133 n.

Guinness, Bewley and Nevill, Guinness agents in Liverpool 1824, 138

Guinness Brewery, Dublin, see James's Gate Brewery

Gweedore, Co. Donegal, Lord George Hill's estate, 12

'Half and half', 39

Hall, F. G., 26 n., 93 n., 166 n., 169 n., 170 n.

Hand trades, decline in nineteenth century, 31–2

Hannin, Guinness sub-agent at Shannon Harbour, 203–4

'Harp', Guinness's trade-mark label, 214

Hartwell, Dr R. M., viii

Harwood, London brewer, 39

'Head' of porter, characteristic creamy, 150, 220

Heron, Sir R., letter from John Foster 1779, 41

Hibernian Insurance Company, first Arthur and Samuel Guinness founder members, 121

Hibernian Mills, Kilmainham, 5, 73–4, 104; built by first Arthur Guinness, 72, 242; destroyed by fire, 121; importance after 1800, 120–2

Hibernian Temperance Society, attitude to spirits, 88

Highland Economy, 1750–1850, 10 n.

Hill, Lord George, estate at Gweedore, Co. Donegal, 12

History of Ireland (1577), 74 n.

History of Prices and of the State of the Circulation during the Years 1793–1856, 33 n., 34 n., 167 n.

History of the Bank of Ireland, 26 n., 93 n., 166 n., 169 n., 170 n.

History, technical, of brewing, little known of Guinness before 1796, 149

Hoare, The Reverend William Deane, 103

Hobsbawm, E. J., 33 n.

Hogan, John, Manager, Guinness's store at Galway, 210

Hogan, Thomas, Manager, Guinness's store at Ballinasloe, 210

Hogshead, 252

Holyhead, Andrews and Arthur Guinness consider setting up brewery there, 55

Home Rule, Irish, 187–8

Hop merchants, London, 129–30

Hop rate, 129, 218, 219; fall during Napoleonic Wars, 152; high in Keeping Beer, 150; variations in, 152–3

Hopback, 252

Hop duty increased in 1840, 141

Hops: and flavour of beer, 149, 155; British monopoly of trade after 1710, 50; cultivation encouraged by Dublin Society, 41, 43; duties on, 41, 146; Guinness expenditure on, 223; 'extravagantly dear' 1812–16, 157; Flemish, 130, 153; Kent, 130; price rises during Napoleonic Wars, 152; source, 130, 222; substitutes, 157–60

Housing, Royal Commission on Working-Class, 168

Howell, George, 31 n.

Huddersfield, one of original Guinness agencies in Britain, 231

Hudson, L. E., viii

'Huff-cup', 38

Hughes, Dr A. H., vii

Ice: importation ceases, 220; use at James's Gate, 156

Imports of British beer into Ireland: 1719, 1720, 1740, 1760, 1772, 52; 1793, 2; 1813, 3; decline of, 3

Imports, prohibition of Irish provisions 1778, 19

Indian Army, John Grattan Guinness joins, 103

Industrial development in Ireland, lack of, 31

Industrial Revolution in Britain, 13

Inflation in Ireland, 5; after 1797, 3; 1810–15, 30

269

Index

Inglis, Dr Brian, vii
Insurance, fire, at James's Gate 1803, 120
Investment, 252: in Ireland, 16; in James's Gate, 183, 224; net, 253
Ireland, Industrial and Agricultural, 92 n.
Irish Historical Studies, 15 n.
Irish Pound, 26 n., 34 n., 35 n.
'Irish Seasonal Migration to Great Britain, 1800–1838', 15 n.
Iron foundry, Edward Guinness and, 4, 108–9
Isinglass, 251
Isle of Man, Edward Guinness in, 111–12, 234; sales there, 123
Iveagh, Countess of, vii
Iveagh, Earl of (1847–1927), *see* Guinness, Sir Edward Cecil
Iveagh, Earl of (1874–), vii, born, 189: presents Iveagh House to Irish Government, 182 n.
Iveagh House, 80 St Stephen's Green, Dublin, 182 n.

James, F. E., viii
James, N., Bristol, consignee Guinness porter 1815, 132
Jameson, James, Dublin distiller, 88 n.
Jameson, Pim & Co., Dublin brewers: absorb North Anne Street Brewery, Thunder & Co., and Ally & Co., 93; sign Dublin Brewers' Agreement 1859, 208
James's Gate Brewery, 74–7, 182–3: capacity inadequate, 220–1; establishment 1759, 8; incorporation 1886, 8; largest porter brewery in world, 183, 240–1; lease obtained by first Arthur Guinness, 69–70; valuation, 192, 195
James's Street, Dublin, no. 101, 240
Jersey, one of original Guinness agencies, 231
Journals, Conversations and Essays Relating to Ireland, 17 n., 168 n.

Kavanagh and Brett, owners of Anchor Brewery, Dublin, 92
Kearney, Dr Hugh, viii
Keeping Beer, Guinness's, 122, 128, 152, 157, 218–19: first brewed 1801, 150
Kennedy, F. W., Guinness agent at Limerick, 7, 208–13
Kennedy, J. G., Dublin ale brewer, 64
Kenny, J., Dublin publican, 216
Kerr, Barbara M., 15 n.
Kieve, 154, 252–3

Kieves at James's Gate, number increased, 239–40
Kildare Street Club, Dublin, 248
Kilderkin, 253
Kilmainham, Guinness Flour Mills, *see* Hibernian Mills
Kingstown (Dún Laoghaire), 167, 248
Kington, John Barnett, 131 n.
'Knockdown', 38

Laboratory analysis at James's Gate, need for, 220
Labour Department, James's Gate, 237
Labour force: characteristics of, 14; migration to Britain, 14–15; supply of, 17
Labourers, Guinness, 237
Lady's Well Brewery, Cork, 93
Land Acts, Irish, 1870, 1881, 172
Land-holding system, 11, 12, 15–16; and Great Famine, 164; after Great Famine, 168–9, 171
Landlords, 168, 171–2: absentee, 15; improving, 12, 16; rents of, 27
Large-scale production of beer in London in eighteenth century, 3, 13, 42
Latimer, John, 131 n.
LaTouche, Christopher Digges, 237
LaTouche family, 71 n.
'Leakes' at James's Gate, 154
Lee, Benjamin, 104
Leeson, Hon. John, presents petition, 79
Leeson family, formerly brewers, Earls of Milltown, 37
Leicester, one of original Guinness agencies in Britain, 231
Leith, Guinness agency, 122
Leixlip, 69, 243
Letters of D. H. Lawrence, 198
Letters on the Condition of the People of Ireland, 11 n., 12 n., 164 n., 170 n.
Letters to the Rt Hon. the Chancellor of the Exchequer, 67 n.
'Liberal', second Arthur Guinness so called, 106–8
Licensing-system, in eighteenth century, 47–8; not stringent, 227
Liffey, River, Dublin, 75
Limerick, 9: Guinness agency, 122–3; trade 1868, 211 n.; trade 1874, 213 n.
Linen industry, 24
Liquor, 253
Liquor interest, Conservatives and, 179
Lisbon, Guinness exports to, 124
Liverpool: first steamer service with Dublin, 124; Guinness agency, 119, 123, 137–40, 231; trade with, 147, 211

270

Index

Meux, London brewers, 222
Midland Great Western Railway, 147, 205
Midleton maltings, 129
Milburn and Prestwick, London hop merchants, 129–30
Milesian Magazine, 143
Mill, Dr C. K., vii
Mills, flour, Guinness's, *see* Hibernian Mills
Milltown, Earls of, Leeson family, formerly brewers, 37
Mitchell, John, and export of food during Great Famine, 164
Moline, Sparkes, 6, 140, 147, 209: Guinness's warehouse-keeper in London 1834–5, 134 n.; made London agent (with S. Waring) 1833, 137
Monasterevan Brewery, 96
Monetary Economy, 173
Money, in Ireland, 11, 13, 25, 163–4: and financial relations with Great Britain, 26–8; increased use after Great Famine, 169–70; paper, suppression of, 26; transfers to Ireland during Great Famine, 166
Moore, Thomas, 144
Morewood, Samuel, 52 n., 79 n., 155 n., 220 n.
Morning Post, 145
Mortality Rates, Irish, lowered by potato diet, 11
Morton, Lee, 234, *see also* Boursiquot, D. L.
Morton, R. G., vii
Mountjoy Brewery, Dublin, 93, 240
Mountmellick maltings, 129, 221; source of malt, 202
Moyne, The Lord, vii
Muckross Estate, Co. Kerry, bought by Sir Arthur Guinness, 196
Mullingar, Guinness agency, trade 1874, 213 n.
Munster Bank, its failure, Munster and Leinster Bank founded, 93
Murdock, H., viii
Murphy, J., proprietor of Lady's Well Brewery, Cork, 93: role in banking history, 93

Napoleonic Wars: fall in hop rates during, 152; Guinness sales during, 120; lack of capital following, 125
National Library of Ireland, viii
Nationalism, Irish, and Sir Arthur Guinness, 196
Nell, Miss J. M., viii
Nevill and Frankland, Guinness agents in Liverpool 1834, 138

New Ross maltings, 222
Newbridge, Co. Kildare, Guinness agency opened, 203; Guinness agree not to undersell D'Arcy, 208; Phoenix Brewery and army canteen, 215
Newcastle-upon-Tyne, one of original Guinness agencies in England, 231
Newmarch, J. J. and W., 33 n., 34 n., 167 n.
Newry, Co. Down, Guinness agency opened, 203
Nicholson's Superior Dublin Porter, 138
'Night clerk' system at James's Gate, 233, 235
North Anne Street Brewery, Dublin, absorbs Robert Manders & Co., 93
Northcott, Miss K., viii
Northern Ireland Public Records Office, Belfast, viii
Nottingham, one of original Guinness agencies in England, 231
Nowlan, Dr K., viii, 161 n., 165 n., 166 n.

O'Brien, Dr Conor Cruise, viii
O'Brien, Professor George, vii, 11 n., 27 n., 34 n.
O'Brien, Sir Lucius, 45
Ó Broin, León, viii
O'Connell, Daniel, junior, acquires Phoenix brewery, 91
O'Connell, Daniel, Liberator: and exports of food during Great Famine, 161, 164; and second Arthur Guinness, 144–5; supported by second Arthur Guinness, but later opposed, 106–7
O'Connell's Brewery, Dublin, 91, 144. *See also* Phoenix Brewery
O'Connor, Valentine, 73
Offices, James's Gate, 240
Official Illustrated Guide to Midland Great Western, Great Southern and Western and Dublin and Drogheda Railway, 156
'Old Cheese' ballad, 40
O'Neill, T. P., 163 n.
Oranmore, Guinness agency, trade 1874, 213 n.
Oriel, Lord, *see* Foster, John
'Organization and Administration of Relief', 163 n.
O'Sullivan, Sean, viii
O'Sullivan, W., viii
Oughterard, Co. Kildare, burial place of first Arthur Guinness, 74
Output: Dublin brewers 1766, 70; fall in Guinness's after 1815, 124; Guinness

Index

Index

Index

276

Index

Trade-mark label, Guinness's 'Harp', 214
Tradesmen, Guinness, 237
Trading centres, Guinness's, opened, 119
Transport: of beer, 198; canals, 21–5; Guinness's policy, 225, 229; improvements after 1840, 218; in eighteenth century, 40; steamship, 6
Trinity College, Dublin, Edward Cecil Guinness as undergraduate, 185, 236
Triple Stout, Guinness's, 151, 218–19. *See also* West Indies Porter
Trollope, Anthony, at Banagher, 23
Trough, beer held in at James's Gate, 156–7
Truman, London brewer, 222
Tuam, Guinness agency, trade in 1874, 213 n.
Tuckett, Henry, and Guinness's London agency, 6, 119, 132–7, 151
Tullamore Brewery, 96
Tunnage, 254
Tuns, fermenting, 156, 239–41, 254
Twining and Keogh, Dublin, output 1810, 80
'Twopenny', 39
'Two-thirds' or 'Three threads', 39

Ulster: absence of brewing there, 98; largely exempt from effects of Great Famine, 26
Union, Act of, 20: blamed for Irish difficulties, 29, 36; economic significance, 25; effects on economic development, 19; repeal of, opposed by second Arthur Guinness, 106
Unionism: Sir Arthur Edward Guinness's, 196; Benjamin Lee Guinness's, 179; Edward Cecil Guinness's, 188
University College, Dublin, 182 n.
Ussher, Captain R. B., 147, 234
Ussher, Simeon, 235

Vaizey, John, 226 n.
Vartry, River, water supply to James's Gate, 240
Vats, 157, 239–41, 254
Veto controversy, 144
Viceregal court, 189
'Vicinity' of Dublin, 147, 203, 208, 211, 225
Vinosity, 254

Wages, levels of Guinness's: 1849 and 1854, 146; 1879, 237–8
Wakefield, Edward, 89 n., 90 n.
Wall, Mrs Maureen, viii

Waller, Edmund, 103, 236
Waller, George (land agent), 169 n.
Waller, George (Guinness brewer), 236
Walsh, D. B., viii
Waring, Edward, Guinness agent in Bristol: joins his father in agency 1837, 133; succeeds his father 1838, 134, 140
Waring, Samuel, Guinness agent in Bristol, 6, 132, 135, 209, 210, 245: and Guinness's Extra Superior Porter, 151; founds Bristol agency, 119; founds London agency, 133; threatened with bankruptcy, 133
Waring and Moline, Guinness agents in London after 1834, 134
Waring and Tuckett, Guinness agents in London 1828, 151
Waring, Tuckett and Foster, Guinness agents in London 1831–3, 134 n.
Waste, its importance, 130
Water rights in James's Gate, 75–7
Water supply, and localization of brewing industry, 75; James's Gate, 239, 240.
Waterford, Guinness agency reorganized, 210; petition by brewers in, 79; trade with Bristol, 131
Watkins, Dublin brewer, signs Brewers' Agreement 1859, 208
Wealth of Nations, 51 n.
Wellington, Duke of, 9, 124 n.
Welsh Ale, 138
Wesley, John, probable influence on first Arthur Guinness's religious views, 73
West Indies Porter, Guinness's, 122–3, 150–1, 153, 219. *See also* Triple Stout
Westmorland, Earl of, correspondence with Lord Grenville, 59–60
Wetherman, M. A. & Co., 235; become Guinness's agents in Bristol 1850, 134 n.
Wexford maltings, 221
Whigs, Grattan's association, 20
Whiskey, alleged cause of turbulence, 65: duty increased 1858, 198; rival to beer 84–5; staple drink of peasantry, 49; victim of the excise and public opinion, 78
Whisky, Scotch, consumption in Belfast 1841, 88
Whitbread, London brewer, 56, 222; London Porter, 131
White, Lady Olivia Charlotte, marries Sir Arthur Guinness, 190
Whitehaven, Guinness agency 1819, 124
Whitmore, Olivia, marries first Arthur Guinness, 71
Wigin, Guinness agent at Cork 1858–9, 209

277

Will, Sir Benjamin Lee Guinness, 194; extract, 184
Williams, D. O., vii
Williams, Professor T. D., viii, 161 n., 162 n., 163 n., 165 n., 166 n.
Woods, Thomas, viii
Works Department, James's Gate, 237

Wort, 149, 154, 219, 251–4: hopped, 155, unfermented, 220

Yeast, 155–6, 220, 251, 254
Young, Arthur, 41 n.
Young, John, East Anglian maltster, 82

For EU product safety concerns, contact us at Calle de José Abascal, 56–1°,
28003 Madrid, Spain or eugpsr@cambridge.org.

www.ingramcontent.com/pod-product-compliance
Ingram Content Group UK Ltd.
Pitfield, Milton Keynes, MK11 3LW, UK
UKHW042212180425
457623UK00011B/169